THE PHILO OF ALEXANDRIA
SCRIPTURE INDEX

STUDIA PHILONICA MONOGRAPHS

Editor
Michael B. Cover

Number 9

THE PHILO OF ALEXANDRIA
SCRIPTURE INDEX

Sean A. Adams and Zanne Domoney-Lyttle

SBL PRESS

 **PRESS**

Atlanta

Copyright © 2023 by Sean A. Adams and Zanne Domoney-Lyttle

Library of Congress Control Number: 2023942610

Contents

Scripture Index

Acknowledgments

Some colleagues have assisted in the creation of this index by making comments or giving us access to current work. We would like to thank William D. Ashworth, Adam Kamesar, Justin Rogers, James R. Royse, Gary Edward Schnittjer, Joan E. Taylor, and Abraham Terian. Substantial feedback was given by the Studia Philonica series editors, especially Michael Cover, Gregory E. Sterling, and David T. Runia. Their comments have made substantial improvement to this project.

We dedicate this book to our nieces and nephews, who bring us joy:

> Elizabeth Alexandria Adams
> Ethan James Adams

and

> Willow Anja Tunnock
> Jack Paul Crawford
> Nell Zanne Law-Lyttle

Abbreviations

Philonic Works

Abr.	*De Abrahamo*
Aet.	*De aeternitate mundi*
Agr.	*De agricultura*
Anim.	*De animalibus*
Cher.	*De cherubim*
Conf.	*De confusione linguarum*
Congr.	*De congressu eruditionis gratia*
Contempl.	*De vita contemplativa*
Decal.	*De decalogo*
Deo	*De Deo*
Det.	*Quod deterius potiori insidior soleat*
Deus	*Quod Deus sit immutabilis*
Ebr.	*De ebrietate*
Flacc.	*In Flaccum*
Fug.	*De fuga et inventione*
Gig.	*De gigantibus*
Her.	*Quis rerum divinarum heres sit*
Hypoth.	*Hypothetica*
Ios.	*De Iosepho*
Leg.	*Legum allegoriae*
Legat.	*Legatio ad Gaium*
Migr.	*De migratione Abrahami*
Mos.	*De vita Mosis*
Mut.	*De mutatione nominum*
Opif.	*De opificio mundi*
Plant.	*De plantatione*
Post.	*De posteritate Caini*
Praem.	*De praemiis et poenis*

Prob.	*Quod omnis probus liber sit*
Prov.	*De providentia*
QE	*Quaestiones et solutiones in Exodum*
QG	*Quaestiones et solutiones in Genesin*
Sacr.	*De sacrificiis Abelis et Caini*
Sobr.	*De sobrietate*
Somn.	*De somniis*
Spec.	*De specialibus legibus*
Virt.	*De virtutibus*

Other Primary Resources

De or.	Cicero, *De oratore*
Inst.	Quintilian, *Institutio oratoria*
Prog.	Theon, *Progymnasmata*

Secondary Resources

ALGHJ	Arbeiten zur Literatur und Geschichte des hellenistischen Judentums
CCS	Cambridge Classical Studies
CCSG	Corpus Christianorum: Series Graeca
CRINT	Compendia Rerum Iudaicarum ad Novum Testamentum
EstBib	*Estudios bíblicos*
FIOTL	Formation and Interpretation of Old Testament Literature
FR(H)	fragment from James Rendel Harris, *Fragments of Philo Judeaus*. Cambridge: Cambridge University Press, 1886.
FR(L)	fragment from Hans Lewy, "Neue Philontexte in der Überarbeitung des Ambrosius: Mit einem Anhang; Neu gefundene griechische Philonfragmente." *SPAW* 4 (1932): 23–84.
FR(P)	fragment from Françoise Petit, *Quaestiones et solutiones in Genesim et in Exodum, Fragmenta Graeca: Introduction, texte critique et notes*, PAPM 33. Paris: Cerf, 1978.
FR(M)	fragment from Ralph Marcus, ed. and trans., *Questions on Exodus*, LCL 401. Cambridge: Harvard University Press, 1953.
JAJSup	Journal of Ancient Judaism Supplements

JSJSup	Supplements to Journal for the Study of Judaism
LCL	Loeb Classical Library
LES	Penner, Ken M., ed. *The Lexham English Septuagint*. Bellingham, WA: Lexham, 2019.
NETS	Pietersma, Albert, and Benjamin G. Wright, eds. *A New English Translation of the Septuagint*. Oxford: Oxford University Press, 2007.
NIV	New International Version
NRSVue	New Revised Standard Version, Updated Edition
OBO	Orbis Biblicus et Orientalis
PACS	Philo of Alexandria Commentary Series
PAPM	*Les oeuvres de Philon d'Alexandrie*. French edition and translation under the general editorship of Roger Arnaldez, Jean Pouilloux, and Claude Mondésert. Paris: Cerf, 1961–1992.
Phil	*Philologus*
PLCLSup	supplement volumes to Francis H. Colson, George H. Whitaker, and Ralph Marcus, trans. and eds., *Philo in Ten Volumes (and Two Supplementary Volumes)*. LCL. Cambridge: Harvard University Press, 1929–1962.
SBB	Stuttgarter biblische Beiträge
SC	Sources chrétiennes
SPAW	*Sitzungsberichte der preussischen Akademie der Wissenschaften*
SPhA	Studies in Philo of Alexandria
SPhiloA	*Studia Philonica Annual*
SVTG	Septuaginta: Vetus Testamentum Graecum
Text	*Textus*
TSAJ	Texte und Studien zum antiken Judentum
TUGAL	Texte und Untersuchungen zur Geschichte der altchristlichen Literatur
VTSup	Supplements to Vetus Testamentum
WUNT	Wissenschaftliche Untersuchungen zum Neuen Testament
ZRGG	*Zeitschrift für Religions- und Geistesgeschichte*

Introduction

This *instrumentum* is an index of identified allusions to and citations of Scripture in the extant corpus of Philo of Alexandria. Components of this work have been undertaken previously by scholars, particularly J. W. Earp, in the Loeb Classical Library; Jean Allenbach and his colleagues, as a supplement to *Biblia Patristica*; and Hans Leisegang, in volume 7 of the critical edition published by de Gruyter.[1] We appreciate their work and have drawn from their scholarship. In previous indices, Philo's scriptural references have been organized by biblical book, and although this organizational structure is useful, it does not allow for the study of Philo's engagement with Scripture in individual treatises or to interrogate how intertexts are collected and grouped by Philo. For this reason, in this study we provide two indices. The first is structured on Philo's treatises

---

1. J. W. Earp, "Indices to Volumes I–X," in *Philo in Ten Volumes (and Two Supplementary Volumes)*, ed. Francis H. Colson, George H. Whitaker, and Ralph Marcus, 12 vols., LCL (Cambridge: Harvard University Press, 1929–1962), 10:189–520; Jean Allenbach et al., eds., *Biblia Patristica: Supplément, Philon d'Alexandrie* (Paris: Centre National de la Recherche Scientifique, 1982). See Hans Leisegang, *Indices ad Philonis Alexandrini opera*, vol. 7 of *Philonis Alexandrini opera quae supersunt* (Berlin: de Gruyter, 1926), 29–43; Günter Mayer, *Index Philoneus* (Berlin: de Gruyter, 1974). One of the earliest collections is Herbert Edward Ryle, *Philo and Holy Scripture: Or, the Quotations of Philo from the Books of the Old Testament, with Introduction and Notes* (London: MacMillan, 1895). On the problems of index making, see Wolfgang Reister, "Zur Problematik eines Philo-Index," *ZRGG* 27 (1975): 166–68.

We have taken as our starting point Allenbach's index and are deeply indebted to him and his team. However, we have also evaluated each entry to determine its veracity and have added new entries identified by us and other scholars. We have also added references to *De animalibus*, which were not included in Allenbach's study. These are taken from Abraham Terian, *Philonis Alexandrini De Animalibus: The Armenian Text with an Introduction, Translation, and Commentary*, Studies in Hellenistic Judaism 1 (Chico, CA: Scholars Press, 1981). We also note that no allusions or citations have been found in *De numeris*.

and organized by corpus (*Quaestiones et solutiones*, Allegorical Commentary, Exposition of the Law, and Philosophical/Historical Works), and the second is organized by biblical book.[2] We hope that having two different arrangements will facilitate the study of Philo not only in identifying which passages are referenced but also how they are grouped together and arranged in the construction of each treatise.

There are some important limitations to this work. First, we do not engage with the *catenae* or the *florilegia*.[3] Second, we did not provide references to works wrongfully attributed to Philo, such as the Latin *Liber antiquitatum biblicarum* and the Armenian sermons De Sampsone and De Jona.[4] Third, we limit our study to the critical edition of Philo and do not specifically evaluate the manuscripts. This final decision, we think, has a minimal impact for this project but is important to take into account as the diversity of manuscripts and their impact on readers is becoming more recognized in scholarship.[5]

---

2. We have also included allusions found in Philo's fragments edited by Harris, Lewy, Petit, and Marcus: James Rendel Harris, *Fragments of Philo Judeaus* (Cambridge: Cambridge University Press, 1886); Hans Lewy, "Neue Philontexte in der Überarbeitung des Ambrosius: Mit einem Anhang; Neu gefundene griechische Philonfragmente," *SPAW* 4 (1932): 23–84; Françoise Petit, *Quaestiones in Genesim et in Exodum, Fragmenta Graeca: Introduction, texte critique et notes*, PAPM 33 (Paris: Cerf, 1978); Ralph Marcus, ed. and trans., *Questions on Exodus*, LCL 401 (Cambridge: Harvard University Press, 1953), 234–37. Fragments from each are marked in the indices by FR(H), FR(L), FR(P), and FR(M), respectively, and use the edition or page number and line of the respective work.

3. On which, see James R. Royse, *The Spurious Texts of Philo of Alexandria: A Study of Textual Transmission and Corruption with Indexes to the Major Collections of Greek Fragments*, ALGHJ 22 (Leiden: Brill, 1991), 14–25 and 26–58, respectively. For a critical edition, see Françoise Petit, *Catena Sinaitica*, vol. 1 of *Catenae Graecae in Genesim et in Exodum*, 2 vols., CCSG 2 (Turnhout: Brepols, 1977).

4. See Pierre-Maurice Bogaert, Charles Perrot, Jacques Cazeaux, and Daniel J. Harrington, *Les Antiquités Bibliques*, 2 vols., SC 229–230 (Paris: Cerf, 1976); Johann Baptist Aucher, *Philonis Judaei paralipomena Armena: Libri videlicet quatuor in Genesin; Libri duo in Exodum; Sermo unus de Sampsone, alter de Jona, tertius de tribus angelis Abraamo apparentibus* (Venice: Lazari, 1826).

5. Sean A. Adams, "Treatise Order in the Greek Codices of Philo of Alexandria: Lists, *Pinakes*, and Manuscripts," *SPhiloA* 34 (2022): 1–31; see also James R. Royse, "The Biblical Quotations in the Coptos Papyrus of Philo," *SPhiloA* 28 (2016): 49–76. For the critical editions of the Greek, see Leopold Cohn, Paul Wendland, and Siegfried Reiter, eds., *Philonis Alexandrini opera quae supersunt*, 6 vols. (Berlin: Reimer,

An index appears deceptively straightforward, but there are many theoretical decisions that need to be made in its creation. For example, to which biblical text does Philo allude, and what referencing system should we employ? Given that Philo made almost exclusive use of Greek Scripture, we have decided to use Septuagint references rather than those assigned to the Hebrew.[6] As a result, some of the references below do not align with chapter and verse numbers in English translations (e.g., NIV, NRSVue). For most of the biblical books, including the Pentateuch, the chapter and verse numbers are identical. However, there are some sections of Exodus, Deuteronomy, Jeremiah, and Psalms that are markedly different. We encourage readers to keep this in mind when using this tool.[7]

Which Greek text(s) Philo had access to further complicates this study.[8] Although he cites Greek Scripture, Philo's quotations do not always align with those found in modern critical editions. The foundational work in this regard is *Philo's Bible*, in which Peter Katz identifies "aberrant" readings in Philo, the consistency of which suggests that Philo had an alternate form of the Pentateuch.[9] More recently, Gregory Sterling has returned to the question of Philo's Septuagint text; taking *Legum allegoriae* as his test corpus, he argues that Philo knew a different, freer version of the Septuagint than that reconstructed by John W. Wevers.[10] Although we are not

---

1896–1915); Leopold Cohn et al., eds., *Philo von Alexandria: Die Werke in deutscher Übersetzung*, 7 vols. (Berlin: de Gruyter, 1909–1964).

6. In some places the allusion is not found in the LXX but in the Hebrew. We have signaled this with [MT].

7. For a complete list of differences, see appendix B (pp. 265–68) in *The SBL Handbook of Style*, 2nd ed. (Atlanta: SBL Press, 2014). For those who do not read Greek, we suggest the use of an English translation of the Septuagint in which the Septuagint verse numbering is retained (e.g., LES or NETS).

8. For a summary of the modern debate over septuagintal origins and revisions, see Emanuel Tov, "The Septuagint," in *Mikra: Text, Translation, Reading and Interpretation of the Hebrew Bible in Ancient Judaism and Early Christianity*, ed. Martin Jan Mulder, CRINT 2.1 (Assen: Van Gorcum, 1988), 161–88.

9. Peter Katz, *Philo's Bible: The Aberrant Text of Biblical Quotations in Some Philonic Writings and Its Place in the Textual History of the Greek Bible* (Cambridge: Cambridge University Press, 1950), 96.

10. Gregory E. Sterling, "Which Version of the Greek Bible Did Philo Read?," in *Pentateuchal Traditions in the Late Second Temple Period: Proceedings of the International Workshop in Tokyo, August 28–31, 2007*, ed. Akio Moriya and Gohei Hatta, JSJSup 158 (Leiden: Brill, 2012), 89–127; Olivier Munnich, "Les retouches faites aux lemmes bibliques dans le Commentaire allégorique de Philon d'Alexandrie: Bilan et

able to reconstruct Philo's scriptural text with certainty, we can say with confidence that he does not always choose to quote the Septuagint exactly. In other words, Philo felt free to make changes to the scriptural text (e.g., omitting words, changing word order) in order to suit his exegetical purpose. Subsequent studies have sought to identify specific recensions expressed in surviving Philonic texts.[11] Although this is a valid line of scholarly inquiry, it does not feature in the indices. Ultimately, we took the Göttingen Septuagint volumes, including their references to manuscript variants, as our primary point of comparison and depended on Rahlfs-Hanhart's *Septuaginta* for books not yet published in that series, such as 1–4 Kingdoms.[12]

Another decision that needed to be made was the criteria by which we would identify quotations of Scripture. Definitions of and criteria for determining quotations vary among scholars.[13] Our intention in this study

---

proposition," in *Les études philoniennes: Regards sur cinquante ans de recherche (1967–2017)*, ed. Olivier Munnich and Sébastien Morlet, SPhA 13 (Leiden: Brill, 2021), 137–83. John W. Wevers is responsible for editing the Greek Pentateuch for the Göttingen series. For Genesis, see John W. Wevers, ed., *Genesis*, SVTG 1 (Göttingen: Vandenhoeck & Ruprecht, 1974).

11. E.g., Paul Wendland, "Zu Philos Schrift *de posteritate Caini* (nebst Bemerkungen zur Rekonstruktion der Septuaginta)," *Phil* 57 (1898): 248–88, especially 284–87 (Lucianic); Dominique Barthélemy, "Est-ce Hoshaya Rabba qui censura le 'Commentaire allégorique'? A partir des retouches faites aux citations bibliques, étude sur la tradition textuelle du Commentaire Allégorique de Philon," in *Philon d'Alexandrie: Lyon 11–15 Septembre 1966, colloques nationaux du Centre National de la Recherche Scientifique*, ed. Roger Arnaldez, Claude Mondésert, and Jean Pouilloux (Paris: Centre national de la recherche scientifique, 1967), 45–78, repr. in Dominique Barthélemy, *Études d'histoire du texte de l'Ancient Testament*, OBO 21 (Göttingen: Vandenhoeck & Ruprecht, 1978), 140–73, with additional notes on 390–91.

12. For a recent summary of this series and a discussion on its future, see Felix Albrecht, "Report on the Göttingen Septuagint," *Text* 29 (2020): 201–20. See also Alfred Rahlfs and Robert Hanhart, eds., *Septuaginta: Id est Vetus Testamentum graece iuxta LXX interpretes*, 2nd ed. (Stuttgart: Deutsche Bibelgesellschaft, 2006).

13. Jacques T. A. G. M. van Ruiten, "Der alttestamentliche Hintergrund von Apocalypse 6:12–17," *EstBib* 53 (1995): 243–44 (minimum two words); Beate Kowalski, *Die Rezeption des Propheten Ezechiel in der Offenbarung des Johannes*, SBB 52 (Stuttgart: Katholisches Bibelwerk, 2004), 61–62 (two words minimum, except for *hapax legomena* between the citing and anterior texts); Armin Lange and Matthias Weigold, *Biblical Quotations and Allusions in Second Temple Jewish Literature*, JAJSup 5 (Göttingen: Vandenhoeck & Ruprecht, 2011), 25 (minimum three words). For an important differentiation and comparison of shared versus nonshared lan-

is not to contribute to this debate but to identify places in Philo's corpus where he clearly cites the biblical text. In what follows we have marked with an asterisk (*) instances where Philo signals that he is drawing from Scripture and/or when there are, at a minimum, two words from the source text cited together in Philo's text.[14] Placing a word limit on Philo's citations is problematic because he regularly uses one Greek word to refer-

---

guage, see Jeffery M. Leonard, "Identifying Inner-Biblical Allusions: Psalm 78 as a Test Case," *JBL* 127 (2008): 241–65. Important discussions are currently being undertaken on the nature of paraphrase and intertextuality, including one's ability to differentiate paraphrase and citation. See, for example, Maren R. Niehoff, *Jewish Exegesis and Homeric Scholarship in Alexandria* (Cambridge: Cambridge University Press, 2011), 38–57; Richard A. Zaleski, "Both Literal and Allegorical: Paraphrastic Biblical Exegesis in Gregory of Nyssa's and Philo of Alexandria's *Lives of Moses*" (PhD diss., University of Chicago, 2020), 33–58. Paraphrase also constituted an important element in literary education. For examples, see Cicero, *De or.* 1.154; Theon, *Prog.* 1, 15; Quintilian, *Inst.* 1.9.2–3. See also Teresa Morgan, *Literate Education in the Hellenistic and Roman Worlds*, CCS (Cambridge: Cambridge University Press, 1998), 202–26.

14. To be clear, these two Greek words need to match exactly with the source text (as reconstructed) and do not include lexical variations (such as paraphrase). The two words include nouns, verbs, adjectives, and some particles (e.g., prepositions and negations) but not articles or conjunctions. References that lack an asterisk include instances where there are one or zero words/lexemes from the source text.

The two-word criterion is primarily for Philo's Greek texts. For texts extant primarily or exclusively in Armenian (i.e., *QG, QE, De Deo, De animalibus*), we have depended on quotation indications from the translators. For Philo's use of titles for scriptural books, including the Pentateuch (*Aet.* 19), see Helmut Burkhardt, *Die Inspiration heiliger Schriften bei Philo von Alexandrien*, 2nd ed., TVG Monographien und Studienbücher 340 (Giessen: Brunnen, 1992), 73–74, 136–37, preceded by B. Pick, "Philo's Canon of the Old Testament and His Mode of Quoting the Alexandrian Version," *Journal of the Society of Biblical Literature and Exegesis* 4 (1884): 126–43. For example, to reference the Psalms, Philo identifies them as "Hymns" (e.g., ἐν ὕμνοις εἴρηται or ἐν ὕμνοις λέγεται; see *Conf.* 52; *Migr.* 157; *Fug.* 59). See also Christiane Böhm, *Die Rezeption der Psalmen in den Qumranschriften, bei Philo von Alexandria und im Corpus Paulinum*, WUNT 2/437 (Tübingen: Mohr Siebeck, 2017), 100–103. In the index we note instances where Philo references the book as a whole with the entry "title."

Philo's citation practice assumes that his readers are acquainted with the Pentateuch. Rarely is the name of Moses mentioned prior to a citation or allusion, but most citations are simply introduced by the words "he says" or "it is said," if they are introduced at all. In contrast, Philo introduces the author of the Psalms as a "divinely inspired man" (ὁ θεσπέσιος ἀνήρ, *Plant.* 29; cf. *Spec.* 1.8) and "a member of the sacred band of Moses" (ὁ τοῦ Μωυσέως δὴ θιασώτης, *Plant.* 39). See Jutta Leonhardt, *Jewish*

ence a passage (e.g., referencing Jer 3:4 in *Cher.* 51 through the mention of παρθενία). Indeed, there are many instances in Philo's corpus in which he is clearly drawing upon and/or citing a biblical text but in a way that disperses words from his source text, namely using two or more words but separating them. A good example is Philo's use of Gen 11:30 in *Mut.* 143. Although there is a clear signal for the reader ("the Scriptures introducing…") and two words are cited (Σάρρα … στεῖρα), we have not marked this as a citation because the words are separated. This lack of citation mark is not meant to imply that Philo did not intentionally draw from Gen 11:30 or that he did not signal his use to his reader. Rather, the complexity of citation and determining its limitation is challenging. Setting the bar at two consecutive words is not ideal, but we thought that a consistent criterion was preferable to not having one.[15]

One challenge for anyone considering Philo's engagement with Scripture is ambiguity. This is a substantial issue for any intertextual endeavor, especially when discussing Jewish Scripture, as many verses in the Pentateuch are similar, sometimes identical.[16] For example, in *Agr.* 82 Philo quotes a phrase from Exodus, but the same words are found in Exod 15:1 and 15:21.[17]

Worship in Philo of Alexandria, TSAJ 84 (Tübingen: Mohr Siebeck, 2001), 148–49; David T. Runia, "Philo's Reading of the Psalms," *SPhiloA* 13 (2001): 111–12.

Philo also uses genre expectations as a means of signaling quotations, specifically the practice of introducing a lemma at the beginning of a commentary. For example, in *Leg.* 1.1 Philo does not introduce the initial citation of Gen 2:1. Similarly, *Leg.* 1.2 does not introduce the citation of Gen 2:2. Rather, the citation is formally signaled by the genre of the text and the silences around the citation's borders. For a discussion of ancient commentaries, see Sean A. Adams, *Greek Genres and Jewish Authors: Negotiating Literary Culture in the Greco-Roman Era* (Waco, TX: Baylor University Press, 2020), 92–110.

15. Our decision to mark citations with an asterisk is not meant to elevate citation over other forms of intertextuality (e.g., allusion, paraphrase, rewriting), nor does it imply that allusion is the norm for Philo. Rather, the use of the asterisk for citations is for convenience; there are fewer citations than allusions.

16. E.g., the Ten Commandments in Deut 5:6–21 and Exod 20:1–17. Another example is Isa 48:22 and 57:21, the words of which are cited in *Mut.* 169. Here Naomi Cohen has rightly argued that Isa 57:21 is to be preferred as the likely source, but we have included both for consistency. See Naomi G. Cohen, *Philo's Scriptures: Citations from the Prophets and Writings; Evidence for a Haftarah Cycle in Second Temple Judaism*, JSJSup 123 (Leiden: Brill, 2007), 84–85.

17. This overlap is not noted by Colson. Geljon and Runia note it in Philo's dif-

Agr. 82
ἔστι δὲ τοιόσδε· <u>ᾄσωμεν τῷ κυρίῳ, ἐνδόξως γὰρ δεδόξασται· ἵππον</u>
<u>καὶ ἀναβάτην ἔρριψεν εἰς θάλασσαν·</u>
It is of this sort: "Let us sing unto the Lord, for gloriously he has
been glorified; horse and rider he threw into the sea."

Exod 15:1
τότε ᾖσεν Μωυσῆς καὶ οἱ υἱοὶ Ἰσραὴλ τὴν ᾠδὴν ταύτην τῷ θεῷ καὶ
εἶπαν λέγοντες <u>ᾄσωμεν τῷ κυρίῳ, ἐνδόξως γὰρ δεδόξασται· ἵππον</u>
<u>καὶ ἀναβάτην ἔρριψεν εἰς θάλασσαν.</u>
The Moses and the sons of Israel sang this song to God and said,
"Let us sing unto the Lord, for gloriously he has been glorified;
horse and rider he threw into the sea."

Exod 15:21
ἐξῆρχεν δὲ αὐτῶν Μαριὰμ λέγουσα <u>ᾄσωμεν τῷ κυρίῳ, ἐνδόξως γὰρ</u>
<u>δεδόξασται· ἵππον καὶ ἀναβάτην ἔρριψεν εἰς θάλασσαν.</u>
And Miriam took their lead, saying "Let us sing unto the Lord,
for gloriously he has been glorified; horse and rider he threw into
the sea."

This lexical overlap poses a challenge for scholars seeking to tally the
number of allusions and citations within an author's corpus. Another
example is the substantial overlap between Exod 31:2–4 and 35:30–31,
the former of which is cited (almost) exactly by Philo (*Gig.* 23, 27, and
47; *Plant.* 26–27). The way that Allenbach treats this overlap implies that
there are two quotations rather than one. This practice creates a numeri-
cal problem for modern scholars but was not an issue for ancient authors.

ferentiation in *Agr.* 80 and their translation on *Agr.* 82 but not in the commentary on
that verse. See Albert C. Geljon and David T. Runia, *Philo of Alexandria, On Cultivation: Introduction, Translation, and Commentary*, PACS 4 (Leiden: Brill, 2013), 177.
In *Agr.* 82, Philo assigns the song to both choirs, which minimizes the ambiguity of
reference and indicates his intention to reference both verses, a "double reference."
The hymn is also referenced in *Leg.* 2.102 (although this passage specifically mentions
Moses, which would incline the reader to identify Exod 15:1 as the text alluded to and
so resolve the possible ambiguity) and *Somn.* 2.269 (which makes no specification and
so has maximum ambiguity). Another example is the overlap between Lev 17:11 and
14 (ἡ γὰρ ψυχὴ πάσης σαρκὸς αἷμα αὐτοῦ ἐστιν), cited in *Det.* 80. Here Philo marks the
ambiguity of his reference with the adverb πολλαχοῦ.

Rather, it is a distinctive element of intertextual signaling that an author could exploit.[18] The way that our first index is organized allows for multiple citations/allusions to be grouped in order to show the possible impact of Philo's compositional practice. In the second index, the overlap will appear as separate entries. This could lead to errors when attempting to tally the number of times Philo cites or alludes to a specific biblical book (discussed below).[19]

Sometimes Philo uses legal phrases from the Pentateuch that could activate a number of intertextual passages. For example, in *Leg.* 1.107 Philo states that Moses "says 'by death dying'" (λέγῃ θανάτῳ ἀποθανεῖν), a phrase that does not specifically align with any phrase in the Pentateuch but is a variant of the Greek rendering of a Hebrew infinitive absolute. The discussion is in the context of Gen 2:17 (θανάτῳ ἀποθανεῖσθε) but could be thought to include similar renderings, such as θανάτῳ θανατούσθω (Exod 21:12 and passim). In these cases, we have limited our index to only the first reference (Gen 2:17) because of contextual constraints and the closer similarity of language. However, we recognize that additional connections could be made by readers both modern and ancient.

The nature of Philo's use of Scripture is complex, and identifying allusions can be challenging. For instance, should one identify a scriptural allusion in a passage when Philo makes an allusion to Scripture on that topic in a different treatise? A concrete example of this is Philo's declaration in *Virt.* 6 that the virtuous person will be supplied with the "wealth of nature" (τῆς φύσεως ... πλοῦτον). In this section there is not a clear allusion to Scripture. However, in his parallel discussion in *Somn.* 1.124–226, Philo explicitly alludes to Gen 28:20. The attentive reader of Philo (cf. *Virt.* 17) will make this connection, but it might not be clear from the localized context. To avoid overcomplication, we decided not to pursue or include serial allusions/citations in this project. The interconnectivity of Philo's corpus, however, lends itself to seeing such connections, and through subsequent studies new allusions can be added to this tool.

---

18. See Don Fowler, "On the Shoulders of Giants: Intertextuality and Classical Studies," *Materiali e discussioni per l'analisi dei testi classici* 39 (1997): 13–34, esp. 16 and the possibility of one-to-one or one-to-many intertextual connections.

19. E.g., Gregory E. Sterling, "The People of the Covenant or the People of God: Exodus in Philo of Alexandria," in *The Book of Exodus: Composition, Reception, and Interpretation*, ed. Thomas B. Dozeman, Craig A. Evans, and Joel N. Lohr, VTSup 164 (Leiden: Brill, 2014), 404–39, esp. 412.

Another challenge of indicating passages alluded to and cited is specificity. In the following lists we provide the full range of verses when a
whole story is referenced as well as specific verses referenced or quoted.
Indeed, Philo does not need to use many words to create a textual connection but can refer to an event or story in a single word. Both specificity
and generality can be present in a section. For example, in *Det.* 14 Philo
references Abraham's defeat of the kings (Gen 14:1–16) but specifically
discusses Abraham's three-hundred-plus servants (14:14). As a result, the
entry in the first index reads: Gen 14:1–16, 14. Both entries are included
in the second index, resulting in an inflated number of citations/allusions
attributed to each book.

We decided to be inclusive in two other regards. First, passages that
contain allusions to or citations of Scripture but are thought by scholars to
be interpolations into Philo's text are included but placed in square brack-
ets (e.g., *Virt.* 208, Gen 27:[16], [23]). Second, we have kept references to
Sirach and Wisdom of Solomon in the index.[20] Scholars have rightfully
identified content or contextual overlap, but we are not always convinced
that Philo alluded to them intentionally. Nevertheless, we retain them in
order to facilitate subsequent research and have not made localized judg-
ments.

Although we think this volume makes an important contribution, we
recognize that this index is an artificial separation of Philo's intertextual
practices. We would posit that Philo was an equally close reader of all texts
and did not differentiate his citation and allusion practices based on the
sacredness of the text under consideration. However, this is not part of
the argument of this work. Rather, this index can contribute to the debate
by making comparisons more accessible. As a result, the fullest picture
of Philo's practice of allusions and citations necessitates the combination
of this index with those produced by others on Philo's use of "secular" or
nonscriptural texts.[21] Accordingly, we direct the reader to use this index in
conjunction with those of his nonscriptural texts.

---

20. For other possible parallels to the deuterocanonical books, derived from the
edition of Thomas Mangey, see Ryle, *Philo and Holy Scripture*, 303–5. See also Thomas
Mangey, *Philonis Judaei opera quae reperiri potuerunt omnia*, 2 vols. (London: William
Humphrey, 1742).

21. See Earp, "Indices," 269–433 (index of names) and 434–86 (translators'
notes); Leisegang, *Indices*, 3–26 (*index nominum*); David Lincicum, "A Preliminary
Index to Philo's Non-biblical Citations and Allusions," *SPhiloA* 25 (2013): 139–67;

Overall, we have identified 2,203 citations and 5,628 allusions, for a total of 7,831 intertextual biblical references (see table 1). These numbers are a fair representation, although one should recognize several caveats. First, allusions and citations are based on their placement within Philo's treatises and are constrained by modern section breaks. As a result, if an allusion is situated on both sides of a break, it is counted twice. Second, as discussed above, this number is inflated, since a word or phrase can activate multiple source texts. Third, these numbers differ, sometimes substantially, from previous tallies due to the adoption of different approaches. For example, Allenbach's index identifies 4,303 intertextual connections for Genesis, 1,755 for Exodus, 737 for Leviticus, 586 for Numbers, and 834 for Deuteronomy.[22] Allenbach's higher tally is a result of listing multiple allusions/citations for a Philonic section. Such additional information can be helpful, especially for Philo scholars, but it does raise the question of where the influence of an allusion ends and where a second allusion begins. We are not convinced that such a level of granularity was present in Philo's compositional awareness. As a result, we identify only passages in which an allusion/citation occurs. Another factor for higher tallies is that Allenbach regularly has two entries for allusions from *QG* and *QE* due to multiple extant versions. This also results in a higher number of references in these treatises. Our decisions result in a decrease in the number of Philo's references to Genesis and Exodus, especially because multiple instances were found in Philo's *QG* and *QE*. On the other hand, the number of explicit links to Leviticus, Numbers, and Deuteronomy—works for which Philo did not compose a questions-and-answers treatise—are slightly higher in this index than Allenbach's. The reason for this is not clear, although it is likely to be because scholars continue to identify new possible allusions, and these have been incorporated in this index.

A second difference between this work and Allenbach's is that we combine ranges of allusions into one entry. To illustrate: Allenbach iden-

---

Erkki Koskenniemi, *Greek Writers and Philosophers in Philo and Josephus: A Study of Their Secular Education and Educational Ideals*, SPhA 9 (Leiden: Brill, 2019); James R. Royse, "Some Overlooked Classical References in Philo," *SPhiloA* 32 (2020): 249–55.

22. These tallies from Allenbach et al. were provided by Gregory E. Sterling, "When the Beginning Is the End: The Place of Genesis in the Commentaries of Philo of Alexandria," in *The Book of Genesis: Composition, Reception, and Interpretation*, ed. Craig A. Evans, Joel N. Lohr, and David L. Petersen, VTSup 152 (Leiden: Brill, 2012), 436–38; and Sterling, "People of the Covenant," 410.

tifies allusions to Gen 1:1, 2, and 3 in *Opif.* 29. We agree, but instead of having these as three separate entries we combine them into one entry: Gen 1:1–3.[23] Given that Philo's Bible did not have the verse differentiations common today, we think that a range sufficiently communicates the content without inflating the numbers.

Table 1: Quotations and Allusions in Philo's Corpus

	Quotations	Allusions	Total
Genesis	1,297	2,399	3,696
Exodus	413	1,191	1,604
Leviticus	119	644	763
Numbers	128	517	645
Deuteronomy	188	672	860
Joshua[24]	0	4	4
Judges	1	5	6
1 Kingdoms	12	21	33
3 Kingdoms	1	6	7
4 Kingdoms	0	2	2
1 Chronicles	0	16	16
2 Chronicles	0	2	2
Esther	0	1	1
Job	1	6	7
Psalms[25]	21	30	51

---

23. In contrast, when completing our scriptural index, we did not condense the Philonic ranges but gave them separately. This was primarily to allow for the differentiation between citation and allusion. For example, there are allusions to Gen 2:8 identified in *Leg.* 1.45 and 1.46 but a citation in *Leg.* 1.47. An entry of *Leg.* 1.45–47 would not allow for differentiation, so we decided to leave all identifications as individual entries.

24. For nonpentateuchal citations, see Burkhardt, *Die Inspiration heiliger Schriften*, 134–37.

25. For other tallies of Psalms quotations in Philo, see Runia, "Philo's Reading of the Psalms," 104–9, who counts twenty citations of Psalms (two are combined in *Migr.* 157); Böhm, *Die Rezeption der Psalmen*, 86–91.

	Quotations	Allusions	Total
Proverbs	5	22	27
Ecclesiastes	0	2	2
Isaiah	8	17	25
Jeremiah	5	16	21
Ezekiel	0	7	7
Daniel[26]	0	1	1
Hosea	3	4	7
Zechariah	1	1	2
Wisdom of Solomon	0	32	32
Sirach	0	10	10
Total	2,203[27]	5,628	7,831

---

26. This allusion is cautiously proposed by Van der Horst, who recognizes that this would be the only identified allusion to Daniel in Philo's corpus. See Pieter Willem van der Horst, *Philo's Flaccus: The First Pogrom; Translation, Introduction, and Commentary*, PACS 2 (Leiden: Brill, 2003), 239.

27. Compare with 1,161 biblical citations in Philo according to Burkhardt, *Die Inspiration heiliger Schriften*, 134.

Scriptural Citations and Allusions in Philo's Treatises

Quaestiones et solutiones in Genesin et Exodum		

	Quaestiones et solutiones in Genesin 1–4	1.25	Gen 1:27; 2:21–22*
		1.26	Gen 2:22*; Prov 31:10–31
		1.27	Gen 2:7, 22*, 24
1.1	Gen 1; 2:1–3, 4*	1.28	Gen 2:7, 22, 23*
1.2	Gen 2:5*	1.29	Gen 2:24*
1.3	Gen 2:6*	1.30	Gen 2:7, 25*
1.4	Gen 1:27; 2:7*	1.31	Gen 3:1*
1.5	Gen 2:7*	1.32	Gen 3:1*; 6:4
1.6	Gen 1; 2:1–3, 8*, 9	1.33	Gen 3:1*, 2–5
1.7	Gen 2:8*; 3:23–24	1.34	Gen 2:16–17; 3:1*
1.8	Gen 1:27; 2:7, 8*	1.35	Gen 2:16–17; 3:3*
1.9	Gen 2:9*	1.36	Gen 3:5*
1.10	Gen 2:9*	1.37	Gen 3:6*
1.11	Gen 2:9*	1.38	Gen 3:6*
1.12	Gen 2:10*, 11, 13–14	1.39	Gen 2:7, 20; 3:7*
1.13	Gen 2:11, 13–14, 14*	1.40	Gen 3:6, 7*
1.14	Gen 2:8, 15*	1.41	Gen 3:7*
1.15	Gen 2:16*, 17	1.42	Gen 3:6, 8*
1.16	Gen 2:17*	1.43	Gen 3:6, 8*
1.17	Gen 2:18*	1.44	Gen 3:6, 8*
1.18	Gen 2:18*, 19*, 20; 9:2–3	1.45	Gen 2:17; 3:6, 9*
1.19	Gen 1:20–25; 2:19*	1.46	Gen 3:12–13*
1.20	Gen 1:28; 2:19*, 20	1.47	Gen 3:1–6, 14–17*
1.21	Gen 1:28; 2:19*	1.48	Gen 3:14–15*
1.22	Gen 2:6, 19*, 20	1.49	Gen 2:18; 3:16*
1.23	Gen 1:5, 8, 10, 11–12, 24–25; 2:20*	1.50	Gen 1:29–30; 2:7; 3:14, 16, 17*–19, 17*
1.24	Gen 2:21*	1.51	Gen 2:7, 17; 3:6, 19*

1.52	Gen 2:7, 22; 3:20*	1.86	Gen 5:24*; Deut 34:5–6;
1.53	Gen 2:7; 3:20, 21*		4 Kgdms 2:11–12
1.54	Gen 3:22*	1.87	Gen 2:7; 5:3–29, 29*;
1.55	Gen 1; 2:1–4, 9; 3:6, 22*;		6:5–22, 9
	Exod 3:14; Num 23:19;	1.88	Gen 5:32*
	Deut 8:5	1.89	Gen 6:1*, 5–22; 41:25–31,
1.56	Gen 2:8–9; 3:17–19, 23*		47–49, 53–54
1.57	Gen 3:24*; Wis 7:26	1.90	Gen 6:3*; Exod 31:1–11,
1.58	Gen 4:1*		3; 35:31
1.59	Gen 4:2*	1.91	Gen 6:3*, 5–22; Num 8:24
1.60	Gen 4:3–4*	1.92	Gen 6:4*, 12; Ps 89:7
1.61	Gen 4:1–3, 4–5*	1.93	Gen 2:7; 3:19; 6:6*
1.62	Gen 4:4–5*	1.94	Gen 6:7*
1.63	Gen 4:5*	1.95	Gen 6:7*
1.64	Gen 1:6–10, 11–13, 20–	1.96	Gen 6:5–6, 8*
	25; 4:7*; Deut 26:1–11	1.97	Gen 6:5–6, 9*
1.65	Gen 4:7*	1.98	Gen 6:11*
1.66	Gen 4:7*	1.99	Gen 6:12*; Isa 11:2
1.67	Gen 4:8*, 11–12	1.100	Gen 6:13*; Num 14:9*
1.68	Gen 4:8, 9*	2.1	Gen 6:14*
1.69	Gen 4:1–2, 8, 9*; Job	2.2	Gen 6:14*
	28:24	2.3	Gen 6:14*
1.70	Gen 4:10*	2.4	Gen 6:14*; 7:18; Exod
1.71	Gen 1:1–19; 2:6; 4:11*		25:10–13; 3 Kgdms 8:6
1.72	Gen 4:12*	2.5	Gen 6:15–16*, 19–21;
1.73	Gen 4:13*		Lev 25:8–17
1.74	Gen 4:1, 14*	2.6	Gen 6:16*
1.75	Gen 4:15*	2.7	Gen 6:16*; 7:17–23
1.76	Gen 4:4–5, 8, 15*, 16–24	2.8	Gen 2:7; 6:17*
1.77	Gen 4:8–15, 17–18, 23*, 24	2.9	Gen 2:19–20; 6:17*
1.78	Gen 4:4–8, 25*	2.10	Gen 6:9, 18*; 7:1
1.79	Gen 4:26*	2.11	Gen 7:1*
1.80	Gen 4:26; 5:1*	2.12	Gen 2:7, 9; 6:17; 7:2–3*;
1.81	Gen 2:7; 4:1, 8, 15–24, 26;		Lev 13:15
	5:3*, 6–32	2.13	Gen 2:2–3; 6:5; 7:2–3, 4*,
1.82	Gen 4:15–16; 5:22*		7, 10*
1.83	Gen 5:21–23*	2.14	Gen 7:4*, 12*
1.84	Gen 5:23*	2.15	Gen 7:4*
1.85	Gen 5:23–24*	2.16	Gen 1:3; 6:9; 7:1, 5*

2.17	Gen 1; 2:7, 16; 6:5; 7:11*; 8:1; Lev 23:5–8	2.48	Gen 7:1–4; 8:14, 15–16*
2.18	Gen 1:1; 7:11*	2.49	Gen 7:13; 8:14, 18*
2.19	Gen 7:16*	2.50	Gen 8:20*
2.20	Gen 7:17, 18*	2.51	Gen 1; 2:1–4; 6:17; 8:20*; 9:18–19
2.21	Gen 7:20*		
2.22	Gen 7:21*	2.52	Gen 8:20*
2.23	Gen 7:22*	2.53	Gen 8:20, 21*
2.24	Gen 7:23*	2.54	Gen 2:7; 8:21*; Num 23:19*; Deut 8:5
2.25	Gen 7:23*		
2.26	Gen 8:1*; Isa 51:2*	2.55	Gen 8:22*
2.27	Gen 6:9; 7:1; 8:1*	2.56	Gen 1:26–28, 31; 2:1–7, 5, 7; 6:9, 17; 7:1; 9:1–2*, 18–19
2.28	Gen 8:1*		
2.29	Gen 7:12, 19, 24; 8:2*, 3; Lev 13:23		
		2.57	Gen 9:3*; Lev 11:21, 42
2.30	Gen 7:11; 8:3*, 13	2.58	Gen 9:3*
2.31	Gen 1; 2:1–4; 6:9; 7:1, 11; 8:4*	2.59	Gen 2:7; 9:4*; Lev 17:11*, 14*
		2.60	Gen 2:20; 3:20; 9:5*
2.32	Gen 8:5*	2.61	Gen 3:19; 9:6*
2.33	Gen 6:9; 7:1, 11–12, 24; 8:3–4, 6*, 13–14	2.62	Gen 1:26; 9:6*
		2.63	Gen 9:11*
2.34	Gen 6:9; 7:1; 8:6*	2.64	Gen 7:11*; 9:11, 13–17, 16*
2.35	Gen 8:7*	2.65	Gen 9:18–19*, 22–27; Deut 32:49
2.36	Gen 8:7*		
2.37	Gen 8:7*	2.66	Gen 1:9; 2:7, 15; 3:23; 4:2; 8:16; 9:20*
2.38	Gen 6:9; 7:1; 8:7, 8*, 9; Lev 5:7; 11:13–19; 12:6, 8; Deut 14:11–19		
		2.67	Gen 2:6; 8:13–14; 9:20*
		2.68	Gen 9:21*
2.39	Gen 8:7, 9*	2.69	Gen 9:21*
2.40	Gen 8:8, 9*	2.70	Gen 9:22*
2.41	Gen 1; 2:1–3; 8:10*	2.71	Gen 9:22*
2.42	Gen 8:9, 11*	2.72	Gen 9:23*
2.43	Gen 8:11*; Isa 1:9*	2.73	Gen 9:24*
2.44	Gen 8:12*	2.74	Gen 9:18, 24*
2.45	Gen 6:9, 11; 7:1, 6; 8:13*, 14; 9:18–19; Exod 12:2*	2.75	Gen 1; 2:1–3; 9:26*
		2.76	Gen 9:27*
2.46	Gen 8:13*	2.77	Gen 9:22, 25–27
2.47	Gen 1:11–13; 7:11; 8:4, 13, 14*, 15–17	2.78	Gen 1; 2:1–3; 9:28*; Lev 23:15–16; 25:4, 8–10

2.79	Gen 5:32; 6:10; 10:1*, 2	3.35	Gen 16:7, 14*
2.80	Gen 9:27; 10:4–5*	3.36	Gen 16:14*
2.81	Gen 10:6*	3.37	Gen 16:15*
2.82	Gen 10:8*, 9*; 11:1–9	3.38	Gen 1:31; 16:16*; 21:4, 6;
3.1	Gen 12:1; 15:7*		Exod 7:7
3.2	Gen 15:8*	3.39	Gen 1:11–12; 17:1*; Lev
3.3	Gen 15:9*; Exod 29:36;		25:4, 10; Num 18:26, 32
	Lev 4:3; 16:5	3.40	Gen 17:1–2*
3.4	Gen 15:10*	3.41	Gen 17:1, 3*
3.5	Gen 15:10*	3.42	Gen 17:1, 3–4*
3.6	Gen 15:10*	3.43	Gen 17:5*
3.7	Gen 15:9–10, 11*	3.44	Gen 17:6*
3.8	Gen 15:11*	3.45	Gen 17:8*
3.9	Gen 15:12*	3.46	Gen 17:10–11*; Deut
3.10	Gen 15:11*, 13–14*, 14*		10:16*
3.11	Gen 15:15*	3.47	Gen 17:10*
3.12	Gen 15:16*	3.48	Gen 17:12*
3.13	Gen 15:16*	3.49	Gen 1:31; 2:1–3; 17:12*
3.14	Gen 15:17*	3.50	Gen 17:12*
3.15	Gen 15:17*	3.51	Gen 17:13*
3.16	Gen 15:18*	3.52	Gen 17:12, 14*; Num
3.17	Gen 15:19–21*		35:10–34
3.18	Gen 16:1*; 18:14	3.53	Gen 17:15*, 16
3.19	Gen 16:1*	3.54	Gen 17:16*
3.20	Gen 16:2*	3.55	Gen 17:17*
3.21	Gen 16:3*	3.56	Gen 17:17*; 21:33; Num
3.22	Gen 16:4*		18:26–29
3.23	Gen 16:5*	3.57	Gen 16:15; 17:18*
3.24	Gen 16:4–5, 6*	3.58	Gen 17:19*
3.25	Gen 16:6*	3.59	Gen 17:20*
3.26	Gen 16:6*	3.60	Gen 17:21*
3.27	Gen 16:7*	3.61	Gen 17:24–25*; Deut 16:16
3.28	Gen 16:8*	3.62	Gen 17:27*
3.29	Gen 16:8*	4.1	Gen 3:21; 18:1–2*
3.30	Gen 16:9*	4.2	Gen 18:1, 2*, 3–5, 8–10,
3.31	Gen 16:10*		13, 16; Exod 3:14
3.32	Gen 16:11*	4.3	Gen 18:2*
3.33	Gen 16:12*	4.4	Gen 4:13*; 18:2, 3*; Exod
3.34	Gen 16:13*		3:14; 19:22*

4.5	Gen 1:2; 18:4*	4.39	Gen 19:9*
4.6	Gen 18:2, 5*	4.40	Gen 19:10–11*
4.7	Gen 18:5*; 26:26	4.41	Gen 19:11*
4.8	Gen 18:2, 6–7*; 26:29–30;	4.42	Gen 19:12–13*
	Exod 3:14; 33:13*	4.43	Gen 19:14*
4.9	Gen 18:8*	4.44	Gen 19:16*
4.10	Gen 14:14; 18:2, 8*	4.45	Gen 19:17*
4.11	Gen 18:9*	4.46	Gen 19:17*
4.12	Gen 18:2, 10*	4.47	Gen 19:4–5, 17, 18–20*
4.13	Gen 18:10*	4.48	Gen 19:21*
4.14	Gen 18:11*	4.49	Gen 19:22*
4.15	Gen 18:11*	4.50	Gen 19:22*
4.16	Gen 18:12*; Exod 4:14*	4.51	Gen 2:8; 19:23–24*
4.17	Gen 17:17, 19; 18:12,	4.52	Gen 19:17, 24, 26*
	13–14*; 21:5–6	4.53	Gen 18:22–32; 19:27–28*
4.18	Gen 18:14*	4.54	Gen 19:29*
4.19	Gen 18:15*	4.55	Gen 19:30*
4.20	Gen 18:1–8, 2, 16*	4.56	Gen 19:31–32*
4.21	Gen 18:17*	4.57	Gen 19:37*
4.22	Gen 18:19*; Exod 3:14	4.58	Gen 19:37–38*
4.23	Gen 18:20*	4.59	Gen 20:1*
4.24	Gen 18:21*	4.60	Gen 12:13; 20:2*
4.25	Gen 18:22*	4.61	Gen 20:2*
4.26	Gen 18:23*	4.62	Gen 20:3*
4.27	Gen 18:24–32, 24*, 28*,	4.63	Gen 20:4*
	29*, 31*, 32*; Lev 25:10	4.64	Gen 20:4*
4.28	Gen 2:7; 3:19; 18:27*;	4.65	Gen 20:6*
	Wis 3:6	4.66	Gen 20:2, 4–6, 7*
4.29	Gen 18:24–32, 33*;	4.67	Gen 20:10–11*
	28:11–12; Exod 19:17–25	4.68	Gen 20:12*
4.30	Gen 18:1–2; 19:1*	4.69	Gen 20:16*
4.31	Gen 19:1*	4.70	Gen 20:17–18*
4.32	Gen 19:1*	4.71	Gen 23:1*
4.33	Gen 18:2–5; 19:2*	4.72	Gen 23:2*
4.34	Gen 19:3*	4.73	Gen 23:2–3*
4.35	Gen 18:6; 19:3*	4.74	Gen 23:4*
4.36	Gen 19:4*	4.75	Gen 23:4*
4.37	Gen 19:5*	4.76	Gen 23:5–6*
4.38	Gen 19:7–8*	4.77	Gen 23:6*, 7, 9

4.78	Gen 23:7, 8–9*	4.113	Gen 24:26*
4.79	Gen 23:10*	4.114	Gen 24:27*
4.80	Gen 23:9*, 11*; Exod	4.115	Gen 24:27*
	26:33	4.116	Gen 24:28*
4.81	Gen 23:11*	4.117	Gen 24:16, 29*
4.82	Gen 23:9*, 11*, 17*, 19*	4.118	Gen 24:30, 31*
4.83	Gen 23:19*	4.119	Gen 24:16, 25*, 31*
4.84	Gen 24:1*	4.120	Gen 24:34*
4.85	Gen 24:2*	4.121	Gen 24:35*
4.86	Gen 24:2*, 3–4	4.122	Gen 16:15; 17:15–16;
4.87	Gen 24:3*; Exod 5:2*		24:36*
4.88	Gen 11:31; 12:1–5; 24:2,	4.123	Gen 24:36*; 25:23; Deut
	3*, 4; 28:1		33:6*, 7*
4.89	Gen 24:5–6*	4.124	Gen 18:1–5, 6, 7; 24:16*,
4.90	Gen 24:2, 7*		18*, 20*, 28*, 46*
4.91	Gen 24:8*	4.125	Gen 24:48*
4.92	Gen 24:10*	4.126	Gen 24:49*
4.93	Gen 24:10*	4.127	Gen 24:50*
4.94	Gen 24:11*	4.128	Gen 24:50*
4.95	Gen 24:12–14	4.129	Gen 24:51*; Prov 19:14*
4.96	Gen 24:15*	4.130	Gen 24:52–53
4.97	Gen 24:15*	4.131	Gen 24:51, 55–56*
4.98	Gen 24:15*	4.132	Gen 24:8, 41, 57*; Num
4.99	Gen 24:16*		30:3*
4.100	Gen 24:16*	4.133	Gen 24:2, 58*
4.101	Gen 24:17*	4.134	Gen 24:59*
4.102	Gen 24:17*; Exod 16:16–	4.135	Gen 24:60*
	18, 31; Lev 12:8	4.136	Gen 24:61*
4.103	Gen 24:18*	4.137	Gen 24:61*
4.104	Gen 24:18*	4.138	Gen 17:17; 21:6; 24:62*;
4.105	Gen 24:18–19*		1 Kgdms 9:9
4.106	Gen 24:19*	4.139	Gen 24:62*
4.107	Gen 24:20*	4.140	Gen 24:63*
4.108	Gen 24:2, 21*	4.141	Gen 24:63*
4.109	Gen 24:18, 22*	4.142	Gen 24:64*
4.110	Gen 24:22*; Exod 23:19;	4.143	Gen 24:65*
	30:13–15; Lev 25:9–10	4.144	Gen 24:2–9, 66*
4.111	Gen 24:23*	4.145	Gen 24:67*
4.112	Gen 24:25*	4.146	Gen 24:67*

4.147	Gen 1:31*; 8:21*; 16:15; 17:17; 21:5-6; 25:1*; Ps 68:34*	4.179	Gen 26:3*
		4.180	Gen 26:3*
		4.181	Gen 26:4*
4.148	Gen 21:6; 24:67; 25:5-6*	4.182	Gen 26:4*
4.149	Gen 25:6*	4.183	Gen 26:4*
4.150	Gen 25:7*	4.184	Gen 26:5*
4.151	Gen 25:7*; Num 8:24-26	4.185	Gen 26:6*
4.152	Gen 25:8*	4.186	Gen 26:6, 7*
4.153	Gen 25:8*	4.187	Gen 26:2-3, 8*
4.154	Gen 25:20*; Deut 6:7; 11:19	4.188	Gen 26:8*
		4.189	Gen 26:12*
4.155	Gen 25:22*	4.190	Gen 26:12, 13*
4.156	Gen 25:22*	4.191	Gen 26:15*
4.157	Gen 25:23*	4.192	Gen 26:16*
4.158	Gen 25:24*	4.193	Gen 26:18*
4.159	Gen 25:24*	4.194	Gen 26:18*
4.160	Gen 25:25*	4.195	Gen 25:20; 26:19*, 20-35; 29:35; 30:17-18; Lev 19:24
4.161	Gen 25:25*		
4.162	Gen 25:26*		
4.163	Gen 25:26*	4.195a[1]	Gen 26:20-22
4.164	Gen 1; 25:25-26, 26*	4.195b	Gen 21:22-34; 26:23, 33
4.165	Gen 25:27*	4.195c	Gen 26:24
4.166	Gen 25:28*	4.195d	Gen 26:24
4.167	Gen 25:28*	4.195e	Gen 26:24
4.168	Gen 25:29-34, 29*	4.195f	Gen 12:7-8; 26:25; Exod 33:7-11
4.169	Gen 25:8, 29*		
4.170	Gen 25:30*	4.195g	Gen 21:22, 32; 26:25-26, 33
4.171	Gen 25:30*		
4.172	Gen 25:31*	4.195h	Gen 12:2; 26:29-30, 31
4.173	Gen 25:32*	4.195i	Gen 26:32-33; 29:35; Lev 19:24; Ps 18:8*
4.174	Gen 25:34*		
4.175	Gen 26:1*	4.195j	Gen 26:34
4.176	Gen 26:1*	4.195k	Gen 26:35
4.177	Gen 26:2*	4.196	Gen 27:1*
4.178	Gen 26:2-3*	4.197	Gen 27:1, 3*

---

1. The following ten entries (4.195a-k) are of the Latin version of *QGE*. For the edition, see Françoise Petit, *L'ancienne version latine des Questions sur la Genèse de Philon d'Alexandrie*, 2 vols., TUGAL 113-114 (Berlin: Akademie, 1973), 1:67-73.

4.198	Gen 25:25–28; 27:3–4*	4.227	Gen 27:34*
4.199	Gen 25:25–26; 27:5, 6*	4.228	Gen 27:33, 35*
4.200	Gen 24:15; 25:26; 27:8–	4.229	Gen 27:36*
	10*	4.230	Gen 25:24–26; 27:36–37*
4.201	Gen 27:11–12*	4.231	Gen 27:38*
4.202	Gen 27:6–10, 12–13*	4.232	Gen 27:1, 38*; 35:28; Ps
4.203	Gen 27:15*		64:2
4.204	Gen 25:25; 27:11, 16*	4.233	Gen 27:38*, 39–40; Exod
4.205	Gen 27:17*		2:23–25
4.206	Gen 25:25–27, 25; 27:11,	4.234	Gen 27:39*
	18–19*	4.235	Gen 27:39*
4.207	Gen 25:27; 27:20*	4.236	Gen 27:40*
4.208	Gen 27:20*	4.237	Gen 27:40*
4.209	Gen 27:21*	4.238	Gen 27:41*
4.210	Gen 27:22*	4.239	Gen 27:42, 43*
4.211	Gen 27:23*	4.240	Gen 25:24–26; 27:45*
4.212	Gen 27:23–24*	4.241	Gen 27:46*
4.213	Gen 27:25–27	4.242	Gen 27:46*
4.214	Gen 27:27*	4.243	Gen 28:2*
4.215	Gen 1:1; 27:28*	4.244	Gen 28:7*; Deut 21:18–21
4.216	Gen 27:29*	4.245	Gen 26:34; 28:1–5, 7,
4.217	Gen 27:29*		8–9*
4.218	Gen 27:29*		
4.219	Gen 27:29*		Unlocated Fragments from *QG*[2]
4.220	Gen 27:30*		
4.221	Gen 27:14, 31*	FR(M)16 = FR(P)3	Gen 6:6
4.222	Gen 27:18, 31*	FR(M)17 = FR(P)17	Gen 14:18,
4.223	Gen 27:18, 32*		20; Lev 27:30–33; Num
4.224	Gen 25:29–34; 27:32–33*		18:26–28
4.225	Gen 27:33*	FR(P)13 Deut 32:5*	
4.226	Gen 27:33*; Num 20:17*;	FR(L)8 [*QG* 2]	Gen 15:13
	21:22	FR(L)8 [*QG* 2]	Gen 16:1

---

2. Only a few of the unlocated fragments have identifiable intertexts, which is one of the reasons they are not able to be placed with confidence in the surviving books. The numbering from this section is taken from Marcus FR(M) with reference to fragments in Petit FR(P) and Lewy FR(L). See Harris, *Fragments of Philo Judaeus*, 69–72; Lewy, "Neue Philontexte," 23–84; Marcus, PLCLSup 2:234–37; Petit, *Quaestiones in Genesim*, 214–28.

2.43	Exod 24:12–13	2.77	Exod 25:33–36
2.44	Exod 4:15–16; 24:14	2.78	Exod 25:37
2.45	Exod 3:2; 24:16*	2.79	Exod 25:37*
2.46	Gen 1; 2:7; Exod 2:1–2;	2.80	Exod 25:38*
	24:16*	2.81	Exod 25:10, 23, 29, 31,
2.47	Exod 3:14; 19:18, 23; 24:17*		39*
2.48	Exod 24:16, 18*	2.82	Exod 25:40*
2.49	Exod 20:1–17; 24:18*;	2.83	Exod 25:10, 23; 26:1
	Num 14:32–35; Deut	2.84	Exod 26:1
	5:6–21	2.85	Exod 26:1
2.50	Exod 25:1–2*, 3	2.86	Exod 26:1, 3*
2.51	Exod 3:14; 25:7*	2.87	Exod 26:2
2.52	Exod 24:12, 16; 25:8*	2.88	Exod 26:1, 6*
2.53	Exod 25:9*, 11; Deut 10:5	2.89	Exod 26:18, 20, 28*
2.54	Exod 25:9–10	2.90	Exod 26:28, 30*
2.55	Exod 25:10*	2.91	Exod 26:31*, 33
2.56	Exod 25:11*	2.92	Exod 26:1, 31*
2.57	Exod 25:12*	2.93	Exod 26:18, 20, 32*
2.58	Exod 25:13	2.94	Exod 26:33*
2.59	Exod 25:15*	2.95	Exod 26:35*
2.60	Exod 25:16*	2.96	Exod 26:31, 36*
2.61	Exod 3:14; 25:16	2.97	Exod 26:32, 37
2.62	Exod 3:14; 25:17	2.98	Exod 27:1
2.63	Exod 3:14; 25:17	2.99	Exod 27:1
2.64	Exod 25:17–18	2.100	Exod 20:26; 27:1
2.65	Exod 25:19*	2.101	Exod 27:2*; Deut 14:4–5
2.66	Exod 3:14; 25:19	2.102	Exod 27:3*; Lev 23:10, 13;
2.67	Exod 3:14; 25:21*		Deut 26:2
2.68	Exod 3:14; 25:9, 15–17,	2.103	Exod 27:20*
	21*	2.104	Exod 26:33; 27:21*
2.69	Exod 25:9, 22*	2.105	Exod 27:21*
2.70	Exod 25:23*	2.106	Exod 26:33; 27:21*
2.71	Exod 25:28*	2.107	Exod 28:2*, 27, 39;
2.72	Exod 25:29*		29:29–30
2.73	Exod 25:30*	2.108	Gen 32:28*; Exod 28:7*
2.74	Exod 25:30*	2.109	Exod 28:9*, 9–12
2.75	Exod 25:31*	2.110	Exod 28:15*
2.76	Exod 25:32; Isa 35:1; Hos	2.111	Exod 28:16*
	14:6*	2.112	Exod 28:17*, 17–21

2.113	Exod 28:17–21, 20*	2.122	Exod 3:14; 28:32*
2.114	Gen 35:22; Exod 28:21*	2.123	Exod 28:33*
2.115	Exod 28:21, 26*	2.124	Exod 28:33–34, 36
2.116	Exod 28:26*		
2.117	Exod 28:12, 17–21, 27*		Unlocated Fragments from *QE*[3]
2.118	Exod 28:28*		
2.119	Gen 28:31; Exod 28:29*	FR(M)1 = FR(P)3	Exod 33:20
2.120	Exod 28:6, 30*, 31, 33	FR(M)6 = FR(P)1	Exod 21:13
2.121	Exod 28:32*	FR(M)15 = FR(P)22	Exod 13:2

The Allegorical Commentary

	Legum allegoriae 1–3	1.31	Gen 1:26–27; 2:7*
		1.32	Gen 2:7
1.1	Gen 2:1*	1.33	Gen 1:2*, 26–27
1.2	Gen 1:14; 2:2*	1.36	Gen 2:7*
1.3	Gen 2:2*	1.39	Gen 2:7*
1.6	Gen 2:2*, 3*	1.40	Exod 7:1*
1.16	Gen 2:2*	1.41	Gen 2:8*
1.17	Gen 2:3*; Num 6:2, 9, 12*	1.42	Gen 1:26–27; 2:7
1.18	Gen 2:2, 3*	1.43	Gen 1:1, 26–27; 2:8*;
1.19	Gen 2:4*		32:28, 30; Prov 8:22
1.20	Gen 2:4*	1.45	Gen 2:8
1.21	Gen 2:1, 4–5*	1.46	Gen 2:8
1.22	Gen 2:5	1.47	Gen 2:8*
1.23	Gen 2:5	1.48	Deut 16:21*
1.24	Gen 2:5*	1.49	Lev 13:3–4
1.25	Gen 2:5*	1.51	Exod 20:23*; Deut 16:21*
1.26	Gen 2:5	1.52	Lev 19:23*
1.27	Gen 2:5*	1.53	Gen 1:26–27; 2:7–8, 15*
1.28	Gen 2:6*	1.54	Gen 2:8
1.29	Gen 2:5–6	1.55	Gen 2:7–8, 15*; 3:23–24

---

3. Similar to the fragments from *Quaestiones et solutiones in Genesin*, only a few unlocated fragments have identifiable intertexts. The numbering from this section is taken from Marcus (M) with reference to fragments in Petit (P). See also Harris, *Fragments of Philo Judaeus*, 72–75; Marcus, PLCLSup 2:258–63; Petit, *Quaestiones in Genesim*, 279–306.

1.56	Gen 2:9	1.106	Gen 2:17
1.58	Gen 2:9*	1.107	Gen 2:17
1.59	Gen 2:9	2.1	Gen 2:18*; Isa 46:5
1.60	Gen 2:9*	2.3	Wis 14:8
1.61	Gen 25:26; 27:36; 42:36*	2.4	Gen 1:26–27; 2:7–8, 15,
1.62	Gen 2:9		18
1.63	Gen 2:10–14*	2.5	Gen 2:18
1.65	Gen 2:10*	2.7	Gen 2:18
1.66	Gen 2:11–12*	2.9	Gen 2:18*, 19*
1.67	Gen 2:11*, 12	2.11	Gen 1:24*; 2:19
1.68	Gen 2:13*	2.12	Gen 2:19
1.69	Gen 2:14*	2.13	Gen 1:24*, 27
1.72	Gen 2:14*	2.14	Gen 2:18–20, 22
1.74	Gen 2:11	2.16	Gen 2:7, 19
1.76	Num 12:12*	2.18	Gen 2:19
1.77	Gen 2:11*	2.19	Gen 2:7, 21*
1.78	Gen 2:12*	2.20	Gen 2:21
1.79	Gen 2:12*	2.22	Gen 2:25
1.80	Gen 29:35; 30:18; 49:15*	2.25	Gen 2:21
1.81	Gen 2:12; 35:23; Exod	2.26	Gen 2:21
	28:17–18*	2.27	Deut 23:13*
1.82	Gen 17:17; 21:6	2.28	Deut 23:13
1.84	Gen 2:12; 29:35	2.29	Deut 23:13
1.85	Gen 2:11, 13–14	2.30	Deut 23:13
1.86	Gen 2:14	2.31	Gen 2:21*
1.88	Gen 2:7–8, 15*	2.34	Gen 32:28, 30; Exod
1.90	Gen 1:26–27; 2:7–8,		12:23*
	16–17*	2.35	Gen 2:21*; Num 31:26*
1.92	Gen 1:26–27; 2:16, 20	2.38	Gen 2:21*, 22*
1.94	Gen 1:26–27	2.40	Gen 2:22–23*
1.95	Gen 2:16	2.41	Gen 2:23*
1.96	Gen 3:23*	2.44	Gen 2:23*
1.97	Gen 2:16*	2.46	Gen 30:1*, 2*; 31:34
1.98	Gen 2:16	2.47	Gen 29:31*
1.99	Gen 2:16; Exod 20:12;	2.48	Deut 21:15–16*
	Deut. 5:16	2.49	Gen 2:24*
1.100	Gen 2:17*	2.51	Deut 10:9*; 33:9*
1.101	Gen 2:16*, 17*	2.52	Lev 16:8*
1.105	Gen 2:17*; 4:1–2	2.53	Gen 2:25–3:1*

2.54	Gen 2:25; Exod 33:7*	2.97	Gen 49:17*
2.55	Exod 33:7	2.99	Gen 49:17*
2.56	Lev 16:2–4	2.101	Gen 49:18*
2.57	Lev 10:1–2, 5	2.102	Exod 15:1*, 21*
2.58	Lev 10:1–2, 5	2.103	Gen 49:17*; Exod 15:1, 21
2.59	Gen 12:1*; 26:2; 27:11; 29:23	2.105	Gen 3:1; 49:17; Lev 11:21*
		2.106	Gen 3:1*
2.60	Gen 9:21*	2.108	Gen 3:1
2.61	Gen 9:21	3.1	Gen 3:8*
2.62	Gen 9:23, 25–27	3.2	Gen 25:27*
2.63	Num 30:4–6, 10*	3.3	Exod 1:17*, 21*
2.64	Gen 2:25*	3.4	Gen 3:8; Exod 17:6*; Deut 4:39*
2.65	Gen 2:25*; 3:5		
2.66	Num 12:1–2, 14*	3.6	Gen 3:8*
2.67	Num 12:1, 7*	3.7	Lev 13:9–17; Num 5:2
2.68	Gen 2:25*	3.8	Num 5:2–3*; Deut 23:1–2
2.71	Gen 3:1*	3.9	Gen 3:8; 18:22–23*
2.72	Gen 1:27; 2:7, 22	3.10	Gen 18:23*
2.74	Gen 3:1	3.11	Deut 16:16
2.77	Num 21:4–5, 6*	3.12	Exod 2:15*; 5:2
2.78	Num 21:7*	3.13	Exod 2:15; 14:28
2.79	Gen 3:1; Num 21:8*	3.14	Exod 2:15
2.80	Num 21:9	3.15	Gen 25:26; 27:36; 31:21; 32:28; Lev 15:31*
2.81	Gen 3:1; Num 21:8*		
2.82	Gen 21:3, 6*	3.16	Gen 31:20–21*
2.84	Num 21:4–6; Deut 8:15–16*	3.18	Gen 31:20*, 21
		3.19	Gen 31:21*, 47
2.86	Exod 16:15; Deut 8:15	3.20	Gen 31:20, 23, 26*
2.87	Num 21:6, 9	3.21	Gen 31:26*, 27
2.88	Exod 4:1–5*	3.22	Gen 35:2; Exod 34:17; Lev 19:4
2.89	Gen 25:26; 27:36; 32:10*; Exod 4:2, 5		
		3.23	Gen 35:4*
2.90	Exod 4:3; 33:11	3.24	Gen 14:21, 22*, 23
2.92	Exod 4:3, 4*	3.25	Gen 19:37–38; 35:4*
2.93	Num 21:9	3.26	Gen 48:22; 49:8
2.94	Gen 30:5–6, 9–12, 17–18; 49:16–18*	3.27	Gen 18:17*; 31:26; 35:4
		3.28	Gen 3:8*
2.95	Gen 29:35	3.32	Exod 22:2–3*
2.96	Gen 30:5–6; 49:8–12	3.33	Exod 22:2

3.34	Exod 22:2	3.81	Gen 14:18; Deut 23:3–4*
3.35	Exod 22:3	3.82	Gen 14:18; Deut 4:39*
3.36	Deut 27:15	3.83	Gen 12:1
3.37	Exod 2:12*	3.85	Gen 17:17*, 19*
3.38	Gen 32:30; Exod 2:11; 3:14	3.87	Gen 17:17, 19; 21:6
3.39	Gen 15:5*; Exod 2:15	3.88	Gen 25:22, 23*
3.40	Gen 15:5*	3.89	Gen 25:23
3.42	Gen 24:7*	3.90	Gen 48:13–14, 19*
3.43	Gen 24:63*; Exod 9:29*	3.93	Gen 25:26; 27:36; 41:51;
3.44	Exod 9:29		48:14
3.45	Exod 17:12*; Num 20:25	3.94	Gen 41:51; Num 9:6–13
3.46	Exod 33:7*	3.95	Exod 31:2–5
3.48	Gen 3:8	3.96	Gen 1:27*
3.49	Gen 3:8, 9*	3.101	Exod 33:13*; Lev 1:1
3.50	Gen 3:9	3.102	Exod 25:9*, 40*; 31:2–11;
3.51	Gen 3:8, 9*		35:30–36:1
3.52	Gen 2:9	3.103	Num 12:1, 6–8*
3.53	Gen 3:9*	3.104	Deut 28:12*
3.54	Gen 3:10*	3.105	Deut 32:34–35*
3.55	Gen 3:7*	3.106	Deut 32:34–35
3.56	Gen 3:12*	3.107	Gen 2:9; 3:14*; Deut
3.57	Gen 3:12		27:17*
3.58	Gen 3:12*	3.108	Deut 27:18*, 24*
3.59	Gen 3:13*	3.110	Lev 27:33*
3.60	Gen 3:13	3.111	Gen 3:14
3.61	Gen 3:12–13	3.114	Gen 3:14*
3.64	Gen 3:12–13	3.118	Exod 28:30*
3.65	Gen 3:14–15*; Deut 19:17*	3.119	Exod 28:30
3.66	Gen 3:13*, 14	3.120	Exod 28:30*
3.68	Gen 3:14	3.123	Exod 28:30
3.69	Gen 38:7	3.125	Exod 28:30
3.70	Gen 38:7	3.128	Exod 28:30
3.71	Gen 38:7*	3.129	Exod 28:30; Lev 8:29*
3.73	Gen 38:7	3.130	Lev 8:15
3.74	Gen 38:6*, 7*	3.131	Lev 8:29
3.75	Gen 3:14	3.132	Exod 28:30
3.77	Gen 5:29; 6:8*, 9; 7:1	3.133	Lev 7:34*
3.78	Gen 6:8	3.135	Lev 7:34; 8:29
3.79	Gen 14:18	3.136	Lev 7:34*

3.137	Lev 7:34	3.182	Gen 3:15*
3.138	Gen 3:14	3.184	Gen 3:15*
3.139	Lev 11:42*	3.185	Gen 2:22; 3:15*
3.140	Lev 7:21	3.186	Exod 17:11*
3.141	Lev 9:14*	3.187	Exod 17:14*; Num 24:20*;
3.142	Exod 34:28*		Deut 25:19
3.143	Lev 1:9	3.188	Gen 3:15*
3.144	Lev 1:9*; 9:14*	3.189	Gen 3:15*
3.146	Gen 29:35; 30:5	3.190	Gen 25:26; 32:24–25
3.147	Lev 8:29; 9:14	3.191	Gen 27:36*
3.148	Num 5:27*	3.192	Gen 27:27, 36*
3.150	Num 5:27*, 28*	3.193	Gen 27:40*
3.151	Deut 23:12*	3.194	Deut 23:15–16*
3.153	Deut 23:13*	3.195	Gen 27:36*
3.154	Exod 12:11*	3.196	Num 28:2*
3.157	Deut 23:13*	3.197	Gen 14:21–23; 25:6; Exod
3.158	Deut 23:13*		18:26
3.159	Lev 1:9; 9:14; Deut	3.198	Exod 21:5*
	23:12–13	3.199	Exod 21:6
3.160	Gen 3:14*	3.200	Gen 3:16*
3.161	Gen 2:7*; 3:14*	3.203	Gen 22:16–17*
3.162	Exod 16:4*	3.204	Num 12:7*
3.163	Exod 16:4	3.205	Gen 22:16
3.165	Exod 12:4*	3.206	Gen 22:16*
3.166	Exod 16:4	3.207	Gen 22:16
3.167	Exod 16:4*	3.208	Deut 6:13*; 10:20*
3.169	Exod 16:13–16*	3.209	Gen 22:16*, 17*
3.170	Exod 16:14	3.210	Gen 22:17
3.172	Exod 15:8*; 16:14*	3.211	Gen 3:16
3.173	Exod 16:15–16*	3.212	Exod 2:23*
3.174	Lev 16:29–30; Deut 8:3*	3.213	Gen 19:26
3.175	Exod 16:15*; Num 14:4*,	3.214	Exod 2:23*; 3:9*
	23	3.215	Exod 20:24*
3.176	Deut 8:3*	3.216	Gen 3:16*
3.177	Gen 48:15–16*	3.217	Gen 17:15–16*, 17*
3.179	Gen 45:9*, 11*; 48:15	3.218	Gen 18:11–12*; 21:3
3.180	Gen 25:26; 27:36; 29:31*;	3.219	Gen 21:6*
	30:1*	3.220	Gen 3:16*
3.181	Gen 29:31; 30:22	3.221	Gen 3:16

3.222	Gen 3:17*		FR(H)	8 B10 Deut 30:15, 19

3.225	Num 21:27–30*
3.226	Num 21:27
3.228	Gen 15:6*; Num 12:7*;
	21:27
3.229	Num 21:28*
3.231	Num 21:29*
3.233	Num 21:28–30
3.234	Num 21:30
3.236	Gen 39:1
3.237	Gen 39:7*, 12*
3.238	Gen 39:11*
3.239	Gen 39:7*, 12*
3.240	Gen 39:12*
3.241	Gen 39:12
3.242	Gen 39:12; Num 25:7*, 8,
	12–13
3.243	Exod 1:17, 20*; 5:2*
3.244	Gen 16:1–2; 17:5
3.245	Gen 21:11, 12*
3.246	Gen 3:14*, 17*
3.247	Gen 3:17*
3.248	Gen 3:18*; Exod 22:6*
3.249	Exod 22:6
3.250	Gen 3:18
3.251	Gen 3:18–19*
3.252	Gen 3:19*
3.253	Gen 3:18, 19*

Fragments from (Lost) *Leg.* 4[4]

FR(H) 8 A4	Deut 30:15, 19
FR(H) 8 A14	Num 23:19
FR(H) 8 A15	Deut 8:5
FR(H) 8 B2	Num 23:19
FR(H) 8 B7	Num 16:5

De cherubim

1	Gen 3:23, 24*
3	Gen 16:6–9; 21:14
4	Gen 16:6; 17:5, 15; 21:10
5	Gen 17:15
6	Gen 16:9
7	Gen 17:5, 15; Isa 41:8;
	Wis 7:27
8	Gen 17:19; 18:11; 21:9–14;
	26:8
9	Gen 21:10*, 12
10	Gen 3:24; 17:5, 15; 21:10
11	Gen 3:24
12	Gen 3:23–24; 4:16*
14	Num 5:18*
15	Deut 16:20*
16	Deut 29:29*
17	Num 5:18*, 19–28
18	Gen 3:24; 18:22*, 23*;
	Num 18:2, 4
20	Gen 3:24
21	Gen 3:24
23	Gen 3:24
25	Gen 3:24; Exod 25:18–19;
	38:8
27	Exod 3:14
28	Gen 3:24
30	Gen 3:24
31	Gen 22:6*
32	Num 22:21–26, 29*
33	Num 22:21–26
35	Num 22:30–31
40	Gen 4:1–2*

---

4. Fragments taken from James Harris are signaled by FR(H). See Harris, *Fragments of Philo Judaeus.*

41	Gen 17:15; 25:20; 29:31; Exod 2:21–22		*De sacrificiis Abelis et Caini*
43	Gen 1:27–28	1	Gen 4:2*
45	Gen 21:1	2	Gen 4:1, 4
46	Gen 29:31–32	4	Gen 25:21–23, 23*
47	Gen 25:21; Exod 2:21–22	5	Gen 4:2; 25:8*; 49:33
48	Prov 3:13–14	6	Gen 35:29*
49	Exod 33:11; Jer 1:1–3; 3:4*	7	Gen 25:8; 35:29
50	Gen 18:11	8	Gen 1:1; 25:8; 49:33; Deut 5:31*; 34:5*, 6
51	Jer 3:4		
52	Gen 4:1, 8, 11; Jer 3:4	9	Exod 3:14; 7:1*; Deut 33:5
53	Gen 2:7; 4:1*	10	Gen 4:2; Deut 34:6; Isa 40:13
54	Gen 4:25*		
57	Gen 3:20; 4:1	11	Gen 4:1*, 2
58	Gen 2:18	12	Exod 4:10
60	Gen 2:23; 3:20	14	Gen 4:1–2
62	Gen 1:8, 10, 11–12, 24–25	17	Gen 25:25–26; 32:24–30
65	Gen 4:1	18	Gen 25:33*
67	Gen 31:43*	19	Deut 21:15–17*
68	Gen 31:43	42	Gen 25:23; 33:11*
72	Exod 21:5*, 6	43	Gen 16:1; 25:1, 5
74	Exod 15:9*	44	Gen 16:1; 25:1
75	Exod 15:9	46	Gen 30:36*
77	Exod 15:9*	47	Gen 30:36*
84	Num 28:2*	48	Gen 42:3; 47:3
85	Num 28:1–29:40	49	Gen 47:3
87	Gen 2:2–3; Exod 16:23; 20:8–10, 10*; Lev 26:2; Deut 5:12–15, 13	50	Exod 3:1*
		51	Gen 4:2; 46:34*; Exod 8:22*
90	Num 28:1–29:40	52	Gen 4:3*
96	Lev 22:19–20	53	Deut 23:22*
106	Gen 18:5–8; 21:2	55	Deut 8:12–14*
108	Lev 25:23*	56	Deut 8:17–18*
119	Lev 25:23*	57	Deut 9:5*
120	Lev 25:23	59	Gen 18:6
121	Lev 25:23*; Deut 21:14	60	Gen 18:6*
124	Gen 4:1*; Lev 25:23	62	Exod 12:39*
128	Gen 40:8*	63	Exod 12:11*
130	Exod 14:6–9, 13*	64	Gen 27:20*

66	Num 11:23*	126	Num 3:12–13
67	Exod 17:6*	127	Lev 25:32*; Deut 10:9
69	Exod 7:26–8:11; 8:5*, 6*	128	Lev 25:32; Num 35:1–6;
71	Gen 4:3*		Deut 19:1–13
72	Gen 4:3; Exod 23:19*	129	Deut 33:9
76	Lev 2:14*	130	Exod 32:26–28; 33:11;
77	Exod 33:11; Lev 19:32*;		Num 35:6; Deut 18:15–
	Num 11:16*		16; 19:4
79	Lev 26:10*	132	Num 8:21–22
80	Lev 2:14; Sir 2:5	133	Exod 21:13*; Num 8:21–
81	Gen 25:29		22; 35:6; Deut 19:4
82	Lev 2:14	134	Exod 12:29; Num 3:13*
83	Exod 36:10; 39:3	135	Gen 27:30, 36
84	Lev 1:6*	136	Gen 4:4; Lev 3:3–4
86	Lev 2:14; Num 11:8	139	Lev 4:11–12
87	Gen 4:4; Exod 6:7*; Lev		
	2:14; 26:12*		
88	Gen 4:3–4		*Quod deterius potiori*
89	Exod 13:11–13*		*insidiari soleat*
90	Exod 6:8		
91	Exod 6:8; 13:11	1	Gen 4:8*
94	Num 23:19*	3	Gen 31:4*
97	Exod 13:11–12*	4	Gen 31:2, 5*
101	Deut 1:31*	5	Gen 4:8; 37:13–17*
102	Exod 13:12*	6	Gen 37:3, 13, 15
103	Exod 13:12*	9	Gen 37:13*
104	Exod 13:12*	10	Gen 37:13*, 15
107	Num 15:19–20*	11	Gen 37:13, 14*
108	Num 15:20	12	Gen 37:14
110	Gen 22:1–14	13	Gen 23:6; 30:43; 37:13–14
111	Num 15:20; 28:2*	14	Gen 14:1–16, 14; 37:3
112	Exod 13:13*	15	Gen 37:14*
114	Exod 13:13*	16	Lev 14:37–42
118	Num 3:12–13*	17	Gen 37:14, 15*
119	Gen 32:28; 35:23	18	Deut 16:20*
120	Gen 27:18–29; 29:32;	19	Gen 37:15
	32:27–28; 35:10, 23; Num	21	Gen 37:15
	8:5–26	22	Gen 37:15
122	Gen 18:23–32; Lev 25:10	24	Gen 37:15*
		25	Gen 37:13, 15, 16*

26	Gen 37:36; 39:1; 40:1–4	74	Gen 4:10
27	Gen 37:17*	78	Gen 4:8, 10
28	Gen 18:11*; 37:15, 17*	79	Gen 4:10*
29	Gen 24:63*	80	Gen 2:7*; Lev 17:11*, 14*
30	Gen 24:65*	83	Gen 1:26–27; 2:7; Lev
31	Gen 24:65*		17:11, 14
32	Gen 4:1, 4, 8	84	Gen 2:7; Lev 17:11, 14
37	Gen 4:8	86	Gen 1:26–27; 2:7; Exod
38	Exod 4:10; 6:12; 7:11		33:18–23
39	Exod 4:14, 16, 19; 7:1	91	Gen 4:10*
40	Exod 4:14, 16; 7:1–2	92	Exod 3:14
42	Gen 4:8	93	Exod 2:23–24
44	Exod 4:14–16	94	Exod 2:23*
45	Gen 4:8; 27:41–45	95	Exod 2:24–25
46	Gen 26:2*; 27:41*	96	Gen 4:7, 11*
47	Gen 4:8*	98	Gen 4:11
48	Gen 4:8*, 10	100	Gen 4:11*
49	Gen 4:8, 10	103	Gen 4:4, 11; Num 19:15*
50	Gen 4:17–19, 23*	104	Gen 4:12
51	Gen 27:45	105	Gen 6:9; 7:1; 9:20
52	Gen 4:8; Exod 20:12*;	108	Gen 4:12; 9:20
	Deut 5:16	109	Gen 4:12
54	Gen 1; Prov 3:19; 8:22–23	112	Gen 4:12*; 9:20
57	Gen 4:8, 9*	114	Deut 32:13*
59	Gen 18:9*	115	Deut 32:13*; Sir 15:2–3
60	Gen 18:10; 21:1–3	117	Deut 32:13
61	Gen 4:9–14; 18:9–10; Job	118	Exod 16:31; Num 11:7–8;
	28:24		Deut 32:13*
62	Gen 4:9*; Num 8:20–22	119	Gen 4:12*
63	Num 8:24–26*	121	Gen 5:29*; 6:9; 7:1
64	Num 8:26	122	Gen 5:29*
65	Num 8:26	123	Gen 21:6*
66	Num 8:24–25, 26*	124	Gen 17:17; 18:12; 21:6
67	Deut 33:1, 8, 9*, 10*	126	Exod 4:14*
68	Gen 4:9; Num 8:24–26;	129	Exod 4:14
	Deut 33:9–10	130	Gen 4:12
69	Gen 4:8, 10*	132	Exod 4:14*
70	Gen 4:10*	135	Exod 4:14*
71	Num 23:7–8; Deut 23:6	137	Exod 4:14

138	Gen 4:26*	13	Exod 33:13, 18–23
139	Gen 4:26*; 5:1*; Exod 3:14	14	Exod 20:21
140	Gen 4:8, 12; Exod 4:14	16	Exod 33:13*
141	Gen 4:13*	17	Gen 22:3, 4*
142	Gen 4:13	21	Gen 4:5
144	Gen 4:13	22	Gen 4:16
146	Gen 4:13	24	Deut 28:65*, 66*
147	Num 30:10*	26	Deut 21:23*
149	Num 30:10	27	Gen 18:22–23*
150	Gen 4:13*, 14*	28	Deut 5:31*
151	Gen 1:20–25; 2:7	29	Gen 46:4*
152	Gen 1:20–21; 4:14	30	Gen 46:4; Deut 5:31
153	Gen 4:14	32	Gen 4:16
155	Gen 4:14	33	Gen 2:22–23; 4:17*
156	Gen 4:14*	34	Gen 5:4; Lev 18:9
159	Gen 12:1*, 7*; Exod 3:14	35	Gen 4:17
160	Exod 3:14*; 33:7*	38	Gen 4:8
161	Exod 3:14; 7:1*	40	Gen 4:17–18; 5:18, 21, 25
162	Exod 3:14; 7:1; Deut 33:1	42	Gen 5:3
163	Gen 4:14*, 16*	43	Gen 5:24
164	Gen 4:14*	44	Gen 4:18; 5:21
165	Gen 4:14–15	45	Gen 4:17; 5:3
166	Gen 4:15*	46	Gen 4:18; 5:25
167	Gen 4:15*	47	Lev 13:3
170	Gen 6:9, 13, 17, 19; 7:1, 2*, 7, 23	48	Gen 4:18; 5:25, 28–29; 6:9; 7:1; Lev 23:27
172	Gen 7:2	49	Gen 4:8, 17
173	Gen 7:2	50	Gen 4:17
177	Gen 4:15*; Exod 4:2–3, 6, 9; 7:9–12, 20	51	Gen 4:17
		53	Gen 11:4, 6–9
		54	Exod 1:11, 13
		56	Exod 1:11
	De posteritate Caini	57	Exod 1:11
		59	Gen 31:46–48
1	Gen 4:16*	60	Num 13:23*
5	Gen 4:16	62	Gen 23:9; 49:29–33; Num 13:23
6	Gen 4:16		
10	Gen 3:23–24; 4:16, 25*	63	Gen 32:30; Exod 4:22; Deut 21:17
12	Gen 4:16; Deut 30:20*		

64	Gen 2:2–3*	119	Gen 4:22
65	Gen 2:2, 4; 4:17	120	Gen 4:22
66	Gen 4:18	121	Deut 32:15*
67	Num 27:16–17*	122	Lev 26:11–12; Num 14:9*
69	Gen 4:18; Deut 30:19–20*	123	Lev 3:16–17*
70	Lev 16:10*	124	Gen 4:8, 19–22, 25*
73	Gen 4:18	127	Gen 2:6*
74	Gen 4:18	128	Gen 2:10*
75	Gen 4:19*	130	Gen 16:1; 21:19
76	Gen 11:29*; 28:2; Exod 6:23*	131	Gen 21:20
		132	Gen 24:16–20*
77	Gen 24:67; Exod 2:21	133	Gen 24:16
79	Gen 4:19	134	Gen 18:11*; 24:16
80	Gen 39:3	135	Gen 29:31
81	Gen 11:6*	136	Gen 24:16; Exod 19:24*
83	Gen 4:19–20	137	Gen 21:19; 24:15
84	Deut 27:17*; 30:11–13	138	Gen 24:18
85	Deut 30:14*	139	Gen 24:17, 18
88	Deut 27:17	140	Gen 24:18*
89	Deut 19:14*; 32:7–9*	142	Deut 15:8*
91	Deut 32:7–8	143	Exod 20:19*
92	Gen 32:30; Deut 32:9	146	Gen 24:18
93	Gen 4:20	147	Gen 24:17, 18–19*
94	Lev 27:33	148	Gen 24:19
95	Lev 27:32–33*	150	Gen 24:20
96	Gen 41:49*; Lev 27:32*	151	Gen 24:20
97	Lev 27:32	153	Gen 24:16, 20
98	Gen 4:20	155	Exod 15:23; 16:3
100	Gen 4:21	156	Exod 15:25; Num 14:3–4
101	Num 20:17	158	Exod 32:20*
102	Num 20:17; Deut 17:11; 28:14*	162	Exod 32:20
		163	Exod 32:20
103	Gen 4:21*	164	Exod 32:20
111	Gen 4:21	166	Exod 32:2–4
112	Gen 4:19–22	167	Deut 32:39*
114	Gen 4:22	168	Deut 32:39
115	Exod 5:2	169	Exod 33:18, 23*
116	Gen 4:22*	170	Gen 4:25*
117	Gen 4:22	172	Gen 4:25

173	Gen 4:25; 5; 6:9; 7:1; Exod 6:16–20	50	Exod 18:14*
174	Gen 6:9–10; 7:1	52	Lev 16:2, 34
175	Gen 4:25*; 19:30–32	53	Gen 6:1, 3
176	Gen 19:33*, 35–38	54	Exod 33:7; 34:31–32
177	Deut 23:3*	55	Gen 6:3*; Num 11:17
179	Gen 30:1, 2*, 24*	56	Gen 6:3; Deut 34:7
180	Gen 38:3–4, 9*	58	Gen 6:4*
182	Num 25:7	59	Exod 20:4; Deut 5:8
183	Num 25:8, 12–13	60	Gen 6:4
		61	Deut 33:1
		62	Gen 11:31

De gigantibus

		63	Gen 17:1*, 5; Deut 33:1
		64	Gen 17:1, 5; Num 20:17; 21:22; Deut 33:1
1	Gen 6:1*	65	Gen 2:24*; 6:4
3	Gen 5:28–32; 6:1, 5, 9; 7:1	66	Gen 10:8*, 10
4	Gen 9:20	67	Gen 6:4; 10:8
5	Gen 5:28–32; 6:1, 9; 7:1		
6	Gen 6:2*		

Quod Deus sit immutabilis

16	Gen 6:2		
17	Ps 77:49*		
18	Gen 6:2	1	Gen 6:4*
19	Gen 6:3*	2	Gen 6:3
22	Gen 1:2*	3	Gen 6:4
23	Exod 31:2–3*; 35:30–31*	4	Gen 6:4; 15:6; 22:2–10, 9
24	Num 11:16, 17*	5	1 Kgdms 1:19–20; 1:27–28
26	Num 11:17	6	Num 28:2*; 1 Kgdms 1:11*, 28
27	Exod 31:3; 35:31	7	Gen 22:8; 1 Kgdms 1:11
29	Gen 6:3*	10	1 Kgdms 2:5*
32	Lev 18:6*	11	1 Kgdms 2:5
34	Lev 18:6*	13	1 Kgdms 2:5
35	Lev 18:6*	14	1 Kgdms 2:5
37	Lev 18:6	15	Gen 6:4
39	Lev 18:6	16	Gen 38:9*, 10
40	Lev 18:6*	17	Gen 38:8
45	Lev 18:6*	18	Gen 38:8–10
47	Gen 6:3; Exod 31:3; 35:31; Num 11:17	19	Gen 6:4*
48	Num 14:44*	20	Gen 6:5–7*
49	Deut 5:31*		

21	Gen 6:6	109	Gen 6:8; Exod 33:17*
23	Deut 5:31*	111	Gen 37:36; 39:1, 20–21;
33	Gen 6:6*		Deut 23:1
34	Gen 6:6	113	Gen 39:20–23
49	Gen 6:6*	115	Gen 39:20–23
50	Deut 30:15*, 19*	116	Gen 6:9; 39:21; Exod 33:17
51	Gen 6:7*	117	Gen 6:9*
53	Num 23:19*	119	Gen 6:9; 37:2*
54	Deut 8:5*	120	Gen 37:2
60	Gen 3:8; 19:24; Exod 3:20;	121	Gen 37:2
	9:3; 15:8, 10, 12; 20:5;	122	Gen 6:9, 11*
	24:10–11; 34:14; Deut 5:9;	123	Lev 13:14–15
	29:20–21; 32:39–42	124	Lev 13:15*
62	Num 23:19*	127	Lev 13:11–13
68	Deut 29:20; 32:41–42	128	Lev 13:11, 13
69	Num 23:19; Deut 8:5	129	Lev 13:10–11, 14–15
70	Gen 6:7*, 8*	130	Lev 13:13, 16–17
72	Gen 6:7*	131	Lev 14:34–35*, 36*
74	Gen 6:8; Ps 100:1*	132	Lev 14:36
76	Gen 6:6–7; 7:21–22	133	Lev 14:36
77	Ps 74:9*	136	3 Kgdms 17:10
78	Ps 74:9	137	Gen 38:11, 18, 27–30
81	Ps 74:9	138	3 Kgdms 17:18*
82	Ps 61:12*; 74:9	139	Deut 33:1; 1 Kgdms 9:9
83	Ps 61:12	140	Gen 6:9, 11, 12*; 7:1
85	Gen 6:9; 7:1	141	Gen 6:12
86	Gen 6:8*	142	Gen 6:12
87	Num 6:2–21	144	Num 20:17–21
88	Num 6:5*	145	Num 20:17–20*
89	Num 6:9	148	Num 20:14, 17
90	Gen 6:8; Num 6:12	149	Num 20:17
92	Gen 27:20*	152	Num 20:17
94	Deut 6:10–11*	153	Num 20:17
95	Deut 6:10	156	Deut 28:12
96	Deut 6:11	157	Gen 48:15*; Num 20:17
99	Deut 1:43–44*	158	Num 20:17
100	Deut 1:44	159	Num 20:17
104	Gen 6:8*	161	Gen 18:23, 27
106	Gen 6:8	162	Num 20:17

164	Num 20:17	52	Ps 22:1*
166	Num 20:18*	54	Ps 22:1
167	Num 20:19*	56	Gen 37:2
168	Num 20:19	57	Gen 46:33–34*
169	Num 20:19*	59	Gen 46:34; 47:3*
171	Num 20:19	60	Gen 47:3
179	Num 20:19*	64	Gen 47:3, 4*
180	Num 20:14–21	66	Gen 46:34; 47:3
181	Num 22:22–35, 31*	67	Gen 4:2; 9:20
182	Num 20:17; Ps 90:11–12	78	Deut 20:1*
183	Num 22:22–35; 31:8*	80	Exod 15:1, 20
		82	Exod 15:1*, 21*
	De agricultura	84	Deut 17:15–16*
		86	Deut 17:16
1	Gen 9:20–21*	88	Deut 17:16
2	Gen 6:9; 7:1; 9:20	89	Exod 15:5; Deut 17:16
3	Gen 4:2	92	Deut 20:1
4	Gen 9:20	94	Gen 49:17–18*; Exod 15:1
5	Gen 4:2; 9:20	95	Gen 3:1, 20; 49:17; Num
8	Gen 1:26–29		21:8–9
9	Gen 9:20	96	Gen 3:1, 4–5; Num
10	Deut 20:20*		21:8–9
12	Deut 20:20*	97	Gen 3:20; Num 21:8–9
17	Gen 9:20; Deut 20:20	99	Gen 3:1; 49:17
19	Deut 20:20	100	Gen 49:17*
20	Gen 6:9; 7:1; 9:20*	102	Gen 49:17*
21	Gen 4:2*, 8, 11–12*	105	Gen 49:17
22	Gen 4:2; 9:20	106	Gen 49:17
26	Gen 4:2; 9:20	107	Gen 3:1, 15*; 49:17
27	Gen 46:34; 47:3	108	Gen 3:1
29	Gen 46:34; 47:3	109	Gen 49:17*
39	Gen 46:34; 47:3	122	Gen 49:17*
42	Gen 30:36*	123	Gen 49:18*
43	Exod 3:1*	124	Gen 4:2; 9:20; 46:34; 47:3;
44	Num 27:16–17*		49:17; Deut 20:1
48	Gen 46:34; Num 27:16–	125	Gen 9:20*
	17	127	Gen 4:3, 7*
50	Ps 22:1*	130	Lev 21:17–23; 22:18–25
51	Exod 23:20*; Ps 22	131	Lev 11:4*

De plantatione

111	Lev 13:12*, 13	24	Gen 14:17; Deut 25:18
112	Lev 19:23	25	Exod 23:2*; Deut 21:20
113	Lev 19:23*	27	Deut 21:20
114	Lev 19:23	28	Deut 21:21*
115	Lev 19:23	29	Deut 21:19–20
116	Lev 19:23	31	Prov 8:22–23*
117	Lev 19:24*	33	Deut 21:19
118	Gen 1:14–19	36	Exod 18:1
119	Lev 19:24	37	Exod 18:16*, 17–23
123	Lev 19:24	39	Num 10:29*
125	Lev 19:24*	40	Num 10:30*
126	Lev 19:24	41	Exod 18:11*
132	Lev 19:24, 25*	43	Exod 18:11
134	Gen 29:35*; 30:18*; 35:23	45	Exod 18:11
135	Gen 29:35; Lev 19:24*	47	Gen 29:26*
136	Gen 30:18	48	Gen 29:18
137	Lev 19:25*	50	Gen 29:26
138	Hos 14:9–10*	52	Gen 29:27*
140	Gen 6:9; 7:1; 9:20–21*	53	Gen 29:28
144	Gen 9:21	54	Gen 31:35*
155	Gen 9:21	60	Gen 18:11; 21:3
163	Gen 9:21	61	Gen 20:12*
169	Gen 21:5–6; 26:8*	62	Gen 18:12
170	Gen 26:8	65	Gen 20:12
		67	Exod 32:27–28*, 29*

De ebrietate

		69	Exod 32:27–28
		70	Exod 32:27
2	Lev 10:9; Num 6:2–3	71	Exod 32:27
4	Gen 9:21	72	Deut 33:9*
5	Gen 9:21	73	Num 25:7–8
6	Gen 3:10–11	74	Num 25:12–13
9	Gen 27:30*	77	Exod 5:2*
14	Deut 21:18–21*	79	Exod 14:27–28; 15:4–5
15	Deut 21:20	82	Gen 32:28*, 30
17	Exod 20:12; Deut 5:16;	84	Prov 3:4*; 4:3*
	21:20	85	Exod 25:10; 27:1; 28:4;
19	Exod 5:2*		30:1; 38:2, 22; 39:13
20	Deut 21:20	86	Lev 16:4, 23–24
23	Deut 21:20	93	Deut 21:20*

94	Gen 11:31; 21:3; 29:32–35; 30:18; 49:10; Exod 2:10; Num 35:6; Deut 21:20
95	Exod 32:1–6; Deut 21:18, 20
96	Exod 32:17–19*
98	Exod 32:17*
99	Exod 32:17*
100	Exod 33:7*
101	Exod 9:29*
104	Exod 32:17
105	Gen 14:17, 22–23*; Exod 32:18*
106	Gen 14:22–23
110	Gen 14:22–23
111	Exod 14:7; 15:1*, 4, 21*
113	Num 21:16–18, 18*
114	Num 31:49–50*
115	Num 31:49
118	Num 31:50*
120	Gen 27:20*
121	Exod 32:18
122	Exod 32:18
123	Exod 32:18*
124	Exod 32:19*
125	Exod 32:18
127	Lev 10:8–10*
128	Lev 10:8
129	Lev 10:9
130	Lev 10:9
131	Lev 10:9
132	Lev 10:9
134	Lev 10:9
135	Lev 16:2
136	Lev 16:34
138	Lev 10:9*
139	Lev 10:9
140	Lev 10:9

141	Lev 10:9
143	1 Kgdms 1:11*
144	1 Kgdms 1:20; 2:18
146	1 Kgdms 1:13, 14*
149	1 Kgdms 1:15*
150	1 Kgdms 1:15
151	1 Kgdms 1:15
152	1 Kgdms 1:15*
164	Gen 19:8, 26
165	Gen 19:31
166	Gen 19:33*, 35
203	Gen 19:33*, 35
208	Gen 40:1–3, 20–21
210	Gen 37:36*; 39:1*; 40:2–3*
213	Deut 23:1*
214	Gen 37:36; 39:2; 40:2
216	Gen 37:36; 39:1; 40:2
220	Gen 39:1; 40:2
222	Gen 19:11; Deut 32:32–33*
223	Gen 19:24; Deut 32:33
224	Gen 39:1; 40:2; Deut 32:32

De sobrietate

1	Gen 9:21, 24*
3	Gen 9:24
6	Gen 9:24
8	Gen 17:25; 21:2–3, 8–9, 14*, 15*, 16*
9	Gen 21:14
10	Deut 32:4–6*
11	Deut 32:5
12	Gen 29:16–17; 37:2; 49:22*
13	Gen 41:53–57; Exod 14:27–28; 15:1–18
14	Gen 37:2

15	Gen 49:22*	9	Gen 11:1, 7
17	Gen 24:1*; 25:7	13	Gen 11:7
18	Gen 24:1	15	Gen 11:1*
19	Num 11:16*	23	Gen 7:11*
21	Deut 21:15–17*	24	Gen 6:5*, 7
22	Deut 21:15*	25	Gen 6:17; 7:6
24	Deut 21:15	26	Gen 14:3*
25	Deut 21:17*	27	Gen 19:1, 4, 8
26	Gen 25:25–26, 33–34	28	Gen 19:1, 4*
27	Gen 48:13–14	29	Exod 7:15*
28	Gen 41:51–52; 48:13	30	Exod 7:15
30	Gen 6:9; 7:1; 9:21, 24*	31	Exod 7:15*; Deut 5:31*
31	Gen 9:25	33	Exod 7:15
32	Gen 5:32; 9:22, 25*	36	Exod 14:30
44	Gen 5:32; 9:22	39	Ps 30:19*
47	Gen 6:9; 7:1; 9:22, 25	41	Gen 42:11*
48	Exod 20:5*; Num 14:18*;	44	Jer 15:10*
	Deut 5:9*	49	Jer 15:10*
49	Lev 13:22–23*	50	Num 16:15*
50	Gen 4:7*	51	Jer 15:10*
51	Gen 9:25*, 26*	52	Ps title; 79:7*
53	Gen 9:26	54	Ps 79:7
55	Gen 9:26	55	Gen 25:2; Num 25:3;
56	Gen 18:17*		31:49*
58	Gen 9:26*	56	Exod 24:11*
59	Gen 9:27*	57	Num 25:7–8, 12
61	Gen 9:27	58	Exod 19:8*
62	Gen 9:27	60	Gen 11:2*
65	Gen 9:27; 11:10, 26; 32:1	61	Gen 2:8*
66	Gen 49:28; Exod 19:6*;	62	Zech 6:12*
	23:22	63	Jer 38:9; Zech 12:10
67	Gen 9:27	64	Gen 11:2
68	Gen 9:27; 49:22	65	Num 23:7–8*
69	Gen 9:27	67	Gen 11:2
		68	Gen 11:2

De confusione linguarum

		70	Exod 14:27*
		72	Exod 1:8*; Num 23:7*
1	Gen 11:1–9*	74	Gen 25:5; 31:32–35;
5	Gen 11:4		35:2–3*

75	Gen 11:2	132	Judg 8:9
76	Gen 11:2*	133	Gen 11:4
79	Gen 23:3, 4*, 8	134	Gen 11:5*
80	Gen 47:9*	138	Exod 17:6*
81	Gen 26:2–3*	140	Gen 11:5*
82	Exod 2:22*	141	Exod 23:1*
83	Gen 11:4	142	Gen 11:5*
84	Gen 11:3*	144	Deut 23:2*
87	Gen 11:3	145	Deut 14:1*; 32:6*, 18*
88	Exod 1:8, 11–14	146	Gen 1:27; 32:28, 31; Prov
91	Exod 1:11, 14		8:22
92	Gen 32:28, 30; Exod 1:14	147	Gen 42:11*
93	Exod 2:23*	148	Gen 32:32; Exod 24:7
94	Exod 4:23; 7:26*	149	3 Kgdms 15:11; 4 Kgdms
95	Gen 11:3; 37:36; 39:1; 40:1		18:3[5]
96	Exod 24:10*	150	Gen 11:6*
98	Num 23:19; Ps 98:5; Isa	152	Gen 11:6*
	66:1	154	Gen 11:4, 6*; Exod 22:28
99	Exod 24:10	155	Gen 11:5*, 6
101	Gen 11:3	156	Gen 11:4
102	Gen 11:3*	158	Gen 11:8*, 9
103	Gen 11:3*	159	Num 22:5–6; 23:1–24:25
105	Gen 6:9, 14*; 7:1; 8:18	160	Exod 21:14*
106	Exod 2:2–3, 6	161	Exod 21:14
107	Gen 11:4*	162	Gen 11:6*
111	Gen 11:4*	165	Gen 4:13*
113	Gen 11:4	166	Deut 31:6*; Josh 1:5
115	Gen 11:4	167	Num 19:15*
116	Gen 11:4*	168	Gen 11:7*
118	Gen 11:4*	169	Gen 1:26*; 3:22*
121	Gen 11:4*	173	Deut 4:19; 10:17*
122	Gen 4:15, 17	179	Gen 1:26*
124	Gen 4:2–4	181	Gen 48:15–16*
128	Gen 11:4; Judg title; 8:8–9	182	Gen 11:7*
129	Gen 32:30	183	Gen 11:7, 9
130	Judg 6:32; 8:9*	189	Gen 11:7*
131	Judg 8:9	191	Gen 11:7, 9

---

5. Although see the comment in Cohen, *Philo's Scriptures*, 107–8.

192	Gen 11:7, 9
195	Gen 11:7
196	Gen 11:8*
197	Deut 30:4*
198	Gen 11:9

De migratione Abrahami

1	Gen 12:1–3*
2	Gen 12:1
3	Gen 2:7; 3:19*; 12:1
5	Gen 28:17*
7	Gen 12:1
8	Exod 23:21; 34:12*; Deut 4:9
9	Gen 12:1
10	Gen 12:1
12	Gen 12:1
13	Gen 13:9*
14	Exod title; 1
15	Exod 2:23*
17	Gen 50:25*; Exod 13:19
18	Gen 50:24*, 25; Exod 13:19
19	Gen 37:36; 39:1, 7*, 12; 40:1, 8*
20	Gen 40:15*; 41:41*; 45:8
21	Gen 39:14*, 17*; 42:18*; 45:28*
22	Gen 45:1*, 2, 5, 7*, 8; 50:19*
23	Gen 50:26
25	Exod 12:11*
26	Gen 32:24
27	Gen: 31:3*
28	Gen 31:2
29	Gen 26:2*; 31:3
30	Gen 31:3
35	Gen 12:1

36	Exod 15:25*
37	Gen 2:9*
38	1 Kgdms 9:9*
39	Gen 32:28, 30
40	Gen 12:1
42	Gen 1:31*
43	Gen 12:1*
44	Gen 15:6*; Deut 34:1–3, 4*
47	Exod 20:18*, 22*
48	Deut 4:12*
50	Exod 20:18, 22
53	Gen 12:2
54	Exod 1:9*
55	Exod 1:9
56	Deut 4:6*, 7
58	Deut 4:6
59	Deut 4:7
60	Deut 7:7*, 8
61	Exod 23:2*
62	Deut 20:1*
64	Lev 11:42*
65	Lev 11:42
66	Gen 3:14*
67	Exod 33:11; Lev 8:21*, 29*
68	Num 14:11*, 12
69	Lev 11:42; Deut 23:1*, 2
70	Gen 12:2
74	Gen 4:8
75	Gen 4:8
76	Exod 4:10*; 7:10–12
78	Exod 4:14*
79	Exod 4:14*
80	Exod 4:15*
81	Exod 4:16*
83	Exod 7:12, 22, 8:3
84	Exod 4:16, 7:1*
85	Exod 7:12*; 8:14–15; 31:18; Deut 9:10
86	Gen 12:2*

88	Gen 12:2	149	Gen 12:4
94	Gen 25:5–6*	150	Gen 14:12
95	Gen 30:13*	152	Exod 12:38*
97	Exod 35:22*, 25–26	153	Gen 27:11*
98	Exod 30:19; 38:26	154	Gen 22:3*; Exod 12:38;
99	Gen 30:13; Num 21:30*		Num 32:13
101	Gen 27:28*	155	Num 11:4*
103	Gen 12:15–19; Exod	157	Ps title; 41:4*; 79:6*
	28:29*, 30, 32*	158	Gen 27:11
104	Exod 28:31*	159	Gen 50:7–8
105	Exod 21:10*	160	Gen 41:43*; 50:7*, 8, 19*
107	Gen 12:2*	162	Gen 42:15–16*; 50:8
108	Gen 12:2	163	Exod 12:38
109	Gen 12:3*	164	Gen 14:24*
113	Num 23:1–24:25, 23:19*,	165	Gen 14:24
	24	166	Gen 22:3, 8*
115	Deut 23:5*, 6	168	Exod 24:1*
118	Gen 12:3*	169	Exod 7:1*
122	Gen 12:3; 18:22–32; Num	171	Exod 33:15*
	14:20*	172	Exod 33:15
125	Gen 6:9; 7:1, 7–23; 8	173	Gen 18:16*
126	Gen 18:10*	174	Exod 23:20*, 21
127	Gen 12:4*	175	Gen 13:10–12
129	Gen 12:4	176	Gen 12:4*
130	Gen 26:5*; Deut 33:3*, 4	177	Gen 11:31–32
131	Deut 13:4*	182	Deut 4:39*
132	Gen 18:23*; Deut 10:20*	183	Exod 17:6*
135	Gen 1:31*	187	Gen 11:31
136	Job 38:4	195	Gen 12:4
139	Gen 22:3*, 4; Num	196	1 Kgdms 10:22*
	31:28*, 29	197	1 Kgdms 10:23*
140	Gen 21:7*; 22:9–12	198	Gen 12:4
141	Gen 21:7*; Exod 1:19*	199	Gen 46:27; Exod 1:5*
142	Num 28:2*	200	Gen 25:26; 27:36; Hos 12:4
143	Deut 25:17*	201	Gen 32:28, 30; Exod 24:1;
144	Deut 25:18		Deut 10:22*
145	Gen 29:16	202	Gen 50:3*; Num 7:13,
146	Num 20:17*		29:13*, 36*
148	Gen 12:4*	203	Gen 45:22*

204	Gen 47:24	33	Gen 15:2
205	Gen 41:51–52; 48:17–20;	34	Gen 15:2*
	Num 27:1	36	Gen 15:2
206	Gen 12:4; Num 27:3*	38	Gen 33:5*
208	Gen 27:43–45*	39	Gen 15:2–3
212	Gen 27:43	42	Gen 15:2
213	Gen 29:4*, 5*	43	Gen 31:28*
214	Gen: 30:30*	44	Gen 31:14–15*; Exod
215	Exod 1:21		4:27; 18:7*
216	Gen 12:4, 6*	47	Deut 21:15
219	Gen 12:6	49	Deut 21:15–17*
221	Gen 12:6; 49:15*	51	Gen 29:31*
223	Gen 12:6; 30:21	52	Gen 15:2
224	Gen 34:2, 25–27; Deut	53	Gen 3:20*
	23:17*	54	Gen 15:2
		56	Gen 1:27, 2:7; Lev 17:11*
		57	Gen 1:27*, 2:7*

Quis rerum divinarum heres sit

		58	Gen 15:1–2; Lev 17:11
2	Gen 15:1–3*	59	Exod 18:4*
4	Exod 4:10*	61	Gen 15:2
8	Gen 26:3–5*	62	Gen 20:12*
10	Deut 27:9*	63	Gen 15:2
13	Deut 27:9	64	Gen 2:7
14	Exod 14:14*, 15*	65	Gen 15:3
16	Exod 4:10; 6:12; 14:15	66	Gen 15:4*
17	Exod 19:19*	68	Gen 15:4*
19	Exod 14:15; 19:19; 20:19*	69	Gen 12:1*
20	Exod 5:22–23*; 32:32*;	70	Exod 3:14
	Num 11:12*, 13*, 22*	71	Gen 12:1
21	Exod 33:11*	76	Gen 15:4*, 5; Deut 28:12*
22	Gen 15:2*	78	Gen 12:7; 15:5; 32:28;
24	Gen 15:2		1 Kgdms 9:9*
25	Gen 15:1; Exod 4:12*;	80	Num 11:5–6*
	Isa 50:4*	81	Gen 15:5
26	Gen 12:1; 15:1	82	Gen 15:5
27	Gen 15:2	83	Deut 13:6*
29	Gen 18:27	84	Lev 16:17*
30	Gen 18:23, 27*	85	Gen 12:1; 15:5
31	Gen 15:2	87	Gen 15:5*

90	Gen 15:6*	165	Gen 1:5–31, 5*; 8:22*
94	Gen 15:6*	166	Exod 25:21*
95	Gen 15:6	167	Exod 32:15, 16*
96	Gen 12:1; 15:7*	168	Exod 20:3–17; Deut
99	Gen 15:6		5:7–21
100	Gen 15:8*	169	Exod 20:3–5; Deut 5:7–9
101	Gen 15:6	170	Exod 20:7–11; Deut
102	Gen 15:9*		5:11–15
104	Gen 15:9	171	Exod 20:12; Deut 5:16
106	Gen 15:9*	172	Exod 20:13–17; Deut
108	Gen 15:9		5:17–21
110	Gen 15:9	174	Exod 29:38–39*; Lev
112	Gen 15:9*; Exod 26		6:20*; 24:5–6
113	Exod 25:1–2*; Lev 16:16*;	175	Gen 35:23–36; Lev 24:5–6
	Num 23:19	176	Exod 28:9–12*
117	Exod 13:1–2*; 25:2	177	Deut 27:11–13*
118	Exod 13:2	179	Lev 16:7–10, 8*
120	Num 31:28*	180	Gen 30:42*
122	Gen 1:1; 2:1–2*	182	Exod 24:6*
123	Exod 25:2	184	Gen 2:7; Exod 24:6
124	Num 3:12*; Deut 10:8–9;	186	Exod 21:5*; 30:12–13*
	33:9	187	Lev 16:8
125	Gen 15:9	189	Exod 30:15*
127	Gen 15:9	191	Exod 16:16, 18*
128	Exod 1:15*	193	Exod 12:4*
129	Gen 15:10*	194	Num 35:8*
131	Exod 36:10*	195	Lev 6:40*; Num 7
132	Gen 15:10	196	Exod 30:34–35*
135	Gen 1:10	198	Exod 30:34
139	Gen 1:20–21, 24–25, 27	199	Exod 30:35; Lev 6:20
141	Gen 15:10	201	Num 16:47–48*
143	Gen 15:10	203	Exod 14:19–20*
146	Gen 1:5, 10; 15:10	204	Gen 7:17*
157	Deut 1:17*	206	Deut 5:5*
159	Gen 1:31*	207	Gen 15:10*
162	Lev 19:35–36*; Deut	213	Gen 15:10
	25:13–16*	216	Exod 25:31, 36*; 38:13–15
163	Gen 1:4–5*; Deut 25:16	218	Exod 38:15–17*
164	Gen 1:27*	219	Exod 38:14–15, 17

220	Exod 38:14–17	274	Gen 15:14
221	Exod 38:17	275	Gen 15:15*
225	Exod 25:31; 38:17	277	Gen 12:1–2*; 15:7, 15*
226	Exod 25:22–31; 30:34*;	278	Gen 12:2
	37: 25[MT]; 38:12–13;	279	Lev 26:10*
	Lev 24:5–6; Num 4:7	280	Gen 15:15
227	Exod 25:22, 30–31; 30:1–	281	Gen 15:15
	2; 37:10[MT], 25[MT]	284	Gen 15:15
230	Gen 15:10*	285	Gen 15:15
231	Gen 1:27*	286	Gen 14:13–16
233	Gen 15:10	287	Gen 12:4–5, 10*
234	Gen 15:9	288	Gen 14:13–16; 15:15
237	Gen 15:10, 11*	290	Gen 15:15; Ps 83:11*;
239	Lev 11:21*		Wis 4:8
240	Gen 15:11	291	Gen 15:15; 25:7–8
242	Gen 15:11	293	Gen 15:16*
243	Gen 15:11*	296	Gen 8:21*; Exod 22:6*
247	Gen 15:11	298	Gen 15:16
249	Gen 15:12*	299	Gen 15:16*
250	Deut 28:28–29*	300	Gen 15:16
251	Gen 27:33*; 45:26*; Exod	302	Gen 15:16
	19:18*; Lev 9:1, 24*	303	Exod 28:30*; Lev 8:8
252	Gen 25:26; 27:5, 33, 36;	304	Gen 15:16
	Hos 12:4	306	Gen 15:16
254	Gen 27:33	307	Gen 15:17*
255	Gen 43:8, 10*; Exod	308	Gen 15:16, 17*
	5:6–14, 6*; 12:11*	309	Lev 10:2*
256	Gen 45:26*	310	Gen 15:17
257	Gen 2:21*, 22	311	Gen 15:17
258	Gen 15:12; 20:2–3, 7*	312	Gen 15:17*
260	Gen 6:9; 7:1; 9:25–27	313	Gen 15:7, 18*
261	Gen 49:1*	315	Gen 15:18*
262	Num 12:6–8*; Deut 34:10*		
263	Gen 15:12		*De congressu eruditionis gratia*
265	Gen 15:12		
266	Gen 15:3*, 13	1	Gen 16:1–2*
268	Gen 15:13	2	Gen 16:1
272	Gen 15:14*	3	Gen 16:1; 17:16; Exod 1:19
273	Lev 25:10	6	Gen 16:1–2

7	Gen 29:31; 30:22	63	Gen 16:2*
8	Exod 25:31, 37, 40; Num 8:3	68	Gen 16:2*
		69	Gen 16:2
9	Gen 16:1	70	Gen 28:6, 7*
11	Gen 16:1	71	Gen 16:3*
12	Gen 16:2*	73	Gen 16:3
13	Gen 16:1, 2*	78	Gen 16:3
14	Gen 16:2*	81	Gen 16:3*
20	Gen 16:1	83	Gen 16:3
21	Gen 16:1	85	Gen 16:3
22	Gen 16:1	86	Lev 18:1–5*
23	Gen 16:3	87	Lev 18:4–5
25	Gen 29:23, 28	88	Gen 16:3*
26	Gen 29:23, 28	89	Exod 12:3; 22:29–30; 26:1–37; Lev 23:13, 17, 27; 25:9–10
30	Gen 29:24, 29		
31	Gen 29:23, 28		
33	Gen 29:24, 29	90	Gen 2:7; 5:28–29; 6:9; 7:1
34	Gen 11:29; 16:3; 24:67; 25:1; 29:23, 28; 30:4, 9	92	Gen 14:1–2, 13–16
		93	Gen 14:20
36	Gen 24:67	94	Lev 27:32*
40	Gen 41:51–52	95	Lev 27:30*, 32*
41	Gen 46:20; 1 Chr 7:14, 23	96	Lev 27:30, 32
42	1 Chr 7:14	98	Num 3:12, 45; 8:16–18
43	Gen 22:23–24; 46:20*; 1 Chr 7:14	99	Gen 14:19, 20*; 28:22*
		100	Exod 16:32–34, 36*
45	Gen 22:20–24	101	Gen 28:20–22
48	Gen 11:27, 31; 22:23	102	Exod 29:40
49	Gen 11:31	103	Lev 6:20
50	Gen 11:29; 22:23	105	Lev 6:20
51	Gen 22:24; 32:28, 30	106	Exod 12:3*
52	Gen 22:24	107	Lev 23:27
54	Gen 36:12*	108	Lev 25:9–10
56	Gen 36:12	109	Gen 18:24, 32; Lev 25:10
57	Gen 4:11–12; 36:12; Exod 15:17*	110	Exod 18:25
		111	Gen 24:10
58	Deut 32:8*	113	Gen 24:22
60	Gen 36:12	114	Num 7:10–11, 14, 20, 26, 32, 38, 44, 50, 56, 62, 68, 74, 80
61	Gen 25:25, 27		
62	Gen 25:27*		

115	Gen 8:21*	169	Lev 2:11
116	Exod 26:1*	170	Deut 8:2–3*
117	Exod 26:1	171	Gen 3:23–24; 4:14, 16
118	Exod 7:14–10:29; 12:29–	172	Deut 8:2–3
	30	173	Exod 16:4; Deut 8:3*; Wis
119	Gen 15:18–21		16:20, 24
120	Exod 20:1–17; Deut 5:6–21	174	Wis 16:25
121	Gen 16:3*, 4	176	Gen 27:40*
122	Gen 16:4*	177	Prov 3:11–12*; 1 Chr 22:9
123	Gen 30:16*	178	Exod 22:22*
124	Gen 38:14–15	180	Gen 16:6
125	Gen 38:16*		
126	Gen 16:4; 38:18		
128	Gen 16:4*		*De fuga et inventione*
129	Gen 21:20; 25:23	1	Gen 16:6–9*, 11–12*
130	Gen 16:4; 25:21	2	Gen 16:6*
131	Exod 2:1–2*	4	Gen 27:41–45; 31:20–21
132	Exod 2:1–2	5	Gen 16:6–9, 11*
134	Deut 10:9*; 18:2; 30:20	6	Gen 16:6
135	Gen 16:4*; 25:21	7	Gen 31:20–21*
137	Exod 21:22–23*	9	Gen 30:42
138	Gen 16:4; 21:22*; 25:21	10	Gen 1:2; 30:39–40
139	Gen 16:4*, 5*	14	Gen 31:21
145	Gen 16:4–5	15	Gen 31:14–16*
151	Gen 16:4–5	16	Gen 31:16
153	Gen 16:5*, 6*	18	Exod 8:22*
155	Gen 16:6*	19	Exod 12:35–36
156	Gen 16:6*	20	Gen 31:21, 27*
158	Gen 16:6*	22	Gen 31:27
159	Exod 20:23; Deut 32:15	23	Gen 27:42–45*
160	Deut 32:15*	24	Gen 27:42–45
161	Exod 12:2; Deut 16:3*	37	Num 4:3, 23; 8:24–26
162	Exod 12:8*	39	Gen 27:42*, 43
163	Exod 15:23–25*	40	Gen 27:43
164	Exod 15:25*; Num 14:3–4	43	Gen 27:43
166	Exod 15:25*	44	Gen 27:43; 31:20
167	Deut 16:3	46	Gen 27:44*
168	Exod 25:30; 39:18; Lev	47	Gen 27:45
	24:5–6	48	Gen 28:2*

49	Gen 27:43; 31:20	101	Exod 25:21*
50	Gen 28:2	102	Exod 21:13; Num 35:11–
52	Gen 28:2		15; Deut 10:9
53	Exod 21:12–14*	103	Num 35:14
54	Exod 21:12*	106	Num 35:25, 28
56	Deut 4:4*	107	Exod 21:13; Num 35:25,
57	Deut 4:4		28
58	Deut 30:15*, 20*	109	Lev 21:11; Jer 10:12; Prov
59	Lev 10:1, 2*, 3*; Num 3:4;		3:19
	26:61; Ps title; 113:25*, 26	110	Exod 3:14; Lev 21:10*;
60	Gen 4:8, 11, 15*		Num 35:25, 28
64	Gen 4:15; Exod 21:12*	111	Lev 21:10*
65	Exod 21:13*	112	Exod 3:14
67	Gen 48:15–16*	113	Lev 21:11*
68	Gen 1; 1:26*	114	Lev 21:13–14*
71	Gen 1:26*, 27*	115	Num 6:9*
72	Gen 1:26*, 27*	116	Num 35:25, 28
73	Gen 29:32; 30:5–12, 20;	119	Gen 16:7*
	Deut 27:12–13	121	Gen 19:26*
75	Exod 21:13	122	Gen 19:26
76	Exod 21:13	123	Deut 29:4*
77	Exod 21:13, 14*; Deut 19:5*	124	Exod 7:23*
78	Exod 21:14	127	Gen 37:15–17*
80	Exod 21:14	128	Gen 18:11*; 25:8*, 17;
83	Exod 21:14, 15*, 16*		37:15, 17
86	Num 35:6–34	131	Gen 37:15, 17
87	Num 35:6, 13–14, 25, 28	132	Gen 22:7*, 8*, 13*
89	Deut 33:9*	133	Gen 22:7
90	Exod 32:4, 27*, 28	135	Gen 22:8*, 13*
91	Exod 32:27	136	Gen 22:8*
93	Exod 21:13*; Num 8:14–	137	Exod 16:4*, 15*
	16; 16:8–9; 18:21–24	138	Exod 16:15*, 31
94	Num 35:6, 13	139	Exod 16:15*, 16*; Wis
96	Num 35:11–15		6:12
97	Num 35:11–15	140	Exod 3:11*, 12*
99	Num 35:11–15	141	Exod 3:6*; Deut 4:30
100	Exod 25:17–20; 38:6–8;	142	Deut 4:29*
	Num 35:6, 12–13; Deut	143	Gen 31:33–34, 35*
	10:2, 5	144	Gen 19:11*

145	Num 16	195	Gen 24:16*
147	Exod 2:15	196	Gen 14:7*
148	Exod 2:11, 12*, 13*	197	Jer 2:13*
149	Gen 38:20–23*	199	Jer 2:13
150	Gen 38:18, 20	200	Gen 21:30; 26:18–22
151	Gen 38:20	201	Jer 2:13
153	Gen 38:20*, 21	202	Gen 16:7*
154	Gen 38:23	203	Gen 16:7*, 8*
155	Gen 38:23	204	Gen 16:11*, 12
157	Lev 10:16	205	Gen 16:8
158	Lev 10:16*	207	Gen 16:9*
159	Lev 10:19*, 20*	208	Gen 16:11; 32:28, 30
161	Exod 3:2–3*	209	Gen 16:12*
162	Exod 3:5*	211	Gen 16:11, 12*, 13*
163	Exod 3:5*	212	Gen 16:14*
165	Exod 33:23*	213	Gen 16:14*
166	Exod 16:4		
167	Gen 18:11*; 21:2*, 3		

De mutatione nominum

168	Gen 27:20*; Exod 1:19*		
170	Lev 25:11*	1	Gen 17:1*; 21:5
171	Lev 25:11*	2	Num 18:26*
173	Gen 2:2–3	6	Gen 17:1
174	Lev 25:6*	7	Exod 20:21
175	Deut 6:10–11*	8	Exod 33:13*
176	Deut 6:10–11	9	Exod 33:23*
177	Gen 16:7*	11	Exod 3:13, 14*
178	Gen 2:6*	12	Exod 3:15*
179	Gen 2:6	13	Exod 6:3*
181	Gen 2:6*	14	Gen 32:24, 29*
183	Exod 15:27*	15	Gen 17:1*
185	Gen 49:28; Exod 25:30;	16	Gen 11:31
	28:15–21; Lev 24:5–6	17	Gen 17:1*
186	Exod 15:27; Num 11:16;	18	Gen 17:1*
	29:12–34	19	Exod 7:1*
188	Lev 20:18*	20	Exod 6:29*; 7:17*
189	Lev 20:18	21	Exod 9:29*, 30
190	Lev 20:18*	23	Gen 17:1*; 35:11*; Exod
192	Gen 7:11*		20:2*; Deut 4:1*; 5:6*
193	Lev 18:7*	25	Deut 33:1*

26	Deut 33:1	89	Gen 30:24; 41:45
27	Gen 17:1*	90	Gen 41:48
29	Gen 17:1*	91	Gen 41:45
30	Gen 2:7, 17; 3:22	92	Gen 35:18
31	Gen 1:26*; 17:1*	94	Gen 35:18
32	Gen 48:15–16	96	Gen 35:16, 19
34	Gen 5:24*	97	Gen 48:5*
38	Gen 5:24*	101	Gen 48:5
39	Gen 17:1*	103	Exod 2:18; 3:1
40	Gen 17:1	104	Exod 18:20–26; Deut
41	Gen 48:15*		1:17; 24:13–16
42	Deut 12:25, 28*	105	Exod 2:18
43	Exod 25:9–10; 26:33; 28:4;	106	Exod 2:16
	Lev 6:10; 16:4	107	Num 25:1–3
44	Gen 32:28*	108	Num 25:7–8, 12–13
47	Gen 17:1*	109	Exod 24:11; Num 31:49
48	Job 14:4–5*	110	Exod 2:16*
51	Gen 17:1*	111	Exod 2:16*
52	Gen 17:2*	112	Exod 2:17
54	Gen 17:3*	113	Exod 2:16–17
56	Gen 17:3*	114	Exod 2:16, 18
57	Gen 17:4*	115	Ps 22:1*
58	Gen 17:4; Exod 3:14	116	Exod 2:16, 18*
60	Gen 17:5*	117	Exod 2:19
61	Gen 17:5, 15	118	Exod 2:19
63	Gen 2:19*	119	Exod 2:20
66	Gen 17:5	120	Exod 2:20*, 21
67	Gen 17:5	121	Num 13:18
68	Gen 17:5	123	Num 14:24*
69	Gen 17:5	125	Exod 7:1; Deut 33:1
71	Gen 17:5	126	Exod 24:1, 4
77	Gen 17:15	128	Exod 7:1; Deut 33:1
79	Gen 17:15	129	Exod 9:29
81	Gen 25:26; 27:36; 32:28,	130	Gen 17:15, 16*
	30; Hos 12:4	131	Gen 21:6
82	Exod 3:14	132	Gen 29:31*
83	Gen 17:5; 32:28	134	Gen 38:15, 25*; Exod 3:6
87	Gen 17:5; 32:27–30	135	Gen 38:25
88	Gen 21:3	136	Gen 38:26*

137	Gen 21:6*
138	Gen 21:6*
139	Hos 14:9–10*
141	Gen 17:16*
143	Gen 11:30; 1 Kgdms 2:5*
144	1 Kgdms 2:5
145	Gen 17:16*
147	Gen 17:16
148	Gen 17:16*
150	Gen 17:16
151	Gen 17:16*
152	Gen 23:6*
154	Gen 17:17
156	Gen 17:17
157	Gen 21:5
166	Gen 17:17*; 18:12*
168	Gen 17:17; Exod 4:14*
169	Isa 48:22*; 57:21*
171	Gen 45:16*
173	Gen 37:36; 39:1, 20; 45:18*
174	Gen 45:18*
175	Gen 17:17*
176	Gen 17:17*
177	Gen 15:4*, 6*
178	Gen 17:17*
182	Deut 32:4*
186	Gen 15:6*
187	Gen 32:25*, 31
188	Gen 17:17
189	Gen 6:9–10; 11:10*
190	Gen 21:33*; 26:12; Exod 27:9; 37:7
191	Num 18:28
192	Exod 26:33
193	Gen 17:17*; 34:2
194	Gen 34:1–2, 3*
195	Gen 4:7*; 34:2–3
200	Gen 34:25; 49:5–7; Deut 33:8

201	Gen 15:6; 17:17*, 18*
202	Gen 16:11; Num 24:16*
203	Num 22:4–20; 31:8*
204	Gen 17:18; Deut 23:2
205	Deut 23:1–2
206	Deut 21:20*
207	Exod 6:26*, 27*
208	Exod 4:14–16; 6:26; 7:2, 11, 22; 8:3
209	Gen 17:18; Exod 6:26
210	Deut 33:6*
213	Gen 17:18
215	Gen 46:30*
216	Gen 17:18*
218	Gen 15:6; 17:18
220	Num 6:21
223	Gen 1:26–27; Wis 7:26
224	Num 13:18, 24–25
228	Gen 18:24–32; Lev 25:10
230	Gen 27:38*
232	Num 11:23*
233	Lev 5:6*, 7
234	Lev 5:11–12
237	Deut 30:12–14*
240	Deut 30:14
245	Lev 5:6–7, 11
247	Lev 5:7
248	Lev 5:7
249	Lev 5:11, 12*
250	Lev 5:7*, 11*
252	Gen 17:18
253	Gen 17:19*
254	Gen 29:16, 31
255	Gen 16:1–2, 12; 17:19; 29:31
259	Exod 16:4*
260	Lev 25:4–6
261	Gen 17:17, 19; 21:6
263	Gen 17:20–21*

264	Gen 17:21*	1.34	Gen 2:7*
265	Num 14:9*	1.35	Lev 19:24
266	Lev 26:12*	1.36	Exod 34:28; Deut 9:9, 18
267	Gen 17:21*	1.37	Gen 29:35*
268	Gen 26:12*	1.38	Gen 26:32
270	Gen 17:22*	1.39	Gen 26:19–25

De Deo[6]

2	Gen 18:2*; 1 Kgdms 9:9
3	Gen 18:2*; Exod 3:14
4	Exod 3:14
5	Exod 25:21*; 1 Chr 28:18
6	Isa 6:1–2*
7	Deut 4:24*
9	Isa 6:2*
11	Exod 19:4*; Deut 32:10–12*

De somniis 1–2

1.3	Gen 28:12–15*
1.4	Gen 28:10–11*
1.5	Gen 28:10*, 11
1.8	Gen 26:32
1.11	Gen 26:32
1.12	Gen 26:33
1.14	Gen 21:25–31; 26:19–25, 32–33
1.24	Gen 26:32–33
1.33	Lev 19:24*

1.40	Gen 26:20–22, 32–33
1.41	Gen 28:10
1.42	Gen 26:32
1.46	Gen 27:43–44*
1.47	Gen 12:4*
1.48	Gen 11:32*
1.50	Prov 9:1–5; Sir 24:21
1.52	Gen 11:31
1.55	Gen 11:31
1.58	Gen 11:31
1.59	Gen 12:4
1.61	Gen 28:10, 11*
1.62	Exod 20:24*; Deut 12:5*
1.63	Gen 28:11
1.64	Gen 22:3–4*
1.67	Gen 22:3–4
1.68	Gen 22:3–4; 26:33; 28:10–11
1.70	Gen 18:33*
1.71	Gen 28:11; Exod 19:17*
1.72	Gen 28:11*
1.73	Gen 28:11
1.74	Gen 1:27*; 9:6*
1.75	Gen 1:3*; Ps 26:1*
1.76	Gen 1:4*

---

6. Developed with reference to Folker Siegert, *Philon von Alexandrien: Über die Gottesbezeichnung "wohltätig verzehrendes Feuer" (DE DEO)*, WUNT 46 (Tübingen: Mohr Siebeck, 1988); Siegert, "Le fragment philonien *De Deo*: Première traduction française avec commentaire et remarques sur le langage métaphorique de Philon," in *Philon d'Alexandrie et le langage de la philosophie*, ed. Carlos Lévy, Monothéismes et Philosophie 1 (Turnhout: Brepols, 1998), 183–227; and Abraham Terian, "*Philonis De visione trium angelorum ad Abraham*: A New Translation of the Mistitled *De Deo*," *SPhiloA* 28 (2016): 77–107.

1.77	Gen 1:4; Exod 1:11	1.159	Gen 28:13*; Deut 10:9*;
1.78	Gen 41:45*		18:2
1.79	Gen 32:31*	1.161	Gen 11:31
1.81	Lev 11:24; 22:6–7*	1.163	Gen 28:13, 21
1.85	Gen 19:23–24*; 28:11	1.166	Gen 28:13*
1.87	Gen 28:11	1.170	Gen 28:13
1.89	Num 25:1*, 4*	1.171	Gen 25:26; 27:36; 32:28,
1.90	Num 25:4		30; Hos 12:4
1.92	Exod 22:26–27*	1.172	Gen 28:13; 46:1*
1.98	Exod 22:26–27	1.173	Gen 28:13*
1.99	Exod 22:27	1.174	Gen 28:13
1.100	Exod 22:26–27	1.175	Gen 28:14*
1.101	Exod 22:27*	1.176	Gen 28:14*
1.104	Exod 22:27	1.179	Gen 28:15*
1.107	Exod 22:26, 27*	1.180	Gen 28:15*
1.109	Exod 22:27*	1.183	Gen 28:16*
1.112	Exod 22:26*	1.184	Gen 28:17*
1.113	Exod 22:26–27	1.185	Gen 28:16*, 17*
1.114	Exod 10:21	1.186	Gen 28:17*
1.116	Gen 28:11*	1.189	Gen 31:11–13*
1.117	Exod 10:23*	1.190	Gen 28:12; 31:11
1.118	Gen 28:11	1.192	Gen 3:9*
1.120	Gen 28:11*	1.193	Deut 27:9*
1.126	Gen 28:11, 20	1.194	Exod 3:4*
1.127	Gen 28:11	1.195	Gen 22:1–2*, 9*, 11–12*
1.128	Gen 28:11	1.196	Gen 31:11*
1.130	Gen 32:25*, 28, 30	1.197	Gen 31:12*
1.133	Gen 28:12–13*	1.199	Gen 31:12
1.134	Gen 28:12	1.200	Gen 31:10*, 12
1.135	Gen 1:16, 20–21, 24–25	1.202	Gen 30:42; 31:10, 12;
1.141	Gen 28:12		Exod 36:15
1.142	Gen 28:12	1.206	Exod 31:2
1.143	Exod 20:19*	1.207	Exod 26:36; 31:2–3
1.144	Gen 28:12	1.208	Gen 31:10, 12
1.146	Gen 28:12	1.209	Gen 31:10, 12
1.148	Gen 28:12; Lev 26:12*	1.210	Gen 2:7; Exod 29:4
1.150	Gen 28:12	1.213	Gen 31:10, 12
1.152	Gen 28:12	1.214	Exod 18:27; 28:4; 29:4–5
1.157	Gen 28:12–13	1.215	Exod 28:4; 29:5

1.216	Gen 31:10, 12; Lev 16:4	2.25	Gen 17:13; Num 6:2*
1.219	Gen 31:10, 12	2.26	Gen 23:6, 9
1.220	Gen 37:3	2.29	Lev 19:9*; 23:22*; Num
1.221	Gen 37:31		31:28*
1.225	Gen 31:12; 37:31; Exod	2.30	Gen 37:7*
	29:5	2.31	Gen 37:7
1.227	Gen 31:12*, 13*	2.33	Gen 29:32; 37:7*
1.228	Gen 31:13*	2.34	Gen 29:33–35; 30:18, 20
1.229	Gen 31:13*	2.35	Gen 30:6, 11, 13
1.230	Exod 6:3	2.36	Gen 30:8; 35:18
1.231	Exod 3:14*	2.37	Gen 29:32–34; 37:7
1.234	Exod 3:14	2.38	Gen 29:35; 30:18
1.237	Num 23:19*; Deut 8:5*	2.39	Gen 30:6, 20
1.238	Gen 31:13*	2.40	Gen 30:11, 13
1.240	Gen 16:1, 13*	2.41	Gen 35:18; 37:7
1.241	Gen 31:13; Exod 17:6	2.42	Gen 37:7
1.242	Gen 31:13	2.43	Gen 41:41
1.244	Gen 31:13	2.44	Gen 32:28, 30; 38:18;
1.245	Deut 16:22*		41:42*
1.247	Gen 19:26	2.45	Gen 38:18
1.248	Gen 19:26	2.46	Gen 41:43, 48–49
1.249	Gen 31:13*	2.47	Gen 30:24
1.252	Gen 31:13*	2.63	Gen 30:24
1.253	Num 6:5*	2.65	Gen 37:33*
1.254	1 Kgdms 1:11, 20, 28	2.66	Gen 37:34–35
1.255	Gen 31:12	2.67	Exod 20:26; Lev 10:1–11
1.256	Gen 31:13	2.69	Deut 25:11–12
2.3	Gen 28:12	2.70	Gen 2:7, 9, 17; 3:3, 19
2.6	Gen 37:7*, 9*	2.71	Lev 2:1*, 2*
2.7	Gen 37:8*, 10*	2.72	Lev 2:1
2.10	Gen 21:8	2.73	Lev 2:1
2.16	Gen 30:22–24; 37:36;	2.74	Lev 2:2
	39:1; 40:1–2; 41:43	2.75	Lev 23:10*
2.17	Gen 37:7*	2.76	Lev 23:10
2.18	Gen 37:7	2.77	Lev 23:10*
2.19	Gen 28:12*; 31:10*; 37:7	2.78	Gen 37:7
2.21	Gen 37:7	2.80	Gen 37:7*
2.23	Lev 23:22*	2.89	Gen 23:7
2.24	Deut 1:17*	2.90	Gen 23:9

2.93	Gen 37:8*	2.195	Gen 40:2, 7, 9–11
2.94	Gen 37:8	2.197	Gen 40:10
2.95	Gen 37:8	2.199	Gen 40:10*
2.96	Gen 37:8*	2.200	Gen 40:11*
2.100	Gen 37:8	2.203	Gen 40:11
2.106	Gen 39:7–12	2.207	Gen 40:16*; 42:36*
2.107	Gen 50:19*	2.210	Gen 40:16
2.109	Exod 13:19	2.211	Gen 40:17
2.111	Gen 37:9–11*	2.212	Gen 40:17
2.113	Gen 37:9	2.213	Gen 40:19
2.132	Gen 37:7, 9	2.215	Gen 40:9–11, 16–17
2.133	Gen 37:9, 20	2.216	Gen 41:17–19*
2.135	Gen 37:10*	2.217	Gen 41:20–21*
2.140	Gen 37:9–10	2.218	Gen 41:22–24*
2.141	Gen 37:11*	2.219	Gen 41:17*
2.142	Exod 2:4*	2.221	Exod 17:6*
2.155	Gen 40:9–11, 16–17	2.222	Exod 24:10*; Deut 8:15*
2.156	Gen 40:8–11, 16–17	2.223	Gen 9:11*
2.158	Gen 40:9–11, 16–17	2.224	Gen 9:11*
2.159	Gen 40:9–11*	2.226	Gen 18:22*
2.160	Gen 40:9*	2.227	Exod 3:14; Deut 5:31*
2.163	Gen 40:9*	2.229	Deut 5:5*
2.169	Gen 40:9	2.231	Lev 16:17*
2.170	Num 13:18–21	2.235	Num 16:48*
2.171	Num 13:24	2.236	Num 16:48*
2.172	Isa 5:7*	2.237	Exod 3:14
2.173	Gen 32:28, 30	2.238	Gen 41:17*
2.175	Deut 30:9–10*	2.241	Gen 2:10*
2.180	Deut 30:12–14	2.242	Ps 36:4*
2.181	Gen 40:9–11	2.243	Gen 2:10*
2.182	Exod 5:2*	2.244	Gen 23:6*
2.184	Gen 40:2, 7; Deut 23:1*	2.245	Ps 64:10*
2.185	Gen 18:11; Lev 21:13–14	2.246	Ps 45:5*
2.186	Exod 28:1; Lev 10:1–2	2.248	Lev 26:12*; Ps 45:5
2.189	Exod 7:1; Lev 16:17*	2.250	Ps 45:5
2.190	Gen 40:9–11	2.253	Ps 45:5
2.191	Deut 32:32–33*	2.255	Gen 15:18*
2.192	Deut 32:32	2.257	Gen 15:18
2.193	Deut 25:13–15*	2.258	Gen 15:18*

2.259	Exod 7:20; 8:2	2.277	Exod 7:15*
2.260	Exod 7:21	2.278	Exod 7:15
2.261	Gen 41:17	2.280	Exod 14:30*
2.263	Deut 27:9*	2.284	Gen 11:1*, 4
2.265	Exod 14:14*	2.286	Gen 11:9
2.266	Exod 11:5; 12:29	2.290	Gen 11:9
2.267	Exod 11:7*	2.292	Exod 3:14
2.269	Exod 15:1*, 21*	2.296	Lev 5:4*, 5*
2.271	Num 21:17*	2.297	Deut 32:39*
2.272	Deut 26:2, 4, 13*	2.299	Lev 5:5
2.273	Deut 26:13	2.300	Exod 7:15*

The Exposition of the Law

	De vita Mosis 1–2	1.58	Exod 2:18–20
		1.59	Exod 2:21
1.5	Gen 46:6–7; Exod 2:2	1.60	Exod 3:1
1.7	Exod 2:1; 6:16–20	1.65	Exod 3:2
1.8	Exod 1:9–10, 16	1.67	Exod 1:14
1.9	Exod 2:2	1.68	Exod 3:2
1.10	Exod 2:3	1.71	Exod 3:7–10
1.11	Exod 2:2	1.72	Exod 3:7, 16
1.12	Exod 2:4	1.73	Exod 2:15, 23; 3:10, 16, 18
1.14	Exod 2:5	1.74	Exod 3:13
1.15	Exod 2:6	1.75	Exod 3:14
1.16	Exod 2:7	1.76	Exod 3:15; 4:1
1.17	Exod 2:8–10	1.77	Exod 4:2–3
1.34	Gen 46:6–7	1.78	Exod 4:4
1.36	Exod 1:8–13	1.79	Exod 4:6–7
1.37	Exod 3:7	1.81	Exod 4:9
1.38	Exod 1:11, 13–14; 5:6–14	1.83	Exod 4:10
1.44	Exod 2:11–12	1.84	Exod 4:11, 14–16
1.45	Exod 2:15	1.85	Exod 4:20, 27–28
1.47	Exod 2:15	1.86	Exod 4:29–31
1.52	Exod 2:16	1.87	Exod 5:1
1.53	Exod 2:17	1.88	Exod 5:2
1.54	Exod 2:17	1.89	Exod 5:6–18
1.57	Exod 2:17	1.90	Exod 5:20–21

1.91	Exod 7:10	1.167	Exod 14:5–8
1.92	Exod 7:11–12	1.169	Exod 14:9
1.93	Exod 7:12	1.170	Exod 14:10
1.94	Exod 7:13	1.171	Exod 14:11–12
1.96	Exod 7:14–12:36	1.173	Exod 14:13–14
1.99	Exod 7:19–21	1.175	Exod 14:13–14
1.101	Exod 7:25	1.176	Exod 14:21
1.103	Exod 7:26–8:3	1.177	Exod 14:16, 21
1.105	Exod 8:4–9	1.178	Exod 14:19–20, 24–25
1.107	Exod 8:12–14	1.179	Exod 14:26–28
1.109	Wis 11:17–19	1.180	Exod 15:1–21
1.110	Exod 9:15	1.181	Exod 15:22
1.112	Exod 8:15*	1.182	Exod 15:23
1.118	Exod 9:23–25	1.183	Exod 15:24
1.120	Exod 9:34–35; 10:13	1.184	Exod 15:25
1.121	Exod 10:12–15	1.185	Exod 15:25
1.122	Exod 10:7*, 16–19	1.186	Exod 15:25
1.123	Exod 10:22–23	1.188	Exod 15:27
1.126	Exod 9:22–25; 10:12–15, 22–23	1.189	Gen 46:27; Num 11:16–17
1.127	Exod 9:8–10	1.191	Exod 16:3
1.130	Exod 8:16–20	1.192	Num 20:5; Deut 8:14–15
1.133	Exod 9:1–7	1.193	Exod 16:3; Num 11:4–5
1.134	Exod 12:29–30	1.200	Exod 16:13–15
1.135	Exod 12:29	1.201	Exod 16:15
1.136	Exod 12:30	1.203	Exod 16:20
1.139	Exod 12:33	1.204	Exod 16:20–21
1.141	Exod 12:35–36	1.205	Exod 16:22–25; 20:10
1.144	Exod 7:14–8:11	1.206	Exod 16:35
1.145	Exod 8:13, 17–20; 9:8–10, 22–26; 10:12–15, 21–23; 12:29–30	1.207	Exod 16:20–23
		1.208	Num 11:8–9
		1.209	Exod 16:13; Num 11:31–32
1.147	Exod 12:37–38	1.210	Exod 17:1–6; Num 20:2–11; Dcut 8:15; Wis 11:4
1.149	Exod 2:5–12, 15; 19:6		
1.150	Exod 18:3–4		
1.156	Exod 33:11		
1.158	Exod 20:21	1.211	Exod 15:25
1.164	Exod 13:17–18	1.216	Exod 17:8–9; Deut 25:17–19
1.166	Exod 13:21–22		

1.217	Exod 17:11–12	1.274	Num 22:35
1.218	Exod 17:13	1.275	Num 22:36–40
1.219	Exod 17:15	1.276	Num 22:41
1.220	Num 13:3	1.277	Num 23:1–3, 6
1.221	Num 13:2–4	1.278	Num 23:7–9
1.222	Num 13:18	1.279	Num 23:10
1.224	Num 13:19–21	1.280	Num 23:11
1.226	Num 13:21	1.281	Num 22:12; 23:12
1.228	Num 13:18	1.282	Num 23:13–14
1.229	Num 13:29, 33–34	1.283	Num 23:18–20
1.230	Num 13:24	1.284	Num 23:21–24
1.231	Num 13:24	1.285	Num 23:25, 27–28
1.233	Num 13:31–34	1.286	Num 23:26
1.234	Num 14:6–9	1.287	Num 23:28–24:1
1.235	Num 14:10	1.288	Num 24:2
1.236	Num 14:36–38	1.289	Num 24:3–6
1.237	Num 14:25	1.290	Num 24:7–8
1.238	Num 14:33	1.291	Num 24:9
1.240	Gen 25:24–26	1.292	Num 24:10
1.242	Gen 25:29–34; 27:41	1.293	Num 24:11
1.243	Num 20:14–21	1.296	Num 25:1–2; 31:16
1.246	Num 20:21	1.301	Num 25:6–7
1.248	Num 20:14–16	1.302	Num 25:6, 8
1.250	Num 21:1	1.303	Num 25:4–5
1.252	Num 21:2–3	1.304	Num 25:8–13
1.253	Num 21:3	1.305	Num 31:16
1.255	Num 21:16–17	1.306	Num 31:4–6
1.256	Num 21:18	1.309	Num 31:7
1.258	Num 21:21–23	1.311	Num 31:15–18
1.259	Num 21:24	1.313	Num 31:19
1.262	Num 21:25–26, 31	1.315	Num 31:25–31
1.263	Num 22:2–4	1.316	Num 31:47
1.266	Num 22:5–13	1.317	Num 31:48–54
1.267	Num 22:14–17	1.320	Num 32:1–5
1.268	Num 22:20–21	1.321	Num 32:6–7
1.269	Num 22:22	1.325	Num 32:8–9, 12–13
1.270	Num 22:23	1.326	Num 32:23
1.271	Num 22:24–27	1.330	Num 32:16–19
1.273	Num 22:31–34	1.331	Num 32:20–21

1.332	Num 32:22	2.97	Exod 16:32–34; 25:15,
1.333	Num 32:25–27		17–19; 38:6–8; 40:18;
1.334	Deut 33:5		Num 17:5
2.3	Deut 33:5	2.101	Exod 30:1–6
2.21	Exod 20:9; Deut 5:13	2.102	Exod 25:30–37; 38:13–17
2.22	Exod 20:10; Deut 5:14	2.104	Exod 25:22, 30; 38:9; Lev
2.23	Lev 16:29–31; 23:26–27		24:7
2.37	Gen 1	2.106	Exod 27:1–8; 38:22–26
2.53	Gen 7:11–24; 19:24–25	2.110	Exod 39:13
2.55	Gen 19:24–25	2.111	Exod 28:5–8; 36:9–12
2.58	Gen 19:9, 29	2.112	Exod 28:9–21, 15*;
2.60	Gen 6:13–7:1		36:13–21
2.61	Gen 1:26–27	2.113	Exod 28:22–28; 36:22–29
2.63	Gen 8:1–14	2.114	Exod 28:32–35; 36:38–40
2.64	Gen 8:18–19	2.116	Exod 26:40
2.65	Gen 1:26	2.118	Exod 28:27; 36:30
2.67	Exod 33:11; Sir 45:1	2.119	Exod 28:29–30; 36:32–34
2.69	Exod 34:28; Deut 9:18	2.122	Exod 28:9; 36:13
2.70	Exod 34:28–35	2.123	Exod 28:10; 36:13
2.77	Exod 26:15–17; 36:20–22[MT][7]	2.124	Exod 28:17–21; 36:16–21
		2.127	Exod 28:16; 36:16
2.78	Exod 26:18–25; 37:8–13	2.128	Exod 28:26
2.80	Exod 26:26–27; 37:6–14	2.130	Exod 28:7; 36:11
2.81	Exod 37:6	2.131	Exod 28:35
2.83	Exod 26:16; 36:21[MT]	2.132	Exod 28:32; 36:38–39
2.84	Exod 26:1–2; 37:1–2	2.133	Exod 28:7, 9, 15–30;
2.85	Exod 26:7–13; 37:2		36:11–13, 15–34
2.87	Exod 26:31–37; 27:16; 37:3–6	2.136	Exod 30:18; 35:22
		2.137	Exod 38:26
2.88	Exod 26:14; 37:3	2.138	Exod 30:18–21
2.89	Exod 27:9–15; 38:9–13	2.142	Exod 28:1
2.90	Exod 27:17–18; 38:18–19	2.143	Exod 28:38–39; 29:4–9;
2.93	Exod 27:16; 38:18–19		Lev 8:6–9, 13
2.94	Exod 40:6, 26	2.146	Exod 30:22–30; Lev
2.95	Exod 25:9–21; 38:1–8		8:10–12

---

7. Some of the details from this section of *De vita Mosis* are not found in the LXX but do appear in the MT. We have left these references in order to facilitate future studies. Unless otherwise marked with [MT], the passages are all from the LXX.

2.147	Exod 29:10–14; Lev 8:14–17	2.219	Exod 16:23; 35:3
2.148	Exod 29:15–18; Lev 8:18–21	2.220	Num 15:32
		2.222	Exod 12:1–2; Num 9:1–2
2.149	Exod 29:25; Lev 8:22	2.224	Exod 12:6; Num 9:3
2.150	Exod 29:20; Lev 8:23–24	2.225	Num 9:6–7
2.152	Lev 8:30	2.226	Num 9:6
2.153	Lev 9:1–22	2.227	Num 9:7
2.154	Lev 9:23–24	2.228	Num 9:8
2.155	Lev 9:24	2.229	Num 9:9
2.159	Num 3:5–8	2.230	Num 9:10
2.161	Exod 32:1–2	2.231	Num 9:11–13
2.162	Exod 32:4–6	2.232	Num 9:14
2.163	Exod 24:2	2.234	Num 27:1
2.165	Exod 32:7–8	2.235	Num 27:3–4
2.166	Exod 32:9–14	2.237	Num 27:5
2.167	Exod 32:19	2.238	Num 27:6–7
2.168	Exod 32:26*	2.239	Num 27:7*
2.170	Exod 32:26	2.242	Num 27:7
2.171	Exod 32:27	2.243	Num 27:8
2.172	Exod 32:28	2.244	Num 27:9–10
2.173	Exod 32:29	2.245	Num 27:10–11
2.175	Num 16:1–3	2.247	Exod 14:2
2.178	Num 17:1–7	2.248	Exod 14:9
2.179	Num 17:8	2.249	Exod 14:10
2.180	Num 17:8	2.252	Exod 14:13–14; 15:10
2.193	Lev 24:10–11	2.253	Exod 14:21
2.196	Lev 24:10–11	2.254	Exod 14:22–27
2.201	Lev 24:12	2.255	Exod 14:27–28
2.202	Lev 24:13–14	2.256	Exod 15:1–21
2.203	Lev 24:15–16, 23	2.257	Exod 15:20
2.205	Lev 24:15	2.258	Exod 16:4–5, 35
2.206	Lev 24:16	2.259	Exod 16:19, 21
2.209	Gen 2:2; Exod 20:11	2.260	Exod 16:20
2.213	Exod 20:18; Num 15:32–33	2.261	Exod 16:20
		2.262	Exod 16:20
2.214	Num 15:32	2.263	Gen 7:1–23; 19:24–25
2.217	Num 15:34–35	2.264	Exod 16:22–26
2.218	Num 15:35	2.266	Gen 1:1; Exod 16:20
		2.267	Gen 1:2

2.268	Exod 16:26	40	Gen 1:11–12
2.269	Exod 16:27	42	Gen 1:11–12
2.270	Exod 32:1–6	45	Gen 1:14–19
2.271	Exod 32:19	46	Gen 1:11–12
2.272	Exod 32:25–26	47	Gen 1:14–19
2.273	Exod 32:26–27	53	Gen 1:14–19
2.274	Exod 32:28–29	55	Gen 1:14–19
2.276	Num 16:1–2	56	Gen 1:16
2.277	Num 16:1–3	57	Gen 1:16
2.279	Num 12:3; 16:15	58	Gen 1:14–15
2.281	Num 16:28–30	59	Gen 1:14*
2.282	Num 16:31–33	60	Gen 1:14–19
2.283	Num 16:35	62	Gen 1:11–23
2.286	Num 16:31–33, 35	64	Gen 1:24*, 25
2.288	Deut 33:1–29	65	Gen 1:20–31
2.289	Deut 33:1–29	66	Gen 1:20–31
2.291	Deut 34:1–8	67	Gen 1:11
		68	Gen 1:20–31

De opificio mundi

12	Gen title; 1:1–2:25, 2:4	69	Gen 1:26
13	Gen 1:1–2:25	71	Gen 1:26
14	Gen 1:1–2:25	72	Gen 1:6–10, 26*
15	Gen 1:1–5	73	Gen 1:11–13, 16, 20–26
22	Gen 1:2	75	Gen 1:26
25	Gen 1:26–27	76	Gen 1:27
26	Gen 1:1*	77	Gen 1:26–31
27	Gen 1:1*	79	Gen 1:26–27
29	Gen 1:1–3, 14–19	82	Gen 1:6–8, 26–31
30	Gen 1:2, 4	83	Gen 1:26, 28
31	Gen 1:3, 14–19	84	Gen 1:28; Ps 8:6–7
32	Gen 1:2*	88	Gen 1:28–29
33	Gen 1:3–5	89	Gen 2:1–3
34	Gen 1:5	114	Gen 1:6–8
35	Gen 1:2, 5	116	Exod 23:16; 34:22; Deut 16:9–17
36	Gen 1:6–7	128	Gen 2:1–3; Exod 20:8–11; Deut 5:12–15
37	Gen 1:8	129	Gen 2:4–5*
38	Gen 1:9	131	Gen 1:9–10; 2:6*
39	Gen 1:10	134	Gen 1:27; 2:7*

135	Gen 2:7	27	Gen 5:29; 6:9; 7:1
136	Gen 1:9–10; 2:7	28	Exod 16:23; 20:9–10;
137	Gen 2:7		Deut 5:13–14
139	Gen 1:26; 2:7	31	Gen 6:9*
140	Gen 2:7	33	Gen 6:9
142	Gen 1:26, 28	34	Gen 6:9
143	Gen 2:7	35	Gen 6:9*
145	Gen 2:7	40	Gen 6:5, 12–13
146	Gen 1:26–27	41	Gen 6:5–7
148	Gen 2:7, 19	42	Gen 7:11, 17–23
149	Gen 2:19	43	Gen 7:19–20
150	Gen 2:20	45	Gen 1:26; 7:21–23
151	Gen 2:22–23	46	Gen 6:8–9; 7:1; 8:18
152	Gen 2:20, 23–24	47	Gen 4:26; 5:24; 6:9
153	Gen 2:8–9	51	Exod 3:15*
154	Gen 2:9	56	Gen 2:7; 6:9; Exod 19:6*
155	Gen 3:1–24	57	Gen 32:28, 30
156	Gen 3:1, 5–6	62	Gen 12:1, 4
157	Gen 3:1, 14	64	Gen 4:12–13
163	Gen 3:1, 14; Lev 11:21*, 22	66	Gen 12:1, 4
		67	Gen 11:31; 12:5–9
165	Gen 3:1–7	72	Gen 11:31
167	Gen 3:16	77	Gen 12:7*
168	Gen 1:16; 3:16–19	79	Gen 12:4
170	Gen 1:1–2:25	80	Gen 12:7*
		81	Gen 17:5
		82	Gen 17:5
	De Abrahamo	83	Gen 17:5
1	Gen title; 1:1–2:1	85	Gen 12:9
7	Gen 4:26	86	Gen 12:1
8	Gen 4:26	91	Gen 12:10
9	Gen 4:26; 5:1*	92	Gen 12:10
11	Gen 5:1	93	Gen 12:11, 14–15
12	Gen 2:7; 4:26	96	Gen 12:17
13	Lev 19:24*	99	Gen 17:15
14	Lev 19:24	107	Gen 18:1–5
17	Gen 5:24*; Sir 44:16	108	Gen 18:6*, 7
19	Gen 5:24	110	Gen 18:8, 10
24	Gen 5:24	111	Gen 17:17; 18:11–12

112	Gen 18:12, 14*, 15	213	Gen 13:7
114	Gen 18:1–8	214	Gen 13:7
118	Gen 18:8	215	Gen 13:8–11
119	Gen 18:1	220	Gen 13:2, 5
121	Exod 3:14	222	Gen 13:7
122	Gen 18:1–3, 9–10	224	Gen 13:9
124	Gen 18:2	226	Gen 14:1–12
131	Gen 18:2	227	Gen 13:10; 14:2, 8
132	Gen 18:3*, 10*	228	Gen 14:4
133	Gen 13:13; 18:20–21, 25	229	Gen 14:5, 11–12
134	Gen 13:10	230	Gen 14:13
138	Gen 19:24–25	232	Gen 14:14
140	Gen 19:28	233	Gen 14:15
142	Gen 18:2; 19:1, 24–25	234	Gen 14:16
145	Gen 14:2, 8; Deut 29:23; Wis 10:6	235	Gen 14:18–20, 22
147	Gen 14:2, 8; Wis 10:6	236	Gen 14:8–9
156	Gen 1:3–4	241	Gen 14:10
158	Gen 1:16	242	Gen 14:9, 15
165	Gen 14:2, 8; Deut 29:23; Wis 10:6	245	Gen 11:31; 12:5, 10–20; 23:2
166	Gen 19:20	247	Gen 16:1
168	Gen 21:2–3; 22:2	248	Gen 16:2
169	Gen 22:1–4	249	Gen 16:2
170	Gen 22:3	251	Gen 16:3
171	Gen 22:4–6	252	Gen 13:2; 24:35
172	Gen 22:8	253	Gen 16:4
173	Gen 22:7*, 9	254	Gen 16:15; 21:2
175	Gen 22:8*	258	Gen 23:2–3
176	Gen 22:9–12	261	Gen 23:6*
181	Deut 12:31*	262	Gen 15:6*
188	Gen 11:31; 22:10	270	Gen 24:1
189	Gen 22:2, 5	271	Gen 24:1
195	Gen 21:5	273	Gen 22:16*
198	Gen 22:10; Lev 1:6	274	Gen 24:1
201	Gen 17:17; 18:12; 21:3, 6	275	Gen 26:5*
206	Gen 18:12, 15		
209	Gen 13:2; 24:35		*De Iosepho*
212	Gen 11:31; 12:4–5	2	Gen 37:2

4	Gen 37:3	61	Gen 37:36; 39:1
5	Gen 37:4	64	Gen 39:7–12
6	Gen 37:5–7	66	Gen 39:7–19
7	Gen 37:8	67	Gen 39:8–9
8	Gen 37:9, 11	72	Lev 19:15; Deut 1:17
9	Gen 37:10	74	Prov 19:18; 23:13–14
10	Gen 37:12	80	Gen 39:16–21
11	Gen 37:13–14	85	Gen 39:21–23
12	Gen 37:15–20	88	Gen 40:1–4
13	Gen 35:23; 37:21–22	89	Gen 40:6–7
14	Gen 37:23–24, 31–32	90	Gen 40:8
15	Gen 35:23; 37:25–28	91	Gen 40:9–11
16	Gen 37:29–30	92	Gen 40:12–13
18	Gen 37:28	93	Gen 40:16–17
22	Gen 37:33	96	Gen 40:18–19
23	Gen 37:34	97	Gen 40:20–22
25	Gen 37:33	99	Gen 40:23
26	Gen 28:5; 31:22–25, 41	100	Gen 41:1
27	Gen 37:33, 36; 39:1	101	Gen 41:1–4
28	Gen 30:24	102	Gen 41:5–7
32	Gen 37:3	103	Gen 41:8
35	Gen 37:28, 36; 39:1	104	Gen 41:9–13
36	Gen 37:28, 36; 39:1	105	Gen 41:14
37	Gen 39:1–6	106	Gen 41:17–24
38	Gen 41:41	107	Gen 41:25
40	Gen 39:6–9	108	Gen 41:26–27
41	Gen 39:10–12	109	Gen 41:28–32
43	Lev 20:10; Deut 22:22–24; 23:17	111	Gen 41:34–36
		114	Gen 41:33
45	Gen 39:7–9	116	Gen 41:37, 38*
46	Gen 39:8–9	117	Gen 41:39–41
48	Gen 39:11	119	Gen 41:41–43
49	Gen 39:12	121	Gen 41:45–46
50	Gen 39:13–18	123	Gen 39:20–22; 41:14, 40–44
52	Gen 37:36; 39:1, 12, 19–20	125	Gen 41:15
54	Gen 37:2; 39:4, 12	126	Isa 6:9
58	Gen 37:36; 39:1	143	Gen 41:15
60	Gen 39:7	144	Exod 20:17; Deut 5:21

148	Gen 41:43	195	Gen 43:14–15
149	Gen 41:42–43	196	Gen 43:16
150	Gen 41:42	197	Gen 43:17–23
151	Gen 41:1–45	199	Gen 43:25–28
152	Gen 37:36; 39:1; 40:1–2	200	Gen 43:29–30
153	Gen 39:1; 40:2, 7	201	Gen 43:23, 31
154	Gen 40:3	202	Gen 43:32
156	Gen 40:20–22	203	Gen 43:33
157	Gen 41:46	205	Gen 43:34
158	Gen 41:34, 47–49	206	Gen 43:34
159	Gen 41:53–54	207	Gen 44:1–2
161	Gen 41:56–57	208	Gen 44:3
163	Gen 35:24; 42:1–4	209	Gen 42:15–16, 20, 24, 27–28, 35
164	Gen 37:5–11; 42:5–6	210	Gen 43:16, 23, 29, 31–34; 44:1
165	Gen 37:28; 42:7–8		
166	Gen 42:9	211	Gen 44:4–6
167	Gen 37:28; 42:10–13	213	Gen 42:9–16; 43:21–22
168	Gen 42:15–16	215	Gen 44:7–8
170	Gen 42:21	216	Gen 44:9
171	Gen 37:5–11	217	Gen 42:36–38; 44:11–13
173	Gen 35:23; 37:21–22, 29–30; 42:22	219	Gen 44:14–16
		220	Gen 44:17
174	Gen 42:22	221	Gen 44:9
175	Gen 35:23–24; 37:28; 42:23–24	222	Gen 35:23; 44:18
		223	Gen 44:19–20
178	Gen 42:25	224	Gen 44:21–24
179	Gen 37:18–35; 42:24	225	Gen 44:22, 25–31
180	Gen 42:27–28	226	Gen 44:34
181	Gen 42:28	227	Gen 44:32
183	Gen 42:29–34	228	Gen 44:33
184	Gen 42:29–30	232	Gen 35:24
185	Gen 42:31–33	233	Gen 42:9–16, 19–20, 24
186	Gen 42:34	234	Gen 35:24; 43:16, 29, 34
187	Gen 35:24; 42:36	235	Gen 44:2, 12
188	Gen 42:37	236	Gen 37:18–28; 45:8
189	Gen 35:23; 42:38–43:10	237	Gen 45:1
191	Gen 43:8	238	Gen 45:2–4
193	Gen 43:11	239	Gen 45:3, 5–8
194	Gen 43:11–13		

241	Gen 45:8	16	Exod 15:23–25; 16:4, 13–15; 17:6; Num 20:11; Deut 8:3, 15
242	Gen 45:8		
244	Gen 37:36; 39:1, 7–20		
245	Gen 45:9	17	Exod 16:17–18; Wis 16:2
246	Gen 45:15	20	Exod 34:28
247	Gen 37:28; 39:20; 41:46	32	Exod 19:16, 19; Deut 4:12; 5:4
248	Gen 40:1–23; 41:1–36, 40–44		
		33	Exod 19:18–19; Deut 4:12, 15; 5:22–26
249	Gen 42:7, 25		
250	Gen 45:16	36	Exod 20:3–17, 13*, 14*, 15*; Deut 5:1, 7–21, 17*, 18*, 19*
251	Gen 45:17–24		
252	Gen 45:25–26		
253	Gen 45:27–28	38	Gen 17:1*
254	Wis 12:27	40	Deut 10:17–19; 17:18–20
255	Gen 46:2–5	44	Exod 19:16–19; Deut 4:11
256	Gen 46:29	45	Exod 19:10–11, 14–15
257	Gen 47:3–11	46	Exod 19:18–19; Deut 4:12
258	Gen 47:14	47	Exod 20:18*
259	Gen 47:13, 15–22	48	Ps 11:7; Wis 3:6–7
260	Gen 47:23–24	50	Exod 31:18; Deut 4:13
261	Gen 50:15, 18	51	Exod 20:2–17; Deut 5:6–21
262	Gen 50:19–21		
265	Wis 7:26; 12:1	59	Exod 20:3–5; Deut 5:7–9
266	Gen 50:19	63	Ps 51:4
267	Gen 47:25	64	Deut 6:5
268	Gen 50:22, 26	65	Exod 20:2–6; Deut 5:6–9
269	Gen 39:6–12; 40:1–23; 41:1–36	66	Wis 13:1–19; 14:1–11; 15:7–19
270	Gen 37:2, 18–28, 36; 39:1, 7–23; 41:40–44, 46	69	Wis 15:14, 16–17
		74	Ps 113:12–16; 134:15–18; Wis 15:15

De decalogo

		76	Wis 15:18–19
		81	Exod 20:4–5; Deut 5:8–9
8	Deut 23:2; Jer 2:27; 3:1–11; 16:20	82	Exod 20:7; Deut 5:11
		86	Lev 19:12
13	Deut 8:2–3, 15–16	92	Sir 23:11; 27:14
14	Deut 4:1–8	95	Sir 23:10–11
15	Exod 15:22–27; Num 20:5; Deut 8:15–18	96	Exod 20:8–11; Deut 5:12–15

97	Gen 2:1–3; Exod 20:11	161	Exod 12:14–27, 45–50;
98	Exod 20:8–11; Deut		13:3–10; 23:16; 34:22; Lev
	5:12–15		23:6, 34; Num 28:17; Deut
100	Exod 20:11		16:13–15
101	Gen 2:2–3; Exod 20:11	162	Exod 23:10–11; Lev
106	Exod 20:8–17; Deut		25:1–5
	5:12–21	164	Lev 25:8–55; 27:17–24
118	Exod 20:12; Deut 5:16	165	Exod 20:12; Deut 5:16
121	Exod 20:12–13; Deut	167	Lev 19:32
	5:16–17	168	Exod 20:2–12, 13;
130	Sir 23:24–25		22:16–17; Lev 18:1–23;
131	Exod 20:13; Deut 5:17		20:10–21; Deut 5:6–17;
132	Exod 20:15; Deut 5:18		22:13–23:1
135	Exod 20:14; Deut 5:19	170	Exod 20:15; 21:12–27;
138	Exod 20:14, 16; Deut		Lev 24:17–22; Deut 5:18;
	5:19–20		19:1–13
141	Exod 20:16; Deut 5:20	171	Exod 20:14; Lev 19:11–13,
142	Exod 20:17; Deut 5:21		35–36; Deut 5:19; 22:1–3;
154	Exod 20:2–17; Deut		24:10–15
	5:6–21	172	Exod 20:16; 23:1–3, 6–8;
155	Exod 20:3; Deut 5:7		Lev 19:11–12; Deut 5:20;
156	Exod 20:4–6; Deut 5:8–10		16:19–20
157	Exod 20:7; Deut 5:11	173	Exod 20:17; Deut 5:21
158	Exod 20:8–11; Deut	175	Exod 20:2–18; Deut
	5:12–14		5:6–21
159	Exod 12:1–20; Lev 23:5–		
	8, 23–32; Num 10:10;		*De specialibus legibus* 1–4
	28:16–17; 29:7–11		
160	Exod 23:16; 34:22; Lev	[1.Title]	Exod 20:3–5; Deut 5:7–9[8]
	23:10–11, 15–22; Deut	1.1	Exod 20:3–17; Deut
	16:9		5:7–21
		1.2	Gen 17:10

---

8. We have included the title of each book of *De specialibus legibus* for thoroughness. The provenance of these longer titles is uncertain: they may come from Philo or a later hand. Early partial evidence for them appears in Eusebius, *Hist. eccl.* 2.18.1. They are found in fuller form in MS Vind. Theol. Gr. 29 (V), an eleventh-century manuscript that has roots in the second half of the fourth century (see David T. Runia, *Philo in Early Christian Literature: A Survey*, CRINT 3 [Assen: Van Gorcum, 1993], 20–21).

1.7	Gen 17:4–6; 22:17; Exod 1:9	1.77	Exod 30:12–16
		1.79	Gen 49:28; Exod 32:1–6, 25–29
1.13	Gen 1:1–2:1; Wis 13:2–3		
1.15	Deut 4:19*	1.80	Lev 21:17–23; 22:4
1.16	Deut 4:19	1.81	Gen 1:27; Exod 3:14
1.22	Exod 20:23*	1.83	Exod 28:36–39
1.25	Exod 20:23; Lev 19:4*	1.84	Lev 16:4
1.28	Lev 19:4	1.85	Exod 28:4, 27; 36:30
1.30	Deut 6:4	1.86	Exod 28:6–9, 12; 36:13–14
1.31	Deut 4:4*		
1.41	Exod 33:18*	1.87	Exod 28:17–21; 36:17–21
1.42	Exod 33:18	1.88	Exod 28:15, 26
1.43	Exod 33:19	1.93	Exod 28:29–30; 36:32–34
1.44	Exod 33:20	1.94	Exod 28:4, 9; 36:13
1.45	Exod 33:18	1.98	Lev 10:9; Ezek 44:21
1.46	Exod 33:22–23	1.100	Lev 10:10*; 21:13–14; Ezek 44:23
1.49	Exod 33:23		
1.51	Lev 19:33–34; Deut 10:18–19	1.101	Lev 21:7
		1.102	Lev 21:7
1.52	Lev 19:33–34; Deut 10:18–19	1.103	Lev 21:17–21
		1.104	Deut 23:18*
1.53	Exod 22:28; Lev 24:15	1.105	Lev 21:13–14
1.55	Deut 13:12–17; 17:6–7	1.106	Lev 21:14
1.56	Num 25:1–3, 6–8	1.108	Lev 21:7
1.57	Num 25:11–13	1.109	Lev 21:7, 13
1.58	Lev 19:28; 21:5; Deut 14:1	1.110	Lev 21:13–14; Ezek 44:22
1.59	Lev 20:6, 27	1.111	Lev 21:7
1.60	Lev 19:26, 31; 20:27; Deut 18:10–12	1.112	Lev 21:1–3
		1.113	Lev 21:11
1.63	Lev 19:26, 31; 20:27; Deut 18:10–13	1.115	Lev 21:10, 12
		1.117	Lev 21:17–22
1.65	Deut 18:15, 18	1.118	Lev 22:4
1.66	Isa 66:1	1.119	Lev 22:4–7
1.67	Deut 12:5–7	1.120	Lev 22:10
1.68	Deut 12:11–14, 17–18	1.122	Lev 22:10
1.72	Exod 30:10; Lev 16:2–3, 12–13, 34	1.123	Lev 22:10
		1.126	Lev 22:11
1.74	Deut 16:21	1.128	Lev 22:11
1.76	Gen 8:21	1.129	Lev 22:13

1.131	Num 18:20; Deut 10:9; 18:1–2	1.179	Num 28:5, 12–14
1.132	Num 15:19–21	1.180	Num 28:11; 29:1–6
1.134	Exod 22:29; 34:26; Num 18:12–13; Deut 18:4; 26:2–4, 10	1.181	Num 28:16–17, 19–24
		1.183	Exod 23:16; Lev 23:15–21; Num 28:26–31
		1.184	Lev 23:19–20; Num 28:27
1.135	Exod 13:12–13; 22:30; 34:19–20; Num 18:15, 17; Deut 15:19	1.185	Lev 23:17, 20
		1.186	Lev 16:29–31; 23:24, 27–32; Num 29:1, 7–11
1.137	Exod 13:13	1.188	Lev 16:5, 7–10; Num 29:8
1.138	Exod 13:13; 22:29	1.189	Lev 23:34–36; Num 29:12–38
1.139	Num 3:46–47; 18:15–16		
1.141	Lev 27:32; Num 18:12; Deut 18:4	1.190	Num 28:15, 22, 30; 29:5, 11, 22, 25, 28, 31, 34, 38
1.145	Exod 29:27; Lev 7:11–14; 10:14–15; Num 18:18	1.194	Lev 1:1–17; 3:1–17; 4:1–35
1.147	Deut 18:3	1.195	Lev 1:1–17
1.150	Deut 18:3	1.196	Lev 3:1–4:35
1.151	Lev 6:38; Deut 18:1–2	1.198	Lev 1:3–4, 10
1.152	Lev 7:19–24; Num 18:9–19	1.199	Lev 1:5–10
		1.200	Lev 1:3, 10
1.156	Num 18:21–24; Ezek 44:10–11, 14	1.202	Lev 1:4
		1.204	Ps 14:5; 23:4
1.157	Num 18:26–32	1.205	Lev 1:5; 17:11, 14
1.158	Num 35:2–8, 11–15	1.206	Lev 1:9
1.160	Num 35:26–27	1.208	Lev 1:6
1.161	Num 35:25–26	1.212	Lev 3:1–17, 1, 3–4, 6, 9–10, 14–15
1.162	Lev 1:14		
1.163	Lev 1:2, 10; 22:19	1.216	Lev 3:3–4, 9–10, 14–15
1.165	Lev 1:2, 10; 22:19	1.218	Lev 3:4, 10, 15
1.166	Lev 22:19–24	1.220	Lev 6:36–38; 19:5–8
1.169	Exod 29:38–42; Num 28:3–8	1.222	Lev 3:1–17; 6:36; 19:6
		1.223	Lev 6:37–38; 19:7–8
1.170	Gen 2:2; Num 28:9–10	1.224	Lev 6:32–34; 22:29
1.171	Gen 1:27; Exod 30:7–8; Lev 17:11	1.225	Lev 6:35; 22:30
		1.226	Lev 4:1–35, 3, 13–14, 22–23, 27–28, 32
1.172	Exod 25:30; Lev 24:5–8		
1.175	Lev 24:7	1.227	Exod 23:8
1.177	Num 28:11	1.228	Lev 4:3, 14, 23, 28, 32

1.230	Lev 4:3*	1.285	Lev 6:9, 12–13
1.231	Lev 4:4–7	1.287	Exod 20:24–25; Deut
1.232	Lev 4:8–21		27:5–6
1.233	Lev 4:22–35	1.288	Lev 6:12–13; Eccl 2:13
1.234	Lev 5:15–16	1.289	Lev 2:13*
1.235	Lev 6:2–3	1.290	Lev 2:12
1.236	Lev 6:4–5	1.291	Lev 2:11
1.237	Lev 6:6–7	1.293	Lev 2:11
1.238	Lev 5:15; 6:6	1.295	Job 1:21; Eccl 5:14
1.239	Lev 1:3–4; 3:3–4; 4:8–9	1.296	Exod 27:21; 30:8; Lev
1.240	Lev 6:19, 22, 36		24:3–4
1.242	Lev 6:19, 22, 36; 21:17–23	1.298	Exod 27:21; 30:8; Lev
1.244	Lev 4:12, 21		24:3–4
1.245	Lev 1:9	1.299	Deut 30:11
1.247	Num 6:2	1.300	Deut 10:12–13
1.248	Exod 13:12–13; 22:29;	1.301	Deut 30:11–14
	34:19–20, 26; Num 6:2;	1.302	Deut 10:14*
	18:12–13, 15, 17–19; Deut	1.303	Deut 8:7; 10:15; 11:11
	15:19; 26:1–4, 10	1.304	Lev 26:41; Deut 32:15; Jer
1.249	Lev 10:9; Num 6:3–4;		9:25
	Ezek 44:21	1.305	Deut 10:16
1.250	Num 6:5–7	1.306	Deut 10:17
1.251	Num 6:13–14	1.308	Deut 10:18
1.252	Num 6:14	1.309	Deut 10:18
1.253	Num 6:14	1.311	Deut 10:21
1.254	Num 6:18	1.312	Deut 10:20; 12:29–31
1.256	Lev 6:13–16	1.313	Deut 6:7; 11:19; 12:31;
1.259	Lev 22:18–25		28:49–57
1.261	Num 19:11–16, 19	1.314	Deut 28:25, 36–37
1.262	Num 19:17–18	1.315	Deut 13:1–11
1.264	Num 19:17	1.316	Deut 13:1–11
1.265	Num 14:11; 15:30*	1.318	Deut 13:18*; 14:1*
1.268	Num 19:2–6, 9	1.319	Lev 19:26
1.271	Lev 5:11; Isa 1:11	1.325	Deut 23:1
1.274	Exod 20:24–25; 27:1–8;	1.326	Deut 23:2, 17
	30:1–7; Deut 27:5–6	1.328	Deut 23:1
1.276	Exod 30:7	1.330	Deut 23:1
1.277	Isa 1:15	1.332	Deut 23:2*
1.280	Deut 23:18	1.333	Deut 23:3

1.344	Deut 23:1–2	2.66	Exod 20:10; Deut 5:14
1.345	Deut 4:4*	2.69	Exod 20:10; 23:12; Deut
[2.Title]	Exod 20:7–12; Deut 5:11–		5:14
	16	2.70	Deut 5:14
2.1	Exod 20:3–6; Deut 5:7–10	2.71	Deut 15:1–3, 7–11
2.2	Exod 20:7; Deut 5:11	2.72	Deut 15:10
2.3	Gen 31:53	2.73	Deut 15:3
2.9	Num 30:3	2.74	Exod 22:25; Lev 25:35–
2.10	Lev 19:12		37; Deut 23:19–20
2.14	Exod 24:3, 7	2.79	Exod 21:2; Lev 25:39–41;
2.24	Num 30:4–17		Deut 15:12*; Jer 41:14
2.25	Num 30:10	2.80	Deut 15:18
2.26	Lev 5:1	2.82	Lev 25:40; Deut 15:18
2.27	Exod 20:7; Deut 5:11	2.84	Exod 21:2; Lev 25:39–41;
2.28	Deut 25:2–3		Deut 15:12, 18; Jer 41:14
2.29	Num 30:4–17	2.85	Deut 15:13–14
2.32	Lev 27:2–8	2.86	Exod 20:8–10; 23:10–11,
2.33	Lev 27:3–7		27–32; Lev 23:27–32;
2.35	Lev 27:9–10		25:2–7; Num 29:7–11;
2.36	Lev 27:11–13		Deut 5:12–14
2.37	Lev 27:14–15	2.87	Exod 23:10–11; Lev
2.38	Deut 23:21		25:2–7
2.39	Exod 20:8–11; Lev 25:2–5;	2.96	Exod 23:10–11; Lev
	Deut 5:12–15; 15:1–2, 12		25:2–7
2.41	Exod 12:14–24; 23:12;	2.104	Exod 23:10–11; Lev
	34:22; Lev 23:40–43; Num		25:2–7
	28:11–15, 26; Deut 16:10	2.105	Exod 23:11; Lev 25:4–6
2.42	Exod 29:38; Num 28:2–3;	2.106	Exod 23:11; Lev 25:6
	Ezek 46:13–14	2.108	Exod 23:11; Lev 25:6
2.50	Lev 18:22; 20:13	2.109	Exod 23:11; Lev 25:7
2.51	Lev 23:2*, 44*	2.110	Lev 25:8–12
2.54	Gen 18:11–15	2.111	Lev 25:10, 13
2.56	Exod 20:8–10; Lev 23:3;	2.112	Lev 25:14–16
	Deut 5:12–14	2.113	Lev 25:14–16, 23; Num
2.58	Gen 2:2; Exod 20:11		36:7, 9
2.60	Exod 20:9; 23:12; 31:17;	2.114	Lev 25:25–28
	Prov 6:9–11; 24:33–34; Sir	2.115	Lev 27:16–21
	33:28	2.116	Lev 25:29–31
2.65	Exod 35:3	2.117	Lev 25:29–30

2.119	Josh 18:10	2.160	Gen 1:29–30; 2:15–16
2.120	Num 18:20; 35:2–8; Deut 10:9	2.161	Exod 12:15; Lev 24:5–6
		2.162	Lev 23:10–14
2.121	Lev 25:32–34	2.168	Gen 23:3–20; Lev 23:10;
2.122	Lev 25:35–43		Deut 26:5
2.123	Lev 25:44–46	2.169	Num 13:24, 28; Deut
2.124	Num 27:8		8:7–10
2.126	Num 36:6–9	2.170	Lev 18:28; Num 13:28–29;
2.127	Num 27:8–11		Deut 4:25–28; 8:19–20;
2.128	Num 36:7, 9		9:1–2
2.129	Num 27:8–11	2.171	Lev 23:10–11
2.132	Num 27:10	2.173	Lev 25:23
2.133	Deut 21:17	2.175	Lev 23:10, 14
2.134	Exod 12:29; 13:2, 15	2.176	Lev 23:10–16; Deut 16:9
2.136	Deut 21:15–17	2.179	Exod 23:16; Lev 23:16–17;
2.138	Deut 21:17		Num 28:26; Deut 16:9–10
2.140	Num 28:11–15	2.182	Lev 2:11; 23:17, 20
2.142	Num 28:11	2.183	Exod 32:25–29; Lev 7:18–
2.145	Exod 12:1–14; Lev 23:5; Num 9:3, 6–11; Deut 16:6		24; 23:20; Num 18:8–20; Deut 10:9; 18:1–5
2.146	Gen 15:13–14; Exod 12:1–14, 21–28, 37; Num 11:21	2.184	Lev 23:17
		2.187	Lev 23:17, 20
		2.188	Lev 23:24; Num 10:10; 29:1
2.148	Exod 12:3–6, 21		
2.149	Exod 12:6; Lev 23:5; Num 9:3	2.189	Exod 19:16, 19
		2.190	Num 10:9; Josh 6:8
2.150	Exod 12:2, 15–20; Lev 23:5; Num 28:16	2.192	Lev 23:24; Num 6:26; 10:10; 29:1; Job 25:2; Isa 45:7
2.151	Gen 1:1–2:1		
2.152	Exod 12:2; Lev 23:5; Num 28:16	2.193	Lev 23:26–32; Num 29:7–11
2.155	Lev 23:6; Num 28:17	2.194	Lev 16:31; 23:32
2.156	Exod 12:15; Lev 23:6; Num 28:17	2.197	Lev 23:26–32; Num 29:7–11
2.157	Exod 12:16	2.199	Exod 15:22–27; 16:4–5, 19–20, 35; 17:1–7; Num 20:2–13; Deut 8:2–3
2.158	Exod 12:8, 34, 39; Deut 16:3		
2.159	Exod 12:15; Lev 23:6; Num 28:17	2.200	Lev 23:27; Num 29:7
		2.201	Lev 23:27; Num 29:7

2.204	Lev 23:34–36, 39–43; Deut 16:13	2.256	Exod 23:13
2.205	Exod 23:16; Lev 23:39; Deut 16:13	2.258	Exod 20:3–7; Deut 5:7–11
		2.259	Exod 20:6; Deut 5:10; Ps 111:1–3
2.206	Lev 23:42	2.260	Gen 2:2; Exod 20:8–11; Deut 5:12–14
2.208	Lev 23:43		
2.210	Lev 23:34, 39; Num 29:12	2.261	Exod 20:12; Deut 5:16
2.211	Lev 23:36; Num 29:35	2.262	Exod 20:12; Deut 5:16
2.215	Deut 26:1–11	[3.Title]	Exod 20:13, 15; Deut 5:17–18
2.216	Deut 26:2–4		
2.217	Deut 26:5–6	3.8	Exod 20:13*; Deut 5:17*
2.218	Deut 26:7–9	3.11	Lev 20:10; Deut 22:22
2.219	Deut 26:10	3.12	Lev 18:6–20
2.222	Lev 7:18–24; Num 18:20; Deut 10:9; 18:1–5; 26:4	3.13	Lev 18:7
		3.14	Lev 18:7
2.223	Exod 20:12; Deut 5:16	3.20	Lev 18:8; 20:11; Deut 22:30; 27:20
2.224	Exod 20:3–12; Deut 5:7–16		
		3.22	Lev 18:9, 11; 20:17; Deut 27:22
2.226	Exod 20:12; Deut 5:16		
2.228	Deut 6:7	3.24	Lev 18:9, 11; 20:17; Deut 27:22
2.232	Deut 21:18–21; Prov 13:24		
2.234	Deut 21:18–21	3.26	Lev 18:10, 12–17; 20:12, 14, 19–21
2.235	Exod 20:12; Deut 5:16		
2.237	Exod 20:12; Deut 5:16	3.27	Lev 18:18
2.238	Lev 19:32	3.29	Exod 34:16; Deut 7:3
2.239	Lev 19:3*	3.30	Deut 24:1–4
2.243	Exod 21:15*; Deut 21:21	3.31	Lev 20:10; Deut 22:22; 24:4
2.248	Exod 21:16; Lev 20:9; Deut 27:16		
		3.32	Lev 18:19; 20:18
2.249	Exod 31:14–15; 35:2	3.37	Lev 18:22; 20:13
2.250	Exod 12:37; Num 15:32	3.38	Deut 23:17
2.251	Exod 35:3; Num 15:33–36; Deut 17:7	3.39	Lev 18:22; 20:13
		3.45	Lev 18:23; 20:15–16
2.252	Exod 20:7; Lev 24:16; Deut 5:11	3.42	Deut 23:1
		3.46	Lev 19:19
2.253	Exod 21:16; Deut 21:18–21	3.47	Lev 19:19
		3.49	Exod 20:15–16; 22:19; Lev 20:15–16
2.255	Deut 4:19, 28; 17:2–5; Ps 113:16; Wis 13:2		
		3.51	Deut 23:17

3.52	Lev 20:10; Deut 22:22; 29:29	3.108	Exod 21:22–23
		3.109	Exod 21:22
3.53	Num 5:12–28	3.110	Exod 21:22
3.55	Num 5:15	3.117	Exod 21:22–23
3.56	Num 5:18	3.120	Exod 21:13
3.57	Num 5:15	3.123	Exod 21:13; Num 35:6,
3.58	Lev 20:10; Num 5:17; Deut 22:22		11–15, 25, 28
		3.124	Exod 32:25–29; Num 35:6
3.59	Num 5:17; 19:17	3.125	Exod 32:1–6
3.60	Num 5:15, 17, 18	3.126	Exod 32:25–29; Num 25:9
3.61	Num 5:19–20, 22	3.127	Exod 32:26, 29
3.62	Num 5:23–28	3.128	Exod 21:13; 32:25–29;
3.63	Lev 15:18		Num 35:6, 11–15
3.65	Exod 22:16–17; Deut 22:28–29	3.129	Exod 21:13–14; Num 35:12
		3.130	Exod 21:14; Num 35:6,
3.70	Exod 22:16–17; Deut 22:28–29		11–15
		3.131	Num 35:25, 28
3.73	Deut 22:23–24	3.132	Num 35:26–28
3.74	Deut 22:23–27	3.133	Num 35:25, 28
3.76	Deut 22:23–27	3.135	Lev 21:11; 22:3–9
3.77	Deut 22:24, 27*	3.136	Exod 21:13
3.78	Deut 22:23–27	3.140	Esth 8:13
3.80	Deut 22:13–17	3.141	Exod 21:20–21
3.81	Deut 22:19	3.142	Exod 21:21
3.82	Deut 22:18–19	3.143	Exod 21:21
3.83	Gen 1:27; 9:6	3.144	Exod 21:28
3.84	Gen 9:6; Exod 21:12; Lev 24:17, 21; Num 35:16–21, 30–31	3.145	Exod 21:29–30, 32
		3.146	Exod 21:35–36
		3.148	Exod 21:33–34
3.86	Exod 21:14	3.149	Deut 22:8
3.88	Exod 21:14	3.150	Num 35:31–33
3.91	Exod 21:14	3.151	Deut 21:22
3.92	Num 35:16–18, 22–23	3.152	Deut 21:23
3.94	Exod 22:18; Deut 18:10	3.153	Deut 24:16
3.102	Exod 22:18; Deut 18:10	3.154	Deut 24:16
3.104	Exod 21:13	3.168	Deut 24:16
3.106	Exod 21:12, 18–19; Num 35:17, 21	3.175	Deut 25:11–12
		3.177	Deut 25:11–12
3.107	Exod 21:19	3.179	Deut 25:11–12

3.180	Deut 25:12	4.29	Exod 22:6
3.182	Exod 21:12, 23–25; Lev	4.31	Lev 6:2, 4
	24:17–21; Deut 19:21	4.33	Exod 22:7
3.183	Exod 21:15	4.34	Exod 22:8
3.184	Exod 21:26	4.36	Exod 22:10–13
3.195	Exod 21:24; Lev 24:20;	4.37	Exod 22:14–15
	Deut 19:21	4.39	Lev 19:11–12*
3.196	Exod 21:26	4.40	Lev 19:11–12
3.197	Exod 21:26	4.41	Exod 20:16*[9]; Lev 19:11;
3.198	Exod 21:27		Deut 5:20*
3.201	Exod 21:26–27	4.42	Exod 20:16; Lev 19:11;
3.202	Exod 21:26–27		Deut 5:20
3.203	Exod 21:27	4.44	Exod 20:16; 23:1–2, 7;
3.204	Deut 24:6		Deut 5:20; 19:16–20
3.205	Num 19:11–13	4.45	Exod 23:1–2
3.206	Num 19:14–15, 19	4.48	Lev 19:26, 31; 20:6; Deut
3.207	Gen 1:27		18:10–12
3.208	Num 19:22	4.49	Deut 18:18
[4.Title]	Exod 20:14, 16–17; Deut	4.50	Lev 19:26, 31; 20:6; Deut
	5:19–21		18:10–12
4.1	Exod 20:13–15; Deut	4.51	Jer 34:9; 36:8
	5:17–19	4.53	Num 35:30; Deut 17:6;
4.2	Exod 22:4, 7, 9		19:15
4.3	Exod 22:3	4.59	Exod 23:1
4.4	Exod 21:2; Deut 15:12	4.60	Exod 23:1
4.5	Exod 22:3–4	4.62	Exod 23:8; Deut 16:19
4.7	Exod 22:1–3	4.64	Exod 23:7–8; Deut
4.10	Exod 22:3		16:18–20
4.11	Exod 22:1, 4	4.66	Exod 23:8; Deut 16:20
4.12	Exod 22:1	4.69	Exod 28:30; Lev 8:8
4.13	Exod 21:16; 22:1, 4; Deut	4.70	Lev 19:15; Deut 1:16–17;
	24:7		16:18–20
4.19	Exod 21:16; Deut 24:7	4.71	Deut 1:17*
4.22	Exod 22:5	4.72	Exod 23:3; Lev 19:15
4.24	Exod 22:5	4.76	Exod 23:3; Lev 19:15
4.26	Exod 22:5–6	4.78	Exod 20:17*; Deut 5:21*

---

9. The placement of the subsection title, which is the quotation, is debated. We place it at *Spec.* 4.41, not 4.40, because of the internal deictic marker τουτί.

4.80	Exod 20:17; Deut 5:21	4.134	Exod 20:3–17; Deut
4.82	Exod 20:17; Deut 5:21		5:7–21
4.83	Exod 20:17; Deut 5:21	4.137	Deut 6:6, 8; 11:18
4.85	Exod 20:17; Deut 5:21	4.138	Deut 6:8; 11:18
4.86	Exod 20:17; Deut 5:21	4.141	Deut 6:7; 11:19
4.92	Exod 20:17; Deut 5:21	4.142	Deut 6:9; 11:20
4.95	Exod 20:17; Deut 5:21	4.143	Deut 4:2; 12:32
4.98	Exod 22:29–30; Num	4.144	Deut 4:2; 12:32
	18:12–13, 31; Deut 18:4–5	4.147	Deut 4:2; 12:32
4.99	Exod 34:26; Num 18:13;	4.149	Deut 19:14*
	Deut 26:2, 10–11	4.157	Deut 17:15*
4.101	Lev 11:7, 10–12; Deut	4.158	Deut 17:16–17
	14:8–10	4.160	Deut 17:18
4.105	Deut 14:4–5	4.161	Deut 17:19
4.106	Lev 11:3–8; Deut 14:4–8	4.163	Deut 17:18
4.108	Lev 11:3; Deut 14:6	4.165	Deut 17:19–20
4.110	Lev 11:9–12; Deut	4.167	Deut 17:20; 28:14
	14:9–10	4.168	Num 20:17; 21:22
4.113	Lev 11:20, 23, 41–43	4.169	Deut 16:20; 17:20;
4.114	Lev 11:21–22		Wis 4:8
4.116	Lev 11:13–19; Deut	4.170	Exod 18:21
	14:12–19	4.171	Exod 18:21
4.117	Deut 14:11, 19	4.173	Exod 18:13–23
4.119	Exod 22:31; Lev 5:2;	4.174	Exod 18:24–26
	17:15; 22:8; Deut 14:20	4.177	Deut 10:17–18*
4.120	Exod 22:31; Lev 5:2;	4.179	Num 23:9; Deut 10:18
	17:15; 22:8; Deut 14:20	4.180	Deut 4:20; Jer 2:3
4.122	Lev 17:11, 14; Deut 12:23	4.183	Lev 19:16*
4.123	Gen 2:7; Lev 3:17; 7:16–	4.190	Deut 17:8–9
	17; 17:11, 14; Deut 12:23	4.191	Lev 10:9
4.124	Lev 3:17; 7:13–15	4.194	Lev 19:35–36; Deut
4.125	Lev 4:7–10; 17:6		25:13–15
4.126	Num 11:4–6	4.195	Lev 19:13; Deut 24:15
4.128	Num 11:31	4.197	Lev 19:14
4.129	Num 11:6–9, 32–33	4.198	Deut 27:18
4.130	Num 11:20, 34	4.200	Lev 19:14; Deut 27:18
4.131	Deut 12:8*	4.202	Lev 19:14
4.133	Exod 20:3–17; Deut	4.203	Lev 19:19; Deut 22:9–11
	5:7–21	4.205	Deut 22:10

4.206	Lev 11:3; Deut 14:4	53	Exod 18:3–4; 28:1; Num
4.207	Lev 19:19; Deut 22:11		31:2
4.208	Lev 19:19; Deut 22:9	55	Exod 33:11
4.211	Lev 19:19; Deut 22:9	58	Num 27:16–17; 3 Kgdms
4.215	Exod 23:10–11; Lev		22:17
	19:19; 25:3–5; Deut 22:9	59	Exod 18:3–4; 28:1
4.217	Lev 19:19; Deut 22:9	62	Prov 8:22–23
4.218	Lev 19:19; Deut 22:9	63	Exod 4:10–13, 19–20;
4.220	Deut 20:10–11		Num 27:17
4.222	Deut 20:12–13	66	Exod 18:3–4; 28:1; Num
4.223	Num 31:10; Deut 13:16;		27:18–21
	20:14	67	Num 27:22–23
4.226	Deut 20:19–20	68	Deut 31:1–3
4.227	Deut 20:19	69	Deut 31:7, 23
4.229	Deut 20:20	70	Num 27:19
		72	Deut 31:30–32:44

De virtutibus

		73	Deut 32:43
		74	Deut 32:1; Ps 104:4
8	Gen 28:20	75	Deut 32:1–43
18	Deut 22:5	77	Deut 33:1–29
20	Deut 22:5	82	Exod 22:25; Lev 25:35–
21	Deut 22:5		37; Deut 23:19–20
23	Deut 20:8	83	Lev 25:35; Deut 15:10
25	Deut 20:8	86	Lev 25:37; Deut 23:19–20
28	Deut 20:5–7; 24:5	88	Lev 19:13; Deut 24:14–15
29	Deut 20:5	89	Deut 24:10–11
30	Deut 20:5–7	90	Lev 19:9; 23:22; Deut
31	Deut 20:5–7		24:19
32	Deut 20:9	91	Lev 19:10; Deut 24:20–21
34	Num 25:1–18; 31:1–18	92	Lev 19:9; 23:22; Deut
35	Num 25:1–2		24:19
40	Num 25:1–2	95	Lev 27:30–33; Num 18:12,
41	Num 25:9		17; Deut 18:4; 26:1–15
42	Num 31:3–6	96	Exod 23:4; Deut 22:1–4
43	Num 31:7–12, 15–18	97	Exod 23:10–11; Lev
44	Exod 24:11; Num 31:49		25:3–7
46	Num 31:5–8, 49	98	Exod 23:10–11; Lev
47	Lev 26:5; Deut 9:1–7;		25:3–7
	11:22–25	99	Lev 25:8–17

100	Lev 25:10, 13	154	Deut 20:19
103	Exod 22:21; Lev 19:33–34; Deut 10:19	156	Lev 19:23
		159	Lev 19:24
104	Exod 12:48; Lev 19:10; 25:6; Num 15:14–16; 25:15; Deut 10:18	160	Exod 22:21; 23:4–5; Lev 19:23–24, 33–34; Deut 10:19; 20:10–11, 19–20; 22:4, 10; 25:4
106	Deut 23:7*	163	Deut 8:11–14
107	Gen 47:4–11; Exod 1:11–14	165	Deut 8:18*
		168	Deut 8:18
108	Deut 23:8	171	Num 15:30*
109	Deut 20:11–15	174	Num 15:30–31
110	Deut 21:10–13	183	Deut 30:11–14
111	Deut 21:12–13	184	Deut 26:17–18*
113	Deut 21:13	199	Gen 2:7; 4:1–2, 8, 10
115	Deut 21:14	200	Gen 4:11–12, 15
116	Exod 23:5; Deut 22:4	201	Gen 6:9; 7:1, 17–23
117	Exod 23:4; Deut 22:1	202	Gen 9:18, 20–25
122	Exod 21:2; Lev 25:39–41; Deut 15:12	203	Gen 2:7
		205	Gen 1:27; 2:17; 3:17–19
124	Deut 23:15–16	207	Gen 11:29; 16:3, 15; 21:2; 24:36; 25:1–2, 5–6
126	Exod 22:30; Lev 22:27		
129	Exod 22:30; Lev 22:27	208	Gen 25:24–34; 27:[16], [23], 41
133	Exod 22:30; Lev 22:27		
134	Lev 22:28	209	Gen 27:27–29, 39–40
136	Lev 22:28	212	Gen 11:31
138	Lev 22:28	214	Gen 12:1
142	Exod 22:30; 23:19*; 34:26*; Lev 22:27; Deut 14:20*	216	Gen 15:6; 23:6
		218	Gen 15:6; 23:6
144	Exod 23:19; 34:26; Deut 14:20; 22:10	221	Gen 38:6
		222	Gen 38:6–10, 29–30
145	Deut 25:4	223	Gen 29:24, 29; 30:3–13
146	Exod 13:13; Lev 17:3; Deut 14:4; 22:10; 25:4	224	Gen 35:22–26
147	Exod 22:21; Lev 19:33–34; Deut 10:19		

De praemiis et poenis

149	Lev 19:9; 23:22; Deut 20:19–20	1	Gen 1:1, 26–27
150	Deut 20:19	2	Exod 20:1–17; Deut 5:6–21

9	Gen 1:28–30
13	Gen 4:26
14	Gen 4:26
16	Gen 5:24*
17	Gen 5:24; 12:1
22	Gen 8:16–19
23	Gen 6:9, 17; 7:1
24	Gen 21:3; 25:26
27	Gen 15:6
28	Gen 15:6
31	Gen 15:6; 21:1–6
35	Gen 21:1–6
36	Gen 32:24–30
39	Gen 32:24–30
44	Gen 32:28, 30
46	Ps 35:10
47	Gen 32:25*
49	Gen 15:6
50	Gen 21:1–6
53	Exod 20:1–17; Deut 5:6–21; 18:18; 33:5; 34:10; Wis 11:1
54	Exod 4:10
55	Exod 20:1–17; Deut 5:6–21; 18:18; 34:10; Wis 11:1
57	Gen 35:22–26
58	Gen 11:31; 12:4; 16:15; 21:1–7; 25:1–4; 1 Chr 1:28, 32, 34
59	Gen 25:24–27
60	Gen 35:22–26
61	Gen 16:15; 21:1–7; 25:1–4; 1 Chr 1:28, 32, 34
63	Gen 25:24
65	Gen 35:22–26
68	Gen 4:1–2, 8, 10–12
70	Gen 4:12
72	Gen 4:12, 15
74	Gen 4:8, 12, 15; Num 16:1–35; 1 Chr 9:19; 26:1–19
77	Num 12:3; 16:8–14
78	Lev 8:1–36; Num 16:3
79	Exod 23:22–23, 27; Lev 26:3–13, 7–8; Deut 28:1–14, 7; 30:7, 16
80	Deut 30:11–14
82	Lev 26:3; Deut 6:6; 11:13; 28:1–2; 30:2, 16–17
83	Deut 4:6
84	Deut 4:7
85	Lev 26:6–8
87	Isa 11:6–8
88	Isa 11:6–8
89	Isa 11:6–8
91	Lev 26:6
93	Lev 26:6*
94	Lev 26:8, 37; Deut 28:7
95	Exod 23:27; Num 24:7*
96	Exod 23:28; Deut 7:20
98	Lev 26:4–5, 10; Deut 28:3–6, 8–14
99	Exod 23:25
101	Lev 26:3–5; Deut 11:14–15, 17; 28:3–5, 8, 12
103	Lev 26:10
104	Deut 28:8
107	Deut 7:13; 15:6; 28:3–4, 12
108	Exod 23:26*; Deut 7:14*
110	Isa 65:20
111	Exod 23:26*
113	Deut 28:6
115	Deut 30:4
118	Exod 15:26; 23:22–23; Lev 26:3–13; Deut 7:15; 28:1–14

119	Exod 15:26; Deut 7:15	146	Deut 28:56
123	Lev 26:12	147	Lev 26:25
124	Lev 26:13; Deut 28:13, 44	148	Lev 26:23, 36–37
125	Lev 26:12	149	Lev 26:22, 39
126	Exod 23:22–23; Lev 26:3–13, 14–46; Deut 28:1–14, 15–69	150	Lev 26:31–32; Deut 28:61
		151	Deut 28:66–67
		152	Deut 28:43–44
127	Lev 26:16; Deut 28:33	153	Exod 23:10–12; Lev 26:33–35
128	Deut 28:38–39		
129	Deut 28:40, 42	154	Exod 23:10–12; Deut 15:1–11
130	Lev 26:16, 20; Deut 28:22		
131	Lev 26:19*; Deut 28:23	157	Lev 26:43
132	Lev 26:19	158	1 Kgdms 2:5*; Isa 54:1
133	Lev 26:31; Deut 28:24	159	1 Kgdms 2:5
134	Lev 26:29; Deut 28:53–57	162	Lev 26:14–46; Deut 28:15–69
136	Lev 26:16; Deut 28:20, 22		
138	Deut 28:48	163	Lev 26:40–45; Deut 30:1–10
139	Deut 28:30–31, 34		
141	Deut 28:16–18	164	Deut 30:3–5
143	Lev 26:16; Deut 28:22, 27–28, 59	165	Isa 11:11–12
		168	Deut 30:5–10
145	Deut 28:35	169	Deut 30:7

The Philosophical Treatises

Quod omnis probus liber sit		*De providentia* 1–2	
13	Prov 9:1–6	1.22	Gen 1:1–2
29	Exod 17:12	1.25	Prov 6:6–8
43	Exod 7:1; Deut 9:26; 10:17	1.47	Exod 9:13–35; 10:1–20
		1.51	Prov 6:6–8
57	Gen 27:40	1.55	Gen 18:23; 19:24
65	Job 28	1.70	Gen 1:11–30
68	Deut 30:11–13, 14*	1.84	Gen 17:9–14; Exod 20:8–11; 31:12–17; Lev 7:9–11; 11; 12:3; Num 15:32–36; Deut 5:12–14; 14:1–21
69	Gen 8:20; 22:2–8; Num 15:3		
		2.29	Deut 29:29; 1 Kgdms 16:7

De animalibus[10]		*De aeternitate mundi*	
16	Gen 1:26–27	1	Gen 1:1; Ps 106:1
[20]	Gen 1:26–29; 9:2–3[11]	19	Gen title; 1:1–2*, 14–18;
22	Lev 11:13–19; Deut 22:6		8:22
25	Exod 23:19; 34:26; Deut		
	22:4–10; 25:4		*De numeris*[12]
31	Lev 11:10–12		
49	Gen 38:9; Exod 20:14; Lev	No allusion or citation to Scripture
	20:10; Deut 5:18; 22:22	are identified in this fragment.
55	Prov 30:30		
66	Lev 19:19		

The Apologetic and Historical Treatises

De vita contemplativa		*Hypothetica*	
2	Exod 3:14	6.1 (427.10)[13]	Gen 11:31
36	Exod 20:8–10; Deut	6.1 (427.11)	Gen 46:6–7;
	5:12–14		Exod 12:37–41
63	Gen 2:21–22	6.1 (427.13)	Exod 3:7–10; 7:3
65	Lev 23:15–16	6.1 (427.17)	Exod 1:7
81	Lev 24:5–9	6.2 (427.22)	Num 20:2–11
85	Exod 15:1–21	6.2 (428.1)	Exod 16:3;
86	Exod 14:15–31		Num 11:4–6
87	Exod 15:1–21	6.3 (428.5)	Exod 17:1–7;
			Num 20:2–11
		6.6 (428.25)	3 Kgdms 6;
			2 Chr 3, 4

---

10. Terian, *Philonis Alexandrini de Animalibus.*

11. This passage with its allusions is thought to be an interpolation by Terian.

12. Abraham Terian, "A Philonic Fragment on the Decad," in Frederick E. Greenspahn, Earle Hilgert, and Burton L. Mack, eds., *Nourished with Peace: Studies in Hellenistic Judaism in Memory of Samuel Sandmel*, Scholars Press Homage Series 9 (Chico: Scholars Press, 1984), 173–82.

13. References are found in Eusebius, *Praep. ev.* 8 and are given in parentheses for the page and line numbers from Karl Mras, ed., *Eusebius' Werke*, vol. 8: *Die Praeparatio evangelica*, GCS 43.1–2, 2nd ed. (Berlin: Akademie Verlag, 1982).

6.8 (429.6)	Num 36:13	177	Dan 4:32
7.1 (429.16)	Exod 21:17		
7.1 (429.19)	Lev 18:22; 20:13		*Legatio ad Gaium*
7.1 (429.20)	Lev 20:10;		
	Deut 22:23–25	4	Gen 32:28, 30
7.1 (429.21)	Exod 21:16–17;	115	Exod 20:3; Deut 5:7
	Deut 23:17	156	Exod 23:16–19; 34:26;
7.2 (429.22)	Deut 24:7		Deut 26:2
7.4 (430.7)	Exod 22:28	202	Deut 7:5; 12:2–3
7.5 (430.12)	Num 30:3–17;	210	Deut 6:7; 11:19
	Deut 23:21–23	289	Deut 21:17
7.6 (430.17)	Lev 19:18	306	Lev 16:34
7.6 (430.18)	Deut 15:14; 22:1–3	307	Lev 16:2, 17
7.6 (430.21)	Ps 40:2; Prov 19:17	353	Exod 20:7; Deut 5:11
7.8 (431.3)	Lev 19:35–36;	361	Lev 11:27
	Deut 25:13–16;		
	Prov 11:1; 16:11		Unplaced Fragments from Harris[14]
7.9 (431.8)	Deut 22:6		
7.12 (431.22)	Exod 20:9–10;		FR(H) 100 A11 Deut 12:8
	Deut 5:13–14		FR(H) 100 B28 Lev 19:32
7.15 (432.11)	Exod 23:11;		FR(H) 106 A23–24 Lev 11;
	Lev 25:4–5		Deut 14:3–20
7.15 (432.12)	Exod 20:9–10;		FR(H) 106 A28 Ps 95:5
	Deut 5:13–14		FR(H) 106 A34 Gen 8:14
7.19 (433.3)	Exod 23:11;		FR(H) 106 A36 Gen 7:11
	Lev 25:4–5		FR(H) 106 A37 Gen 8:3–4
7.20 (433.8)	Exod 20:9–10;		FR(H) 106 B3 Exod 16:35
	Deut 5:13–14		FR(H) 106 B7 Exod 16:31;
			32:25–29
	In Flaccum		FR(H) 106 B8 Exod 16:12, 32;
			Num 11:4
116	Lev 23:34		FR(H) 106 B9 Exod 32:4
121	Prov 24:17–18		FR(H) 106 B10 Num 11:5
123	Gen 1:10		FR(H) 106 B19 Gen 8:14
159	Num 25:12		FR(H) 106 B21 Gen 6:9
167	Deut 28:67		

14. Fragments taken from James Harris are signaled by FR(H). See Harris, *Fragments of Philo Judaeus*. Fragments from QG and QE are located above.

FR(H) 107 B33 Exod 2:14;
       Num 8:16
FR(H) 107 B36 Exod 2:11–12
FR(H) 108 A1 Num 8:15
FR(H) 108 A7 Num 35:6
FR(H) 108 B3 Num 35:6
FR(H) 110 A16 Exod 20:12;
       Deut 5:16

Scripture Index

1:20–25	*QG* 1.19, 64; *Det.* 151	2:1–3	*QG* 1.1, 6; 2.41, 75,
1:20–26	*Opif.* 73		78; 3.49; *Opif.* 89, 128;
1:20–31	*Opif.* 65, 66, 68		*Decal.* 97
1:24	*Leg.* 2.11*, 13*; *Opif.* 64*	2:1–4	*QG* 1.55; 2.31, 51
1:24–25	*QG* 1.23; *Cher.* 62; *Her.*	2:1–7	*QG* 2.56
	139; *Somn.* 1.135	2:2	*QG* 2.13; *QE* 1.9; *Leg.*
1:25	*Opif.* 64		1.2*, 3*, 6*, 16*, 18, 65;
1:26	*QG* 2.62; *Conf.* 169*,		*Post.* 65; *Mos.* 2.209;
	179*; *Fug.* 68*, 71*, 72*;		*Spec.* 1.170; 2.58, 260
	Mut. 31*; *Mos.* 2.65;	2:2–3	*Cher.* 87; *Post.* 64*; *Fug.*
	Opif. 69, 71, 72*, 75, 83,		173; *Decal.* 101
	139, 142; *Abr.* 45	2:3	*Leg.* 1.6*, 17, 18*
1:26–27	*Leg.* 1.31, 33, 42, 43, 53,	2:4	*QG* 1.1*; *Leg.* 1.19*, 20*;
	90, 92, 94; 2.4; *Det.* 83,		*Post.* 65; *Opif.* 12
	86; *Mut.* 223; *Mos.* 2.61;	2:4–5	*Leg.* 1.21*; *Opif.* 129*
	Opif. 25, 79, 146; *Praem.*	2:5	*QG* 1.2*; 2.56; *Leg.* 1.22,
	1; *Anim.* 16		23, 24*, 25*, 26, 27*
1:26–28	*QG* 2.56	2:5–6	*Leg.* 1.29
1:26–29	*Agr.* 8; [*Anim.* 20]	2:6	*QG* 1.3*, 22, 71; 2.67;
1:26–31	*Opif.* 77, 82		*Leg.* 1.28*; *Post.* 127*;
1:27	*QG* 1.4, 8, 25; *Leg.* 2.13,		*Fug.* 178*, 179, 181*;
	72; 3.96*; *Plant.* 19, 44;		*Opif.* 131*
	Conf. 146; *Her.* 56, 57*,	2:7	*QG* 1.4*, 5*, 8, 27, 28,
	139, 164*, 231*; *Fug.*		30, 39, 50, 51, 52, 53, 81,
	71*, 72*; *Somn.* 1.74*;		87, 93; 2.8, 12, 17, 54,
	Opif. 76, 134; *Spec.* 1.81,		56, 59, 66; 4.28; *QE* 2.46;
	171; 3.83, 207; *Virt.* 205		*Leg.* 1.31*, 32, 36*, 39*,
1:27–28	*Cher.* 43		42; 2.16, 19, 72; 3.161*;
1:28	*QG* 1.20, 21; *Opif.* 83,		*Cher.* 53; *Det.* 80*, 83,
	84, 142		84, 86, 151; *Plant.* 18,
1:28–29	*Opif.* 88		19*, 23, 24, 34; *Migr.* 3;
1:28–30	*Praem.* 9		*Her.* 56, 57*, 64, 184;
1:29–30	*QG* 1.50; *Spec.* 2.160		*Congr.* 90; *Mut.* 30;
1:31	*QG* 2.56; 3.38, 49;		*Somn.* 1.34*, 210; 2.70;
	4.147*; *Migr.* 42*, 135*;		*Opif.* 134*, 135, 136, 137,
	Her. 159*		138, 139, 140, 143, 145,
2:1	*Leg.* 1.1*, 21		148; *Abr.* 12, 56; *Spec.*
2:1–2	*Her.* 122*		4.123; *Virt.* 199, 203

2:7–8	*Leg.* 1.53, 55, 88, 90; 2.4	2:18–20	*Leg.* 2.14
2:7–9	*Plant.* 44	2:19	*QG* 1.18*, 19*, 20*, 21*,
2:8	*QG* 1.6*, 7*, 8*, 14; 4.51;		22*; *Leg.* 2.9*, 11, 12, 16,
	Leg. 1.41*, 43*, 45, 46,		18; *Mut.* 63*; *Opif.* 148,
	47*, 54; *Plant.* 32*, 36,		149
	38, 40, 41*; *Conf.* 61*	2:19–20	*QG* 2.9
2:8–9	*QG* 1.56; *Opif.* 153	2:20	*QG* 1.18, 20, 22, 23*,
2:9	*QG* 1.6, 9*, 10*, 11*, 55;		39; 2.60; *Leg.* 1.92; *Opif.*
	2.12; *Leg.* 1.56, 58*, 59,		150, 152
	60*, 62; 3.52, 107; *Plant.*	2:21	*QG* 1.24*; *Leg.* 2.19*,
	36*; *Migr.* 37*; *Somn.*		20, 25, 26, 31*, 35*, 38*;
	2.70; *Opif.* 154		*Her.* 257*
2:10	*QG* 1.12*; *Leg.* 1.65*;	2:21–22	*QG* 1.25*; *Contempl.* 63
	Post. 128*; *Somn.*	2:22	*QG* 1.26, 27*, 28, 52;
	2.241*, 243*		*Leg.* 2.14, 38*, 72; 3.185;
2:10–14	*Leg.* 1.63*		*Her.* 257
2:11	*QG* 1.12, 13; *Leg.* 1.67*,	2:22–23	*Leg.* 2.40*; *Post.* 33; *Opif.*
	74, 77*, 85		151
2:11–12	*Leg.* 1.66*	2:23	*QG* 1.28*; *Leg.* 2.41*,
2:12	*Leg.* 1.67, 78*, 79*, 81,		44*; *Cher.* 60
	84	2:23–24	*Opif.* 152
2:13	*Leg.* 1.68*	2:24	*QG* 1.27, 29*; *Leg.* 2.49*;
2:13–14	*QG* 1.12, 13; *Leg.* 1.85		*Gig.* 54*
2:14	*QG* 1.13*; *Leg.* 1.69*,	2:25	*QG* 1.30*; *Leg.* 2.22, 54,
	72*, 86		64*, 65*, 68*
2:15	*QG* 1.14*; 2.66; *Leg.*	2:25–3:1	*Leg.* 2.53*
	1.53*, 55*, 88*; 2.4	3:1	*QG* 1.31*, 32*, 33*, 34*;
2:15–16	*Spec.* 2.160		*Leg.* 2.71*, 74, 79, 81,
2:16	*QG* 1.15*; 2.17; *Leg.*		105, 106*, 108; *Agr.* 95,
	1.92, 95, 97*, 98, 99,		96, 99, 107, 108; *Opif.*
	101*; *Plant.* 34		156, 157, 163
2:16–17	*QG* 1.34, 35; *Leg.* 1.90*	3:1–6	*QG* 1.47
2:17	*QG* 1.15, 16*, 45, 51;	3:1–7	*Opif.* 165
	Leg. 1.100*, 101*, 105*,	3:1–24	*Opif.* 155
	106, 107; *Plant.* 45; *Mut.*	3:2–5	*QG* 1.33
	30; *Somn.* 2.70; *Virt.* 205	3:3	*QG* 1.35*; *Somn.* 2.70
2:18	*QG* 1.17*, 18*, 49; *Leg.*	3:4–5	*Agr.* 96
	2.1*, 4, 5, 7, 9*; *Cher.* 58	3:5	*QG* 1.36*; *Leg.* 2.65

3:5–6	*Opif.* 156	3:22	*QG* 1.54*, 55*; *Conf.*
3:6	*QG* 1.37*, 38*, 40, 42,		169*; *Mut.* 30
	43, 44, 45, 51, 55	3:23	*QG* 1.56*; 2.66; *Leg.*
3:7	*QG* 1.39*, 40*, 41*; *Leg.*		1.96*; *Cher.* 1
	3.55*	3:23–24	*QG* 1.7; *Leg.* 1.55; *Cher.*
3:8	*QG* 1.42*, 43*, 44*; *Leg.*		12; *Post.* 10; *Plant.* 34,
	3.1*, 4, 6*, 9, 28*, 48, 49,		46; *Congr.* 171
	51; *Deus* 60	3:24	*QG* 1.57*; *Cher.* 1*, 10,
3:9	*QG* 1.45*; *Leg.* 3.49*, 50,		11, 18, 20, 21, 23, 25, 28,
	51*, 53*; *Somn.* 1.192*		30
3:10	*Leg.* 3.54*	4:1	*QG* 1.58*, 74, 81; *Cher.*
3:10–11	*Ebr.* 6		52, 53*, 57, 65, 124*;
3:12	*Leg.* 3.56*, 57, 58*		*Sacr.* 2, 11*; *Det.* 32
3:12–13	*QG* 1.46*; *Leg.* 3.61, 64	4:1–2	*QG* 1.69; *Leg.* 1.105;
3:13	*Leg.* 3.59*, 60, 66*		*Cher.* 40*; *Sacr.* 14; *Virt.*
3:14	*QG* 1.50; *Leg.* 3.66, 68,		199; *Praem.* 68
	75, 107*, 111, 114*, 138,	4:1–3	*QG* 1.61
	160*, 161*, 246*; *Migr.*	4:2	*QG* 1.59*; 2.66; *Sacr.* 1*,
	66*; *Opif.* 157, 163		5, 10, 11, 51; *Agr.* 3, 5,
3:14–15	*QG* 1.48*; *Leg.* 3.65*		21*, 22, 26, 67, 124
3:14–17	*QG* 1.47*	4:2–4	*Conf.* 124
3:15	*Leg.* 3.182*, 184*, 185*,	4:3	*Sacr.* 52*, 71*, 72; *Agr.*
	188*, 189*; *Agr.* 107*		127;
3:16	*QG* 1.49*, 50; *Leg.*	4:3–4	*QG* 1.60*; *Sacr.* 88
	3.200*, 211, 216*, 220*,	4:4	*Sacr.* 2, 87, 136; *Det.* 32,
	221; *Opif.* 167		103
3:16–19	*Opif.* 168	4:4–5	*QG* 1.61*, 62*, 76
3:17	*QG* 1.50*; *Leg.* 3.222*,	4:4–8	*QG* 1.78
	246*, 247*	4:5	*QG* 1.63*; *Post.* 21
3:17–19	*QG* 1.56; *Virt.* 205	4:7	*QG* 1.64*, 65*, 66*; *Det.*
3:18	*Leg.* 3.248*, 250, 253		96; *Agr.* 127*; *Sobr.* 50;
3:18–19	*QG* 1.50; *Leg.* 3.251*		*Mut.* 195*
3:19	*QG* 1.51*, 93; 2.61; 4.28;	4:8	*QG* 1.67*, 68, 69, 76,
	Leg. 3.252*, 253*; *Migr.*		81; *Cher.* 52; *Det.* 1*, 5,
	3*; *Somn.* 2.70		32, 37, 42, 45, 47*, 48*,
3:20	*QG* 1.52*, 53; 2.60; *Cher.*		49, 52, 57, 69, 78, 140;
	57, 60; *Agr.* 95, 97; *Her.*		*Post.* 38, 49, 124; *Agr.*
	53*		21; *Migr.* 74, 75; *Fug.* 60;
3:21	*QG* 1.53*; 4.1		*Virt.* 199; *Praem.* 68, 74

4:8–15	QG 1.77	4:19	Post. 75*, 79
4:9	QG 1.68*, 69*; Det. 57*, 62*, 68	4:19–20	Post. 83
		4:19–22	Post. 112, 124
4:9–14	Det. 61	4:20	Post. 93, 98
4:10	QG 1.70*; Det. 38, 48, 49, 69*, 70*, 74, 78, 79*, 91*; Virt. 199	4:21	Post. 100, 103*, 111
		4:22	Post. 114, 116*, 117, 119, 120
4:10–12	Praem. 68	4:23	QG 1.77*; Det. 50*
4:11	QG 1.71*; Cher. 52; Det. 96*, 98, 100*, 103; Fug. 60	4:24	QG 1.77
		4:25	QG 1.78*; Cher. 54*; Post. 10*, 124*, 170*, 172, 173, 175*
4:11–12	QG 1.67; Agr. 21*; Congr. 57; Virt. 200		
4:12	QG 1.72*; Det. 104, 108, 109, 112*, 119*, 130, 140; Praem. 70, 72, 74	4:26	QG 1.79*, 80, 81; Det. 138*, 139*; Abr. 7, 8, 9, 12, 47; Praem. 13, 14
4:12–13	Abr. 64	5	Post. 173
4:13	QG 1.73*; 4.4*; Det. 141*, 142, 144, 146, 150*; Conf. 165*	5:1	QG 1.80*; Det. 139*; Abr. 9*, 11
		5:3	QG 1.81*; Post. 42, 45
4:14	QG 1.74*; Det. 150*, 152, 153, 155, 156*, 163*, 164*; Congr. 171	5:3–29	QG 1.87
		5:4	Post. 34
		5:6–32	QG 1.81
4:14–15	Det. 165	5:18	Post. 40
4:15	QG 1.75*, 76*; Det. 166*, 167*, 177*; Conf. 122; Fug. 60*, 64; Virt. 200; Praem. 72, 74	5:21	Post. 40, 44
		5:21–23	QG 1.83*
		5:22	QG 1.82*
		5:23	QG 1.84*
4:15–16	QG 1.82	5:23–24	QG 1.85*
4:15–24	QG 1.81	5:24	QG 1.86*; Post. 43; Mut. 34*, 38*; Abr. 17*, 19, 24, 47; Praem. 16*, 17
4:16	Cher. 12*; Det. 163*; Post. 1*, 5, 6, 10, 12, 22, 32; Congr. 171		
		5:25	Post. 40, 46, 48
4:16–24	QG 1.76	5:28–29	Post. 48; Congr. 90
4:17	Post. 33*, 35, 45, 49, 50, 51, 65; Conf. 122	5:28–32	Gig. 3, 5
		5:29	QG 1.87*; Leg. 3.77; Det. 121*, 122*; Abr. 27
4:17–18	QG 1.77; Post. 40		
4:17–19	Det. 50	5:32	QG 1.88*; 2.79; Sobr. 32, 44
4:18	Post. 44, 46, 48, 66, 69, 73, 74		
		6:1	QG 1.89*; Gig. 1*, 3, 5, 53

6:2   *Gig.* 6*, 16, 18
6:3   *QG* 1.90*, 91*; *Gig.* 19*,
           29*, 47, 53, 55*, 56;
           Deus 2
6:4   *QG* 1.32, 92*; *Gig.* 58*,
           60, 65, 67; *Deus* 1*, 3, 4,
           15, 19*
6:5   *QG* 2.13, 17; *Gig.* 3;
           Conf. 24*; *Abr.* 40
6:5–6   *QG* 1.96, 97
6:5–7   *Deus* 20*; *Abr.* 41
6:5–22   *QG* 1.87, 89, 91
6:6   *QG* 1.93*; FR(M)16 =
           FR(P)3; *Deus* 21, 33*,
           34, 49*
6:6–7   *Deus* 76
6:7   *QG* 1.94*, 95*; *Deus* 51*,
           70*, 72*; *Conf.* 24
6:8   *QG* 1.96*; *Leg.* 3.77*, 78;
           Deus 70*, 74, 86*, 90,
           104*, 106, 109
6:8–9   *Abr.* 46
6:9   *QG* 1.87, 97*; 2.10, 16,
           27, 31, 33, 34, 38, 45,
           56; FR(H) 106 B21; *Leg.*
           3.77; *Det.* 105, 121, 170;
           Post. 48, 173; *Gig.* 3, 5;
           Deus 85, 116, 117*, 119,
           122, 140; *Agr.* 2, 20,
           181; *Plant.* 1, 140; *Sobr.*
           30, 47; *Conf.* 105; *Migr.*
           125; *Her.* 260; *Congr.*
           90; *Abr.* 27, 31*, 33, 34,
           35*, 47, 56; *Virt.* 201;
           Praem. 23
6:9–10   *Post.* 174; *Mut.* 189
6:10   *QG* 2.79
6:11   *QG* 1.98*; 2.45; *Deus*
           122*, 140

6:12   *QG* 1.92, 99*; *Deus* 140*,
           141, 142
6:12–13   *Abr.* 40
6:13   *QG* 1.100*; *Det.* 170
6:13–7:1   *Mos.* 2.60
6:14   *QG* 2.1*, 2*, 3*, 4*;
           Plant. 43; *Conf.* 105*
6:15–16   *QG* 2.5*
6:16   *QG* 2.6*, 7*
6:17   *QG* 2.8*, 9*, 12, 51,
           56; *Det.* 170; *Conf.* 25;
           Praem. 23
6:18   *QG* 2.10*
6:19   *Det.* 170
6:19–21   *QG* 2.5
7:1   *QG* 2.10, 11*, 16, 27,
           31, 33, 34, 38, 45, 56;
           Leg. 3.77; *Det.* 105, 121,
           170; *Post.* 48, 173, 174;
           Gig. 3, 5; *Deus* 85, 140;
           Agr. 2, 20, 181; *Plant.* 1,
           140; *Sobr.* 30, 47; *Conf.*
           105; *Migr.* 125; *Her.* 260;
           Congr. 90; *Abr.* 27, 46;
           Virt. 201; *Praem.* 23
7:1–4   *QG* 2.48
7:1–23   *Mos.* 2.263
7:2   *Det.* 170*, 172, 173
7:2–3   *QG* 2.12*, 13
7:4   *QG* 2.13*, 14*, 15*
7:5   *QG* 2.16*
7:6   *QG* 2.45; *Conf.* 25
7:7   *QG* 2.13; *Det.* 170
7:7–23   *Migr.* 125
7:8   *Migr.* 125
7:8–9   *Plant.* 43
7:10   *QG* 2.13*
7:11   *QG* 2.17*, 18*, 30, 31,
           47, 64*; FR(H) 106 A36;

7:11 (*cont.*)
    Conf. 23*; *Fug.* 192*;
    Abr. 42
7:11–12   *QG* 2.33
7:11–24   *Mos.* 2.53
7:12   *QG* 2.14*, 29
7:13   *QG* 2.49
7:14–16   *Plant.* 43
7:16   *QG* 2.19*
7:17   *QG* 2.20; *Her.* 204*
7:17–23   *QG* 2.7; *Abr.* 42; *Virt.*
    201
7:18   *QG* 2.4, 20*
7:19   *QG* 2.19
7:19–20   *Abr.* 43
7:20   *QG* 2.21*
7:21   *QG* 2.22*
7:21–22   *Deus* 76
7:21–23   *Abr.* 45
7:22   *QG* 2.23*
7:23   *QG* 2.24*, 25*; *Det.* 170
7:24   *QG* 2.29, 33
8:1   *QG* 2.17, 26*, 27*, 28*
8:1–14   *Mos.* 2.63
8:2   *QG* 2.29*
8:3   *QG* 2.29, 30*
8:3–4   *QG* 2.33; FR(H) 106
    A37
8:4   *QG* 2.31*, 47
8:5   *QG* 2.32*
8:6   *QG* 2.33*, 34*
8:7   *QG* 2.35*, 36*, 37*, 38,
    39
8:8   *QG* 2.38*, 40
8:9   *QG* 2.38, 39*, 40*, 42
8:10   *QG* 2.41*
8:11   *QG* 2.42*, 43*
8:12   *QG* 2.44*
8:13   *QG* 2.30, 45*, 46*, 47

8:13–14   *QG* 2.33, 67
8:14   *QG* 2.45, 47*, 48, 49;
    FR(H) 106 A34, B19
8:15–16   *QG* 2.48*
8:15–17   *QG* 2.47
8:16   *QG* 2.66
8:16–19   *Praem.* 22
8:18   *QG* 2.49*; *Conf.* 105;
    Abr. 46
8:18–19   *Mos.* 2.64
8:20   *QG* 2.50*, 51*, 52*, 53;
    Prob. 69
8:21   *QG* 2.53*, 54*; 4.147*;
    Her. 296*; *Congr.* 115*;
    Spec. 1.76
8:22   *QG* 2.55*; *Her.* 165*;
    Aet. 19
9:1–2   *QG* 2.56*
9:2–3   *QG* 1.18; [*Anim.* 20]
9:3   *QG* 2.57*, 58*
9:4   *QG* 2.59*
9:5   *QG* 2.60*
9:6   *QG* 2.61*, 62*; *Somn.*
    1.74*; *Spec.* 3.83, 84
9:11   *QG* 2.63*, 64; *Somn.*
    2.223*, 224*
9:13–17   *QG* 2.64
9:16   *QG* 2.64*
9:18   *QG* 2.74; *Virt.* 202
9:18–19   *QG* 2.45, 51, 56, 65*
9:20   *QG* 2.66*, 67*; *Det.* 105,
    108, 112; *Gig.* 4; *Agr.* 2,
    4, 5, 9, 17, 20*, 22, 26,
    67, 124, 125*, 158, 181*;
    Plant. 1*
9:20–21   *Agr.* 1*, 157; *Plant.* 140*
9:20–25   *Virt.* 202
9:21   *QG* 2.68*, 69*; *Leg.*
    2.60*, 61; *Plant.* 144,

9:21 (cont.)
          155, 163; *Ebr.* 4, 5; *Sobr.*
          1, 30
9:22   *QG* 2.70*, 71*, 77; *Sobr.*
          32, 44, 47
9:22–27   *QG* 2.65
9:23   *QG* 2.72*; *Leg.* 2.62
9:24   *QG* 2.73*, 74*; *Sobr.* 1*,
          3, 6, 30*
9:25   *Sobr.* 31, 32*, 47, 51*
9:25–27   *QG* 2.77; *Leg.* 2.62; *Her.*
          260
9:26   *QG* 2.75*; *Sobr.* 51*, 53,
          55, 58*
9:27   *QG* 2.76*, 80; *Sobr.* 59*,
          61, 62, 65, 67, 68, 69
9:28   *QG* 2.78*
10:1   *QG* 2.79*
10:2   *QG* 2.79
10:4–5   *QG* 2.80*
10:6   *QG* 2.81*
10:8   *QG* 2.82*; *Gig.* 66*, 67
10:9   *QG* 2.82*
10:10   *Gig.* 66
11:1   *Conf.* 9, 15*; *Somn.*
          2.284*
11:1–9   *QG* 2.82; *Conf.* 1*
11:2   *Conf.* 60*, 64, 67, 68, 75,
          76*
11:3   *Conf.* 84*, 87, 95, 101,
          102*, 103*
11:4   *Post.* 53; *Conf.* 5, 83, 107*,
          111*, 113, 115, 116*,
          118*, 121*, 128, 133, 154,
          156; *Somn.* 2.284
11:5   *Conf.* 134*, 140*, 142*,
          155*
11:6   *Post.* 81*; *Conf.* 150*,
          152*, 154*, 155, 162*

11:6–9   *Post.* 53
11:7   *Conf.* 9, 13, 168*, 182*,
          183, 189*, 191, 192, 195
11:8   *Conf.* 158*, 196*
11:9   *Conf.* 158, 183, 191, 192,
          198; *Somn.* 2.286, 290
11:10   *Sobr.* 65; *Mut.* 189*
11:26   *Sobr.* 65
11:27   *Congr.* 48
11:29   *Post.* 76*; *Congr.* 34, 50;
          Virt. 207
11:30   *Mut.* 143
11:31   *QG* 4.88; *Gig.* 62; *Ebr.*
          94; *Migr.* 187; *Congr.* 48,
          49; *Mut.* 16; *Somn.* 1.52,
          55, 58, 161; *Abr.* 67, 72,
          188, 212, 245; *Virt.* 212;
          Praem. 58; *Hypoth.* 6.1
          (427.10)
11:31–32 *Migr.* 177
11:32   *Somn.* 1.48*
12:1   *QG* 3.1; *Leg.* 2.59*; 3.83;
          Det. 159*; *Migr.* 2, 3, 7,
          9, 10, 12, 35, 40, 43*;
          Her. 26, 69*, 71, 85, 96;
          Abr. 62, 66, 86; *Virt.*
          214; *Praem.* 17
12:1–2   *Her.* 277*
12:1–3   *Migr.* 1*
12:1–5   *QG* 4.88
12:2   *QG* 4.195h; *Migr.* 53, 70,
          86*, 88, 107*, 108; *Her.*
          278
12:3   *Migr.* 109*, 118*, 122
12:4   *Migr.* 127*, 129, 148*,
          149, 176*, 195, 198, 206,
          216; *Abr.* 62, 66, 79;
          Somn. 1.47*, 59; *Praem.*
          58

12:4–5	*Her.* 287; *Abr.* 212	14:12	*Migr.* 150
12:5	*Abr.* 245	14:13	*Abr.* 230
12:5–9	*Abr.* 67	14:13–16	*Her.* 286, 288; *Congr.* 92
12:6	*Migr.* 216*, 219, 221, 223	14:14	*QG* 4.10; *Det.* 14; *Abr.* 232
12:7	*Det.* 159*; *Her.* 78; *Abr.* 77*, 80*	14:15	*Abr.* 233, 242
12:7–8	*QG* 4.195f	14:16	*Abr.* 234
12:9	*Abr.* 85	14:17	*Ebr.* 24, 105
12:10	*Her.* 287*; *Abr.* 91, 92	14:18	*QG* FR(M)17 = FR(P)17; *Leg.* 3.79, 81, 82
12:10–20	*Abr.* 245		
12:11	*Abr.* 93	14:18–20	*Abr.* 235
12:13	*QG* 4.60	14:19	*Congr.* 99
12:14–15	*Abr.* 93	14:20	*QG* FR(M)17 = FR(P)17; *Congr.* 93, 99*
12:15–20	*Abr.* 103		
12:17	*Abr.* 96	14:21	*Leg.* 3.24
13:2	*Abr.* 209, 220, 252	14:21–23	*Leg.* 3.197
13:5	*Abr.* 220	14:22	*Leg.* 3.24*; *Abr.* 235
13:7	*Abr.* 213, 214, 222	14:22–23	*Ebr.* 105*, 106, 110
13:8–11	*Abr.* 215	14:23	*Leg.* 3.24
13:9	*Migr.* 13*; *Abr.* 224	14:24	*Migr.* 164*, 165
13:10	*Abr.* 134, 227	15:1	*Her.* 25, 26
13:10–12	*Migr.* 175	15:1–2	*Her.* 58
13:13	*Abr.* 133	15:1–3	*Her.* 2*
14:1–2	*Congr.* 92	15:2	*Her.* 22*, 24, 27, 31, 33, 34*, 36, 42, 52, 54, 61, 63
14:1–12	*Abr.* 226		
14:1–16	*Det.* 14		
14:2	*Opif.* 165; *Abr.* 145, 147, 165, 227	15:2–3	*Her.* 39
		15:3	*Her.* 65, 266*
14:3	*Conf.* 26*	15:4	*Her.* 66*, 68*, 76*; *Mut.* 177*
14:4	*Abr.* 228		
14:5	*Abr.* 229	15:5	*Leg.* 3.39*, 40*; *Her.* 76, 78, 81, 82, 85, 87*
14:7	*Fug.* 196*		
14:8	*Opif.* 165; *Abr.* 145, 147, 165, 227	15:6	*Leg.* 3.228*; *Deus* 4; *Migr.* 44*; *Her.* 90*, 94*, 95, 99, 101; *Mut.* 177*, 186*, 201, 218; *Abr.* 262*; *Virt.* 216, 218; *Praem.* 27, 28, 31, 49
14:8–9	*Abr.* 236		
14:9	*Abr.* 242		
14:10	*Abr.* 241		
14:11–12	*Abr.* 229		

15:7	*QG* 3.1*; *Her.* 96*, 277, 313	16:2	*QG* 3.20*; *Congr.* 12*, 13*, 14*, 63*, 68*, 89; *Abr.* 248, 249
15:8	*QG* 3.2*; *Her.* 100*		
15:9	*QG* 3.3*; *Her.* 102*, 104, 106*, 108, 110, 112*, 125, 127, 234	16:3	*QG* 3.21*; *Congr.* 23, 34, 71*, 73, 78, 81*, 83, 85, 88*, 121*; *Abr.* 251; *Virt.* 207
15:9–10	*QG* 3.7		
15:10	*QG* 3.4*, 5*, 6*; *Her.* 129*, 132, 141, 143, 146, 207*, 213, 230*, 233, 237	16:4	*QG* 3.22*; *Congr.* 121, 122*, 126, 128*, 130, 135*, 138, 139*; *Abr.* 253
15:11	*QG* 3.7*, 8*, 10*; *Her.* 237*, 240, 242, 243*, 247	16:4–5	*QG* 3.24; *Congr.* 145, 151
15:12	*QG* 3.9*; *Her.* 249*, 258, 263, 265	16:5	*QG* 3.23*; *Congr.* 139*, 153*
15:13	*QG* FR(L)8; *Her.* 266, 268	16:6	*QG* 3.24*, 25*, 26*; *Cher.* 4; *Congr.* 153*, 155*, 156*, 158*, 180; *Fug.* 2*, 6
15:13–14	*QG* 3.10*; *Spec.* 2.146		
15:14	*QG* 3.10*; *Her.* 272*, 274		
15:15	*QG* 3.11*; *Her.* 275*, 277* 280, 281, 284, 285, 288, 290, 291	16:6–9	*Cher.* 3; *Fug.* 1*, 5
		16:7	*QG* 3.27*, 35; *Fug.* 119*, 177*, 202*, 203*
15:16	*QG* 3.12*, 13*; *Her.* 293*, 298, 299*, 300, 302, 304, 306, 308	16:8	*QG* 3.28*, 29*; *Fug.* 203*, 205
		16:9	*QG* 3.30*; *Cher.* 6; *Fug.* 207*
15:17	*QG* 3.14*, 15*; *Her.* 307*, 308*, 310, 311, 312*		
		16:10	*QG* 3.31*
		16:11	*QG* 3.32*; *Fug.* 5*, 204*, 208, 211; *Mut.* 202
15:18	*QG* 3.16*; *Her.* 313*, 315*; *Somn.* 2.255*, 257, 258*		
		16:11–12	*Fug.* 1*
15:18–21	*Congr.* 119	16:12	*QG* 3.33*; *Fug.* 204, 209*, 211*; *Mut.* 255
15:19–21	*QG* 3.17*		
16:1	*QG* 3.18*, 19*; FR(L)8; *Sacr.* 43, 44; *Post.* 130; *Congr.* 2, 3, 9, 11, 13, 20, 21; *Somn.* 1.240; *Abr.* 247	16:13	*QG* 3.34*; *Fug.* 211*; *Somn.* 1.240*
		16:14	*QG* 3.35*, 36*; *Fug.* 212*, 213*
		16:15	*QG* 3.37*, 57; 4.122, 147; *Abr.* 254; *Virt.* 207; *Praem.* 58, 61
16:1–2	*Leg.* 3.244; *Congr.* 1*, 6; *Mut.* 255	16:16	*QG* 3.38*

17:1	*QG* 3.39*, 41, 42; *Gig.* 63*, 64; *Mut.* 1*, 6, 15*, 17*, 18*, 23*, 27*, 29*, 31*, 39*, 40, 47*, 51*; *Decal.* 38	17:19	*QG* 3.58*; 4.17; *Leg.* 3.85*, 87; *Cher.* 8; *Mut.* 253*, 255, 261
		17:20	*QG* 3.59*
		17:20–21	*Mut.* 263*
17:1–2	*QG* 3.40*	17:21	*QG* 3.60*; *Mut.* 264*, 267*
17:2	*Mut.* 52*		
17:3	*QG* 3.41*; *Mut.* 54*, 56*	17:22	*Mut.* 270*
17:3–4	*QG* 3.42*	17:24–25	*QG* 3.61*
17:4	*Mut.* 57*, 58	17:25	*Sobr.* 8
17:4–6	*Spec.* 1.7	17:27	*QG* 3.62*
17:5	*QG* 3.43*; *Leg.* 3.244; *Cher.* 4, 7, 10; *Gig.* 63, 64; *Mut.* 60*, 61, 66, 67, 68, 69, 71, 83, 87; *Abr.* 81, 82, 83	18:1	*QG* 4.2; *Abr.* 119
		18:1–2	*QG* 4.1*, 30
		18:1–3	*Abr.* 122
		18:1–5	*QG* 4.124; *Abr.* 107
		18:1–8	*QG* 4.20; *Abr.* 114
17:6	*QG* 3.44*	18:2	*QG* 4.2*, 3*, 4, 6, 8, 10, 12, 20; *Deo* 2*, 3*; *Abr.* 124, 131, 142
17:8	*QG* 3.45*		
17:9–14	*Prov.* 1.84		
17:10	*QG* 3.47*; *Spec.* 1.2	18:2–5	*QG* 4.33
17:10–11	*QG* 3.46*	18:3	*QG* 4.4*; *Abr.* 132*
17:12	*QG* 3.48*, 49*, 50*, 52	18:3–5	*QG* 4.2
17:13	*QG* 3.51*; *Somn.* 2.25	18:4	*QG* 4.5*
17:14	*QG* 3.52*	18:5	*QG* 4.6*, 7*
17:15	*QG* 3.53*; *Cher.* 4, 5, 7, 10, 41; *Mut.* 61, 77, 79, 130; *Abr.* 99	18:5–8	*Cher.* 106
		18:6	*QG* 4.35, 124; *Sacr.* 59, 60*; *Abr.* 108*
17:15–16	*QG* 4.122; *Leg.* 3.217*	18:6–7	*QG* 4.8*
17:16	*QG* 3.53, 54*; *Congr.* 3; *Mut.* 130*, 141*, 145*, 147, 148*, 150, 151*	18:7	*QG* 4.124; *Abr.* 108
		18:8	*QG* 4.9*, 10*; *Abr.* 110, 118
		18:8–10	*QG* 4.2
17:17	*QG* 3.55*, 56*; 4.17, 138, 147; *Leg.* 1.82; 3.85*, 87, 217*; *Det.* 124; *Mut.* 154, 156, 166*, 168, 175*, 176*, 178*, 188, 193*, 201*, 261; *Abr.* 111, 201	18:9	*QG* 4.11*; *Det.* 59*
		18:9–10	*Det.* 61; *Abr.* 122
		18:10	*QG* 4.12*, 13*; *Det.* 60; *Migr.* 126; *Abr.* 110, 132*
17:18	*QG* 3.57*; *Mut.* 201*, 204, 209, 213, 216*, 218, 252	18:11	*QG* 4.14*, 15*; *Cher.* 8, 50; *Det.* 28*; *Post.* 134*;

18:11 (cont.)
    Ebr. 60; *Fug.* 128*, 167*;
    Somn. 2.185
18:11–12 *Leg.* 3.218*; *Abr.* 111
18:11–15 *Spec.* 2.54
18:12   *QG* 4.16*, 17; *Det.* 124;
    Ebr. 62; *Mut.* 166*; *Abr.*
    112, 201, 206
18:13   *QG* 4.2
18:13–14 *QG* 4.17*
18:14   *QG* 3.18; 4.18*; *Abr.* 112*
18:15   *QG* 4.19*; *Abr.* 112, 206
18:16   *QG* 4.2, 20*; *Migr.* 173*
18:17   *QG* 4.21*; *Leg.* 3.27*;
    Sobr. 56*
18:19   *QG* 4.22*
18:20   *QG* 4.23*
18:20–21 *Abr.* 133
18:21   *QG* 4.24*
18:22   *QG* 4.25*; *Cher.* 18*;
    Somn. 2.226*
18:22–23 *Leg.* 3.9*; *Post.* 27*
18:22–32 *QG* 4.53; *Migr.* 122
18:23   *QG* 4.26*; *Leg.* 3.10*;
    *Cher.*18*; *Deus* 161;
    Migr. 132*; *Her.* 30;
    Prov. 1.55
18:23–32 *Sacr.* 122
18:24   *QG* 4.27*; *Congr.* 109
18:24–32 *QG* 4.27, 29; *Mut.* 228
18:25   *Abr.* 133
18:27   *QG* 4.28*; *Deus* 161;
    Her. 29, 30*; *Somn.*
    1.214
18:28   *QG* 4.27*
18:29   *QG* 4.27*
18:31   *QG* 4.27*
18:32   *QG* 4.27*; *Congr.* 109
18:33   *QG* 4.29*; *Somn.* 1.70*

19:1   *QG* 4.30*, 31*, 32*;
    Conf. 27, 28; *Abr.* 142
19:2   *QG* 4.33*
19:3   *QG* 4.34*, 35*
19:4   *QG* 4.36*; *Conf.* 27, 28*
19:4–5   *QG* 4.47
19:5   *QG* 4.37*
19:7–8   *QG* 4.38*
19:8   *Ebr.* 164; *Conf.* 27
19:9   *QG* 4.39*; *Mos.* 2.58
19:10–11 *QG* 4.40*
19:11   *QG* 4.41*; *Ebr.* 222; *Fug.*
    144*
19:12–13 *QG* 4.42*
19:14   *QG* 4.43*
19:16   *QG* 4.44*
19:17   *QG* 4.45*, 46*, 47, 52
19:18–20 *QG* 4.47*
19:20   *Abr.* 166
19:21   *QG* 4.48*
19:22   *QG* 4.49*, 50*
19:23–24 *QG* 4.51*; *Somn.* 1.85*
19:24   *QG* 4.52; *Deus* 60; *Ebr.*
    223; *Prov.* 1.55
19:24–25 *Mos.* 2.53, 55, 263; *Abr.*
    138, 142
19:26   *QG* 4.52*; *Leg.* 3.213;
    Ebr. 164; *Fug.* 121*,
    122*; *Somn.* 1.247, 248
19:27–28 *QG* 4.53*
19:28   *Abr.* 140
19:29   *QG* 4.54*; *Mos.* 2.58
19:30   *QG* 4.55*
19:30–32 *Post.* 175
19:31   *Ebr.* 165
19:31–32 *QG* 4.56*
19:33   *Post.* 176*; *Ebr.* 166*,
    203*
19:35   *Ebr.* 166, 203

19:35–38	*Post.* 176	21:12	*Leg.* 3.245*; *Cher.* 9
19:37	*QG* 4.57*	21:14	*Cher.* 3; *Sobr.* 8*, 9
19:37–38	*QG* 4.58*; *Leg.* 3.25	21:15	*Sobr.* 8*
20:1	*QG* 4.59*	21:16	*Sobr.* 8*
20:2	*QG* 4.60*, 61*, 66	21:19	*Post.* 130, 137
20:2–3	*Her.* 258	21:20	*Post.* 131; *Congr.* 129
20:3	*QG* 4.62*	21:22	*QG* 4.195g; *Congr.* 138*
20:4	*QG* 4.63*, 64*	21:22–34	*QG* 4.195b
20:4–6	*QG* 4.66	21:25–31	*Somn.* 1.14
20:6	*QG* 4.65*	21:30	*Fug.* 200
20:7	*QG* 4.66*; *Her.* 258*	21:32	*QG* 4.195g
20:10–11	*QG* 4.67*	21:33	*QG* 3.56; *Plant.* 73*, 74,
20:12	*QG* 4.68*; *Ebr.* 61*, 65;		75, 78, 85*, 86, 89*; *Mut.*
	Her. 62*		190*
20:16	*QG* 4.69*	22:1–2	*Somn.* 1.195*
20:17–18	*QG* 4.70*	22:1–4	*Abr.* 169
21:1	*Cher.* 45	22:1–14	*Sacr.* 110
21:1–3	*Det.* 60	22:2	*Abr.* 168, 189
21:1–6	*Praem.* 31, 35, 50	22:2–8	*Prob.* 69
21:1–7	*Praem.* 58, 61	22:2–10	*Deus* 4
21:2	*Cher.* 106; *Fug.* 167*;	22:3	*Post.* 17; *Migr.* 139*,
	Abr. 254; *Virt.* 207		154*, 166; *Abr.* 170
21:2–3	*Sobr.* 8; *Abr.* 168	22:3–4	*Somn.* 1.64*, 67, 68
21:3	*Leg.* 2.82; 3.218; *Ebr.* 60,	22:4	*Post.* 17*; *Migr.* 139
	94; *Fug.* 167; *Mut.* 88;	22:4–6	*Abr.* 171
	Abr. 201; *Praem.* 24	22:5	*Abr.* 189
21:4	*QG* 3.38	22:6	*Cher.* 31*
21:5	*Mut.* 1, 157; *Abr.* 195	22:7	*Fug.* 132*, 133; *Abr.* 173*
21:5–6	*QG* 4.17, 147; *Plant.* 169	22:8	*Deus* 7; *Migr.* 166*; *Fug.*
21:6	*QG* 3.38; 4.138, 148; *Leg.*		132*, 135*, 136*; *Abr.*
	1.82; 2.82*; 3.87, 219*;		172, 175*
	Det. 123*, 124; *Mut.* 131,	22:9	*Deus* 4; *Somn.* 1.195*;
	137*, 138*, 261; *Abr.* 201		*Abr.* 173
21:7	*Migr.* 140*, 141*	22:9–12	*Migr.* 140; *Abr.* 176
21:8	*Somn.* 2.10	22:10	*Abr.* 188, 198
21:8–9	*Sobr.* 8	22:11–12	*Somn.* 1.195*
21:9–14	*Cher.* 8	22:13	*Fug.* 132*, 135*
21:10	*Cher.* 4, 9*, 10	22:16	*Leg.* 3.205, 206*, 207,
21:11	*Leg.* 3.245		209*; *Abr.* 273*

22:16–17	*Leg.* 3.203*	24:11	*QG* 4.94*
22:17	*Leg.* 3.209*, 210; *Spec.* 1.7	24:12–14	*QG* 4.95
		24:15	*QG* 4.96*, 97*, 98*, 200; *Post.* 137
22:20–24	*Congr.* 45		
22:23	*Congr.* 48, 50	24:16	*QG* 4.99*; 100*, 117, 119, 124*; *Post.* 133, 134, 136, 153; *Fug.* 195*
22:23–24	*Congr.* 43		
22:24	*Congr.* 51, 52		
23:1	*QG* 4.71*	24:16–20	*Post.* 132*
23:2	*QG* 4.72*; *Abr.* 245	24:17	*QG* 4.101*, 102*; *Post.* 139, 147
23:2–3	*QG* 4.73*; *Abr.* 258		
23:3	*Conf.* 79	24:18	*QG* 4.103*, 104*, 109, 124*; *Post.* 138, 139, 140*, 146
23:3–20	*Spec.* 2.168		
23:4	*QG* 4.74*, 75*; *Conf.* 79*		
23:5–6	*QG* 4.76*	24:18–19	*QG* 4.105*; *Post.* 147*
23:6	*QG* 4.77*; *Det.* 13; *Mut.* 152*; *Somn.* 2.26, 244*; *Abr.* 261*; *Virt.* 216, 218	24:19	*QG* 4.106*; *Post.* 148
		24:20	*QG* 4.107*, 124*; *Post.* 150, 151, 153
23:7	*QG* 4.77, 78; *Somn.* 2.89	24:21	*QG* 4.108*
23:8	*Conf.* 79	24:22	*QG* 4.109*, 110*; *Congr.* 113
23:8–9	*QG* 4.78*		
23:9	*QG* 4.77, 80*, 82*; *Post.* 62; *Somn.* 2.26, 90	24:23	*QG* 4.111*
		24:25	*QG* 4.112*, 119*
23:10	*QG* 4.79*	24:26	*QG* 4.113*
23:11	*QG* 4.80*, 81*, 82*	24:27	*QG* 4.114*, 115*
23:17	*QG* 4.82*	24:28	*QG* 4.116*, 124*
23:19	*QG* 4.82*, 83*	24:29	*QG* 4.117*
24:1	*QG* 4.84*; *Sobr.* 17*, 18; *Abr.* 270, 271, 274	24:30	*QG* 4.118
		24:31	*QG* 4.118*, 119*
24:2	*QG* 4.85*, 86*, 88, 90, 108, 133	24:34	*QG* 4.120*
		24:35	*QG* 4.121*; *Abr.* 209, 252
24:2–9	*QG* 4.144		
24:3	*QG* 4.87*, 88*	24:36	*QG* 4.122*, 123*; *Virt.* 207
24:3–4	*QG* 4.86		
24:4	*QG* 4.88	24:41	*QG* 4.132
24:5–6	*QG* 4.89*	24:46	*QG* 4.124*
24:7	*QG* 4.90*; *Leg.* 3.42*	24:48	*QG* 4.125*
24:8	*QG* 4.91*, 132	24:49	*QG* 4.126*
24:10	*QG* 4.92*, 93*; *Congr.* 111	24:50	*QG* 4.127*, 128*
		24:51	*QG* 4.129*, 131

24:52–53	QG 4.130	25:24	QG 4.158*, 159*; *Praem.* 63
24:55–56	QG 4.131*		
24:57	QG 4.132*	25:24–26	QG 4.230, 240; *Mos.* 1.240
24:58	QG 4.133*		
24:59	QG 4.134*	25:24–27	*Praem.* 59
24:60	QG 4.135*	25:24–34	*Virt.* 208
24:61	QG 4.136*, 137*	25:25	QG 4.160*, 161*, 204, 206; *Congr.* 61
24:62	QG 4.138*, 139*		
24:63	QG 4.140*, 141*; *Leg.* 3.43*; *Det.* 29*	25:25–26	QG 4.164, 199; *Sacr.* 17; *Sobr.* 26
24:64	QG 4.142*	25:25–27	QG 4.206
24:65	QG 4.143*; *Det.* 30*, 31*	25:25–28	QG 4.198
24:66	QG 4.144*	25:26	QG 4.162*, 163*, 164*, 200; *Leg.* 1.61; 2.89; 3.15, 93, 180, 190; *Migr.* 200; *Her.* 252; *Mut.* 81; *Somn.* 1.171; *Praem.* 24
24:67	QG 4.145*, 146*, 148; *Post.* 77; *Congr.* 34, 36		
25:1	QG 4.147*; *Sacr.* 43, 44; *Congr.* 34		
25:1–2	*Virt.* 207	25:27	QG 4.165*, 207; *Leg.* 3.2*; *Plant.* 44*; *Congr.* 61, 62*
25:1–4	*Praem.* 58, 61		
25:2	*Conf.* 55		
25:5	*Sacr.* 43; *Conf.* 74	25:28	QG 4.166*, 167*
25:5–6	QG 4.148*; *Migr.* 94*; *Virt.* 207	25:29	QG 4.168*, 169*; *Sacr.* 81
25:6	QG 4.149*; *Leg.* 3.197	25:29–34	QG 4.168, 224; *Mos.* 1.242
25:7	QG 4.150*, 151*; *Sobr.* 17	25:30	QG 4.170*, 171*
25:7–8	*Her.* 291	25:31	QG 4.172*
25:8	QG 4.152*, 153*, 169; *Sacr.* 5*, 7, 8; *Fug.* 128*	25:32	QG 4.173*
		25:33	*Sacr.* 18*
25:17	*Fug.* 128	25:33–34	*Sobr.* 26
25:20	QG 4.154*, 195; *Cher.* 41	25:34	QG 4.174*
25:21	*Cher.* 47; *Congr.* 130, 135, 138	26:1	QG 4.175*, 176*
		26:2	QG 4.177*; *Leg.* 2.59; *Det.* 46*; *Migr.* 29*
25:21–23	*Sacr.* 4		
25:22	QG 4.155*, 156*; *Leg.* 3.88	26:2–3	QG 4.178*, 187; *Conf.* 81*
25:23	QG 4.123, 157*; *Leg.* 3.88*, 89; *Sacr.* 4*, 42; *Congr.* 129	26:3	QG 4.179*, 180*
		26:3–5	*Her.* 8*
		26:4	QG 4.181*, 182*, 183*

26:5	*QG* 4.184*; *Migr.* 130*; *Abr.* 275*	27:11	*QG* 4.204, 206; *Leg.* 2.59; *Migr.* 153*, 158
26:6	*QG* 4.185*, 186	27:11–12	*QG* 4.201*
26:7	*QG* 4.186*	27:12–13	*QG* 4.202*
26:8	*QG* 4.187*, 188*; *Cher.* 8; *Plant.* 169*, 170	27:14	*QG* 4.221
		27:15	*QG* 4.203*
26:12	*QG* 4.189*, 190; *Mut.* 190, 268*	27:16	*QG* 4.204*; [*Virt.* 208]
		27:17	*QG* 4.205*
26:13	*QG* 4.190*	27:18	*QG* 4.222, 223
26:15	*QG* 4.191*	27:18–19	*QG* 4.206*
26:16	*QG* 4.192*	27:18–29	*Sacr.* 120
26:18	*QG* 4.193*, 194*	27:20	*QG* 4.207*, 208*; *Sacr.* 64*; *Deus* 92*; *Ebr.* 120*; *Fug.* 168*
26:18–22	*Fug.* 200		
26:19	*QG* 4.195*		
26:19–25	*Somn.* 1.14, 39	27:21	*QG* 4.209*
26:20–35	*QG* 4.195	27:22	*QG* 4.210*
26:20–22	*QG* 4.195a; *Somn.* 1.40	27:23	*QG* 4.211*; [*Virt.* 208]
26:23	*QG* 4.195b	27:23–24	*QG* 4.212*
26:24	*QG* 4.195, 195d, 195e	27:25–27	*QG* 4.213
26:25	*QG* 4.195f	27:27	*QG* 4.214*; *Leg.* 3.192
26:25–26	*QG* 4.195g	27:27–29	*Virt.* 209
26:26	*QG* 4.7	27:28	*QG* 4.215*; *Migr.* 101*
26:29–30	*QG* 4.8, 195h	27:29	*QG* 4.216*, 217*, 218*, 219*
26:31	*QG* 4.195h		
26:32	*Plant.* 79, 80, 83; *Somn.* 1.8, 11, 36, 42	27:30	*QG* 4.220*; *Sacr.* 135; *Ebr.* 9*
26:32–33	*QG* 4.196i; *Plant.* 78*; *Somn.* 1.14, 24, 38, 40	27:31	*QG* 4.221*, 222*
		27:32	*QG* 4.223*
26:33	*QG* 4.195b, 195g; *Plant.* 82; *Somn.* 1.12, 68	27:32–33	*QG* 4.224*
		27:33	*QG* 4.225*, 226*, 228; *Her.* 251*, 252, 254
26:34	*QG* 4.195j, 245		
26:35	*QG* 4.195k	27:34	*QG* 4.227*
27:1	*QG* 4.196*, 197, 232	27:35	*QG* 4.228*
27:3	*QG* 4.197*	27:36	*QG* 4.229*; *Leg.* 1.61; 2.89; 3.15, 93, 180, 191*, 192*, 195*; *Sacr.* 135; *Migr.* 200; *Her.* 252; *Mut.* 81; *Somn.* 1.171
27:3–4	*QG* 4.198*		
27:5	*QG* 4.199; *Her.* 252		
27:6	*QG* 4.199*		
27:6–10	*QG* 4.202		
27:8–10	*QG* 4.200*	27:36–37	*QG* 4.230*

27:38	QG 4.231*, 232*, 233*; Mut. 230*	28:12–15	Somn. 1.3*
27:39	QG 4.234*, 235*	28:13	Somn. 1.159*, 163, 166*, 170, 172, 173*, 174
27:39–40	QG 4.233; Virt. 209	28:14	Somn. 1.175*, 176*
27:40	QG 4.236*, 237*; Leg. 3.193*; Congr. 176*; Prob. 57	28:15	Somn. 1.179*, 180*
		28:16	Somn. 1.183*, 185*
27:41	QG 4.238*; Det. 46*; Mos. 1.242; Virt. 208	28:17	Migr. 5*; Somn. 1.184*, 185*, 186*
27:41–45	Det. 45; Fug. 4	28:20	Somn. 1.126; Virt. 8
27:42	QG 4.239; Fug. 39*	28:20–22	Congr. 101
27:42–45	Fug. 23*, 24	28:21	Plant. 90*; Somn. 1.163
27:43	QG 4.239*; Migr. 212; Fug. 39, 40, 43, 44, 49	28:22	Congr. 99*
		28:31	QE 2.119
27:43–44	Somn. 1.46*	29:4	Migr. 213*
27:43–45	Migr. 208*	29:5	Migr. 213*
27:44	Fug. 46*	29:16	Migr. 145; Mut. 254
27:45	QG 4.240*; Det. 51; Fug. 47	29:16–17	Sobr. 12
		29:18	Ebr. 48
27:46	QG 4.241*, 242*	29:23	Leg. 2.59; Congr. 25, 26, 31, 34
28:1	QG 4.88		
28:1–5	QG 4.245	29:24	Congr. 30, 33; Virt. 223
28:2	QG 4.243*; Post. 76; Fug. 48*, 50, 52	29:26	Ebr. 47*, 50
		29:27	Ebr. 52*
28:5	Ios. 26	29:28	Ebr. 53; Congr. 25, 26, 31, 34
28:6	Congr. 70		
28:7	QG 4.244*, 245; Congr. 70*	29:29	Congr. 30, 33; Virt. 223
		29:31	Leg. 2.47*; 3.180*, 181; Cher. 41; Post. 135; Her. 51*; Congr. 7; Mut. 132*, 254, 255
28:8–9	QG 4.245*		
28:10	Somn. 1.5*, 41, 61		
28:10–11	Somn. 1.4*, 68		
28:11	Somn. 1.5, 61*, 63, 71, 72*, 73, 85, 87, 116*, 118, 120*, 126, 127, 128	29:31–32	Cher. 46
		29:32	Sacr. 120; Fug. 73; Somn. 2.33
28:11–12	QG 4.29	29:32–34	Somn. 2.37
28:12	Somn. 1.134, 141, 142, 144, 146, 148, 150, 152, 190; 2.3, 19*	29:32–35	Ebr. 94
		29:33–35	Somn. 2.34
		29:35	QG 4.195, 195i; Leg. 1.80, 84; 2.95; 3.146; Plant. 134*, 135;
28:12–13	Somn. 1.133*, 157		

29:35 (cont.)
    Somn. 1.37*; 2.38

30:1   *Leg.* 2.46*; 3.180*; *Post.* 179

30:2   *Leg.* 2.46*; *Post.* 179*

30:3–13 *Virt.* 223

30:4   *Congr.* 34

30:5   *Leg.* 3.146

30:5–6 *Leg.* 2.94, 96

30:5–12 *Fug.* 73

30:6   *Somn.* 2.35, 39

30:8   *Somn.* 2.36

30:9   *Congr.* 34

30:9–12 *Leg.* 2.94

30:11   *Somn.* 2.35, 40

30:13   *Migr.* 95*, 99; *Somn.* 2.35, 40

30:16   *Congr.* 123*

30:17–18 *QG* 4.195; *Leg.* 2.94

30:18   *Leg.* 1.80; *Plant.* 134*, 136; *Ebr.* 94; *Somn.* 2.34, 38

30:20   *Fug.* 73; *Somn.* 2.34, 39

30:21   *Migr.* 223

30:22   *Leg.* 3.181; *Congr.* 7

30:22–24 *Somn.* 2.16

30:24   *Post.* 179*; *Mut.* 89; *Somn.* 2.47, 63; *Ios.* 28

30:30   *Migr.* 214*

30:36   *Sacr.* 46*, 47*; *Agr.* 42*

30:37   *Plant.* 110*

30:39–40 *Fug.* 10

30:42   *Her.* 180*; *Fug.* 9; *Somn.* 1.202

30:43   *Det.* 13

31:2   *Det.* 4; *Migr.* 28

31:3   *Migr.* 27*, 29, 30

31:4   *Det.* 3*

31:5   *Det.* 4*

31:10   *Somn.* 1.200*, 202, 208, 209, 213, 216, 219; 2.19*

31:11   *Somn.* 1.190, 196*

31:11–13 *Somn.* 1.189*

31:12   *Somn.* 1.197*, 199, 200, 202, 208, 209, 213, 216, 219, 225, 227*, 255

31:13   *Somn.* 1.227*, 228*, 229*, 238*, 240*, 241, 242, 244, 249*, 252*, 256

31:14–15 *Her.* 44*

31:14–16 *Fug.* 15*

31:16   *Fug.* 16

31:20   *Leg.* 3.18*, 20; *Fug.* 44, 49

31:20–21 *Leg.* 3.16*; *Fug.* 4, 7*

31:21   *Leg.* 3.15, 18, 19*; *Fug.* 14, 20

31:22–25 *Ios.* 26

31:23   *Leg.* 3.20

31:26   *Leg.* 3.20*, 21*, 27

31:27   *Leg.* 3.21; *Fug.* 20*, 22

31:28   *Her.* 43*

31:32–35 *Conf.* 74

31:33–34 *Fug.* 143

31:34   *Leg.* 2.46

31:35   *Ebr.* 54*; *Fug.* 143*

31:41   *Ios.* 26

31:43   *Cher.* 67*, 68

31:46–48 *Post.* 59

31:47   *Leg.* 3.19

31:53   *Spec.* 2.3

32:1   *Sobr.* 65

32:10   *Leg.* 2.89*

32:24   *Migr.* 26; *Mut.* 14

32:24–26 *Leg.* 3.190

32:24–30 *Sacr.* 17; *Praem.* 36, 39

32:25   *Mut.* 187*; *Somn.* 1.130*; *Praem.* 47*

32:27	*Mut.* 14	35:19	*Mut.* 96
32:27–28	*Sacr.* 120	35:22	*QE* 2.30, 114
32:27–30	*Mut.* 87	35:22–26	*Virt.* 224; *Praem.* 57, 60, 65
32:28	*QE* 2.108*; *Leg.* 1.43; 2.34; 3.15; *Sacr.* 119; *Ebr.* 82*; *Conf.* 92, 146; *Migr.* 39, 201; *Her.* 78; *Congr.* 51; *Fug.* 208; *Mut.* 44*, 81, 83; *Somn.* 1.130, 171; 2.44, 173; *Abr.* 57; *Praem.* 44; *Legat.* 4	35:23	*QG* 4.123; *Leg.* 1.81; *Sacr.* 119, 120; *Plant.* 134; *Ios.* 13, 15, 173, 189, 222
		35:23–24	*Ios.* 175
		35:23–36	*Her.* 175
		35:24	*Ios.* 163, 187, 232, 234
		35:28	*QG* 4.232
		35:29	*Sacr.* 6*, 7
32:29	*Mut.* 14*	36:12	*Congr.* 54*, 56, 57, 60
32:30	*Leg.* 1.43; 2.34; 3.15, 38; *Post.* 63, 92; *Ebr.* 82; *Conf.* 92, 129, 146; *Migr.* 39, 201; *Congr.* 51; *Fug.* 208; *Mut.* 81; *Somn.* 1.171; 2.44, 173; *Abr.* 57; *Praem.* 36, 44; *Legat.* 4	37:2	*Deus* 119*, 120, 121; *Agr.* 56; *Sobr.* 12, 14; *Ios.* 2, 54, 270
		37:3	*Det.* 6, 14; *Somn.* 1.220; *Ios.* 4, 32
		37:4	*Ios.* 5
		37:5–7	*Ios.* 6
		37:5–11	*Ios.* 164, 171
32:31	*Mut.* 187; *Somn.* 1.79*, 130	37:7	*Somn.* 2.6*, 17*, 18, 19, 21, 30*, 31, 33*, 37, 41, 42, 78, 80*, 132
32:32	*Conf.* 148	37:8	*Somn.* 2.7*, 93*, 94, 95, 96*, 100; *Ios.* 7
33:5	*Her.* 38*		
33:11	*Sacr.* 42*	37:9	*Somn.* 2.6*, 113, 132, 133; *Ios.* 8
34:1–2	*Mut.* 194		
34:2	*Migr.* 224; *Mut.* 193	37:9–10	*Somn.* 2.140
34:2–3	*Mut.* 195	37:9–11	*Somn.* 2.111*
34:3	*Mut.* 194*	37:10	*Somn.* 2.7*, 135*; *Ios.* 9
34:25	*Mut.* 200	37:11	*Somn.* 2.141*; *Ios.* 8
34:25–27	*Migr.* 224	37:12	*Ios.* 10
35:2	*Leg.* 3.22	37:13	*Det.* 6, 9*, 10*, 11, 25
35:2–3	*Conf.* 74*	37:13–14	*Det.* 13; *Ios.* 11
35:4	*Leg.* 3.23*, 25*, 27	37:13–17	*Det.* 5*
35:10	*Sacr.* 120	37:14	*Det.* 11*, 12, 15*, 17
35:11	*Mut.* 23*	37:15	*Det.* 6, 10, 17*, 19, 21, 22, 24*, 25, 28; *Fug.* 128, 131
35:16	*Mut.* 96		
35:18	*Mut.* 92, 94; *Somn.* 2.36, 41		

37:15–17	*Fug.* 127*	38:16	*Congr.* 125*
37:15–20	*Ios.* 12	38:18	*Deus* 137; *Congr.* 126;
37:16	*Det.* 25*		*Fug.* 150; *Somn.* 2.44, 45
37:17	*Det.* 27*, 28*; *Fug.* 128,	38:20	*Fug.* 150, 151, 153*
	131	38:20–23	*Fug.* 149*
37:18–28	*Ios.* 236, 270	38:21	*Fug.* 153
37:18–35	*Ios.* 179	38:23	*Fug.* 154, 155
37:20	*Somn.* 2.133	38:25	*Mut.* 134*, 135
37:21–22	*Ios.* 13, 173	38:26	*Mut.* 136*
37:23–24	*Ios.* 14	38:27–30	*Deus* 137
37:25–28	*Ios.* 15	38:29–30	*Virt.* 222
37:28	*Ios.* 18, 35, 36, 165, 167,	39:1	*Leg.* 3.236; *Det.* 26; *Deus*
	175, 247		111; *Ebr.* 210*, 216, 220,
37:29–30	*Ios.* 16, 173		224; *Conf.* 95; *Migr.* 19;
37:31	*Somn.* 1.221, 225		*Mut.* 173; *Somn.* 2.16;
37:31–32	*Ios.* 14		*Ios.* 27, 35, 36, 52, 58, 61,
37:33	*Somn.* 2.65*; *Ios.* 22, 25,		152, 153, 244, 270
	27	39:1–6	*Ios.* 37
37:34	*Ios.* 23	39:2	*Ebr.* 214
37:34–35	*Somn.* 2.66	39:3	*Post.* 80
37:36	*Det.* 26; *Deus* 111; *Ebr.*	39:4	*Ios.* 54
	210*, 214, 216; *Conf.*	39:6–9	*Ios.* 40
	95; *Migr.* 19; *Mut.* 173;	39:6–12	*Ios.* 269
	Somn. 2.16; *Ios.* 27, 35,	39:7	*Leg.* 3.237*, 239*; *Migr.*
	36, 52, 58, 61, 152, 244,		19*; *Ios.* 60
	270	39:7–9	*Ios.* 45
38:3–4	*Post.* 180	39:7–12	*Somn.* 2.106; *Ios.* 64
38:6	*Leg.* 3.74*; *Virt.* 221	39:7–19	*Ios.* 66
38:6–10	*Virt.* 222	39:7–20	*Ios.* 244
38:7	*Leg.* 3.69, 70, 71*, 73,	39:7–23	*Ios.* 270
	74*	39:8–9	*Ios.* 46, 67
38:8	*Deus* 17	39:10–12	*Ios.* 41
38:8–10	*Deus* 18	39:11	*Leg.* 3.238*; *Ios.* 48
38:9	*Post.* 180*; *Deus* 16*;	39:12	*Leg.* 3.237*, 239*, 240*,
	Anim. 49		241, 242; *Migr.* 19; *Ios.*
38:10	*Deus* 16		49, 52, 54
38:11	*Deus* 137	39:13–18	*Ios.* 50
38:14–15	*Congr.* 124	39:14	*Migr.* 21*
38:15	*Mut.* 134	39:16–21	*Ios.* 80

39:17	*Migr.* 21*	40:20–22	*Ios.* 97, 156
39:19–20	*Ios.* 52	40:23	*Ios.* 99
39:20	*Mut.* 173; *Ios.* 247	41:1	*Ios.* 100
39:20–21	*Deus* 111	41:1–36	*Ios.* 248, 269
39:20–22	*Ios.* 123	41:1–45	*Ios.* 151
39:20–23	*Deus* 113, 115	41:1–4	*Ios.* 101
39:21	*Deus* 116	41:5–7	*Ios.* 102
39:21–23	*Ios.* 85	41:8	*Ios.* 103
40:1	*Conf.* 95; *Migr.* 19	41:9–13	*Ios.* 104
40:1–2	*Somn.* 2.16; *Ios.* 152	41:14	*Ios.* 105, 123
40:1–3	*Ebr.* 208	41:15	*Ios.* 125, 143
40:1–4	*Det.* 26; *Ios.* 88	41:17	*Somn.* 2.219*, 238*, 261
40:1–23	*Ios.* 248, 269	41:17–19	*Somn.* 2.216*
40:2	*Ebr.* 214, 216, 220, 224;	41:17–24	*Ios.* 106
	Somn. 2.184, 195; *Ios.*	41:20–21	*Somn.* 2.217*
	153	41:22–24	*Somn.* 2.218*
40:2–3	*Ebr.* 210*	41:25	*Ios.* 107
40:3	*Ios.* 154	41:25–31	*QG* 1.89
40:6–7	*Ios.* 89	41:26–27	*Ios.* 108
40:7	*Somn.* 2.184, 195; *Ios.*	41:28–32	*Ios.* 109
	153	41:33	*Ios.* 114
40:8	*Cher.* 128*; *Migr.* 19*;	41:34	*Ios.* 158
	Ios. 90	41:34–36	*Ios.* 111
40:8–11	*Somn.* 2.156	41:37	*Ios.* 116
40:9	*Somn.* 2.160*, 163*, 169	41:38	*Ios.* 116*
40:9–11	*Somn.* 2.155, 158, 159*,	41:39–41	*Ios.* 117
	181, 190, 195, 215; *Ios.*	41:40–44	*Ios.* 123, 248, 270
	91	41:41	*Migr.* 20*; *Somn.* 2.43;
40:10	*Somn.* 2.197, 199*,		*Ios.* 38
40:11	*Somn.* 2.200*, 203	41:41–43	*Ios.* 119
40:12–13	*Ios.* 92	41:42	*Somn.* 2.44*; *Ios.* 150
40:15	*Migr.* 20*	41:42–43	*Ios.* 149
40:16	*Somn.* 2.207*, 210	41:43	*Migr.* 160*; *Somn.* 2.16,
40:16–17	*Somn.* 2.155, 156, 158,		46; *Ios.* 148
	215; *Ios.* 93	41:45	*Mut.* 89, 91; *Somn.* 1.78*
40:17	*Somn.* 2.211, 212	41:45–46	*Ios.* 121
40:18–19	*Ios.* 96	41:46	*Ios.* 157, 247, 270
40:19	*Somn.* 2.213	41:47–49	*QG* 1.89; *Ios.* 158
40:20–21	*Ebr.* 208	41:48	*Mut.* 90

41:48–49	*Somn.* 2.46	43:10	*Her.* 255*
41:49	*Post.* 96*	43:11	*Ios.* 193
41:51	*Leg.* 3.93, 94	43:11–13	*Ios.* 194
41:51–52	*Sobr.* 28; *Migr.* 205;	43:14–15	*Ios.* 195
	Congr. 40	43:16	*Ios.* 196, 210, 234
41:53–54	*QG* 1.89; *Ios.* 159	43:17–23	*Ios.* 197
41:53–57	*Sobr.* 13	43:21–22	*Ios.* 213
41:56–57	*Ios.* 161	43:23	*Ios.* 201, 210
42:1–4	*Ios.* 163	43:25–28	*Ios.* 199
42:3	*Sacr.* 48	43:29	*Ios.* 210, 234
42:5–6	*Ios.* 164	43:29–30	*Ios.* 200
42:7	*Ios.* 249	43:31	*Ios.* 201
42:7–8	*Ios.* 165	43:31–34	*Ios.* 210
42:9	*Ios.* 166	43:32	*Ios.* 202
42:9–16	*Ios.* 213, 233	43:33	*Ios.* 203
42:10–13	*Ios.* 167	43:34	*Ios.* 205, 206, 234
42:11	*Conf.* 41*, 147*	44:1	*Ios.* 210
42:15–16	*Migr.* 162*; *Ios.* 168, 209	44:1–2	*Ios.* 207
42:18	*Migr.* 21*	44:2	*Ios.* 235
42:19–20	*Ios.* 233	44:3	*Ios.* 208
42:20	*Ios.* 209	44:4–6	*Ios.* 211
42:21	*Ios.* 170	44:7–8	*Ios.* 215
42:22	*Ios.* 173, 174	44:9	*Ios.* 216, 221
42:23–24	*Ios.* 175	44:11–13	*Ios.* 217
42:24	*Ios.* 179, 209, 233	44:12	*Ios.* 235
42:25	*Ios.* 178, 249	44:14–16	*Ios.* 219
42:27–28	*Ios.* 180, 209	44:17	*Ios.* 220
42:28	*Ios.* 181	44:18	*Ios.* 222
42:29–30	*Ios.* 184	44:19–20	*Ios.* 223
42:29–34	*Ios.* 183	44:21–24	*Ios.* 224
42:31–33	*Ios.* 185	44:22	*Ios.* 225
42:34	*Ios.* 186	44:25–31	*Ios.* 225
42:35	*Ios.* 209	44:32	*Ios.* 227
42:36	*Leg.* 1.61*; *Somn.* 2.207*;	44:33	*Ios.* 228
	Ios. 187	44:34	*Ios.* 226
42:36–38	*Ios.* 217	45:1	*Migr.* 22*; *Ios.* 237
42:37	*Ios.* 188	45:2	*Migr.* 22
42:38–43:10	*Ios.* 189	45:2–4	*Ios.* 238
43:8	*Her.* 255; *Ios.* 191	45:3	*Ios.* 239

45:5	*Migr.* 22
45:5-8	*Ios.* 239
45:7	*Migr.* 22*
45:8	*Migr.* 20, 22; *Ios.* 236, 241, 242
45:9	*Leg.* 3.179*; *Ios.* 245
45:11	*Leg.* 3.179*
45:15	*Ios.* 246
45:16	*Mut.* 171*; *Ios.* 250
45:17-24	*Ios.* 251
45:18	*Mut.* 173*, 174*
45:22	*Migr.* 203*
45:25-26	*Ios.* 252
45:26	*Her.* 251*, 256*
45:27-28	*Ios.* 253
45:28	*Migr.* 21*
46:1	*Somn.* 1.172*
46:2-5	*Ios.* 255
46:4	*Post.* 29*, 30
46:4-7	*Mos.* 1.5, 34
46:6-7	*Hypoth.* 6.1 (427.10)
46:20	*Congr.* 41, 43*
46:27	*Migr.* 199; *Mos.* 1.189
46:29	*Ios.* 256
46:30	*Mut.* 215*
46:33-34	*Agr.* 57*
46:34	*Sacr.* 51*; *Agr.* 27, 29, 39, 48, 59, 66, 124
47:3	*Sacr.* 48, 49; *Agr.* 27, 29, 39, 59*, 60, 64, 66, 124
47:3-11	*Ios.* 257
47:4	*Agr.* 64*
47:4-11	*Virt.* 107
47:9	*Conf.* 80*
47:13	*Ios.* 259
47:14	*Ios.* 258
47:15-22	*Ios.* 259
47:23-24	*Ios.* 260
47:24	*Migr.* 204
47:25	*Ios.* 267
48:5	*Mut.* 97*, 101
48:13	*Sobr.* 28
48:13-14	*Leg.* 3.90; *Sobr.* 27
48:14	*Leg.* 3.93
48:15	*Leg.* 3.179; *Deus* 157*; *Mut.* 41*
48:15-16	*Leg.* 3.177*; *Conf.* 181*; *Fug.* 67*; *Mut.* 32
48:17-20	*Migr.* 205
48:19	*Leg.* 3.90*
48:22	*Leg.* 3.26
49:1	*Her.* 261*
49:5-7	*Mut.* 200
49:8	*Leg.* 3.26
49:8-12	*Leg.* 2.96
49:10	*Ebr.* 94
49:15	*Leg.* 1.80*; *Migr.* 221*
49:16-18	*Leg.* 2.94*
49:17	*Leg.* 2.97*, 99*, 103*, 105; *Agr.* 95, 99, 100*, 102*, 105, 106, 107, 109*, 122*, 124
49:17-18	*Agr.* 94*
49:18	*Leg.* 2.101*; *Agr.* 123*
49:22	*Sobr.* 12*, 15*, 68
49:28	*Sobr.* 66; *Fug.* 185; *Spec.* 1.79
49:29-33	*Post.* 62
49:33	*Sacr.* 5, 8
50:3	*Migr.* 202*
50:7	*Migr.* 160*
50:7-8	*Migr.* 159
50:8	*Migr.* 160, 162
50:15	*Ios.* 261
50:18	*Ios.* 261
50:19	*Migr.* 22*, 160*; *Somn.* 2.107*; *Ios.* 266
50:19-21	*Ios.* 262

50:22	*Ios.* 268
50:24	*Migr.* 18*
50:25	*Migr.* 17*, 18
50:26	*Migr.* 23; *Ios.* 268

Exodus

Title	*Migr.* 14
1	*Migr.* 14
1:5	*Migr.* 199*
1:7	*Hypoth.* 6.1 (427.17)
1:8	*Conf.* 72*, 88
1:8–13	*Mos.* 1.36
1:8–21	QE 1.4
1:9	*Migr.* 54*, 55; *Spec.* 1.7
1:9–10	*Mos.* 1.8
1:11	*Post.* 54, 56, 57; *Conf.* 91; *Somn.* 1.77; *Mos.* 1.38
1:11–14	*Conf.* 88; *Virt.* 107
1:13	*Post.* 54
1:13–14	*Mos.* 1.38
1:14	*Conf.* 91, 92; *Mos.* 1.67
1:15	*Her.* 128*
1:16	*Mos.* 1.8
1:17	*Leg.* 3.3*, 243
1:19	*Migr.* 141*; *Congr.* 3; *Fug.* 168*
1:20	*Leg.* 3.243*
1:21	*Leg.* 3.3*; *Migr.* 215
2:1	*Mos.* 1.7
2:1–2	QE 2.46; *Congr.* 131*, 132
2:2	*Mos.* 1.5, 9, 11
2:2–3	*Conf.* 106
2:3	*Mos.* 1.10
2:4	*Somn.* 2.142*; *Mos.* 1.12
2:5	*Mos.* 1.14
2:5–12	*Mos.* 1.149
2:6	*Conf.* 106; *Mos.* 1.15

2:7	*Mos.* 1.16
2:8–10	*Mos.* 1.17
2:10	*Ebr.* 94
2:11	*Leg.* 3.38; *Fug.* 148
2:11–12	*Mos.* 1.44; FR(H) 107 B36
2:12	*Leg.* 3.37*; *Fug.* 148*
2:13	*Fug.* 148*
2:14	FR(H) 107 B33
2:15	*Leg.* 3.12*, 13, 14, 39; *Fug.* 147; *Mos.* 1.45, 47, 73, 149
2:16	*Mut.* 106, 110*, 111*, 114, 116; *Mos.* 1.52
2:16–17	*Mut.* 113
2:17	*Mut.* 112; *Mos.* 1.53, 54, 57
2:18	*Mut.* 103, 105, 114, 116*
2:18–20	*Mos.* 1.58
2:19	*Mut.* 117, 118
2:20	*Mut.* 119, 120*
2:21	*Post.* 77; *Mut.* 120; *Mos.* 1.59
2:21–22	*Cher.* 41, 47
2:22	*Conf.* 82*
2:23	*Leg.* 3.212*, 214*; *Det.* 94*; *Conf.* 93*; *Migr.* 15*; *Mos.* 1.73
2:23–24	*Det.* 93
2:23–25	QG 4.233
2:24–25	*Det.* 95
3:1	*Sacr.* 50*; *Agr.* 43*; *Mut.* 103; *Mos.* 1.60
3:2	QE 2.45; *Mos.* 1.65, 68
3:2–3	*Fug.* 161*
3:4	*Somn.* 1.194*
3:5	*Fug.* 162*, 163*
3:6	*Fug.* 141*; *Mut.* 134
3:7	*Mos.* 1.37, 72

3:7–10	*QE* 1.1, 4, 10, 15; 2.2; *Mos.* 1.71; *Hypoth.* 6.1 (427.13)	4:10–13	*Virt.* 63
		4:11	*Mos.* 1.84
		4:12	*Her.* 25*
3:9	*Leg.* 3.214*	4:14	*QG* 4.16*; *Det.* 39, 40, 126*, 129, 132*, 135*, 137, 140; *Migr.* 78*, 79*; *Mut.* 168*
3:10	*Mos.* 1.73		
3:11	*Fug.* 140*		
3:12	*Fug.* 140*		
3:13	*Mut.* 11; *Mos.* 1.74	4:14–16	*Det.* 44; *Mut.* 208; *Mos.* 1.84
3:14	*QG* 1.55; 4.2, 4, 8, 22; *QE* 1.20; 2.3, 11, 14, 16, 47, 51, 61, 62, 63, 66, 67, 68, 122; *Leg.* 3.38; *Cher.* 27; *Sacr.* 9; *Det.* 92, 139, 159, 160*, 161, 162; *Plant.* 26; *Her.* 70; *Fug.* 110, 112; *Mut.* 11*, 58, 82; *Deo* 3, 4; *Somn.* 1.231*, 234; 2.227, 237, 292; *Mos.* 1.75; *Abr.* 121; *Spec.* 1.81; *Contempl.* 2	4:15	*Migr.* 80*
		4:15–16	*QE* 2.27, 44
		4:16	*Det.* 39, 40; *Migr.* 81*, 84
		4:19	*Det.* 39
		4:19–20	*Virt.* 63
		4:20	*Mos.* 1.85
		4:22	*Post.* 63
		4:23	*Conf.* 94
		4:27	*Her.* 44
		4:27–28	*Mos.* 1.85
		4:29–31	*Mos.* 1.86
3:15	*Mut.* 12*; *Mos.* 1.76; *Abr.* 51*	5:1	*Mos.* 1.87
		5:2	*QG* 4.87*; *Leg.* 3.12, 243*; *Post.* 115; *Ebr.* 19*, 77*; *Somn.* 2.182*; *Mos.* 1.88
3:16	*Mos.* 1.72, 73		
3:18	*Mos.* 1.73		
3:20	*Deus* 60		
4:1	*Mos.* 1.76	5:6	*Her.* 255*
4:1–5	*Leg.* 2.88*	5:6–14	*Her.* 255; *Mos.* 1.38
4:2	*Leg.* 2.89	5:6–18	*Mos.* 1.89
4:2–3	*Det.* 177; *Mos.* 1.77	5:20–21	*Mos.* 1.90
4:3	*Leg.* 2.90, 92	5:22–23	*Her.* 20*
4:4	*Leg.* 2.92*; *Mos.* 1.78	6:3	*Mut.* 13*; *Somn.* 1.230
4:5	*Leg.* 2.89	6:7	*Sacr.* 87*
4:6	*Det.* 177	6:8	*Sacr.* 90, 91
4:6–7	*Mos.* 1.79	6:12	*Det.* 38; *Her.* 16
4:9	*Det.* 177; *Mos.* 1.81	6:16–20	*Post.* 173; *Mos.* 1.7
4:10	*Sacr.* 12; *Det.* 38; *Migr.* 76*; *Her.* 4*, 16; *Mos.* 1.83; *Praem.* 54	6:23	*Post.* 76*
		6:26	*Mut.* 207*, 208, 209
		6:27	*Mut.* 207*

6:29	*Mut.* 20*	8:13	*Mos.* 1.145
7:1	*Leg.* 1.40*; *Sacr.* 9*; *Det.*	8:14–15	*Migr.* 85
	39, 161*, 162; *Migr.* 84*,	8:15	*Mos.* 1.112*
	169*; *Mut.* 19*, 125, 128;	8:16–20	*Mos.* 1.130
	Somn. 2.189; *Prob.* 43	8:17–20	*Mos.* 1.145
7:1–2	*Det.* 40	8:22	*Sacr.* 51*; *Fug.* 18*
7:2	*Mut.* 208	9	*QE* 1.4
7:3	*Hypoth.* 6.1 (427.13)	9:1–7	*Mos.* 1.133
7:7	*QG* 3.38	9:3	*Deus* 60
7:8–29	*QE* 1.4	9:8–10	*Mos.* 1.127, 145
7:9–12	*Det.* 177	9:13–35	*Prov.* 1.47
7:10	*Mos.* 1.91	9:15	*Mos.* 1.110
7:10–12	*Migr.* 76	9:22–25	*Mos.* 1.126
7:11	*Det.* 38; *Mut.* 208	9:22–26	*Mos.* 1.145
7:11–12	*Mos.* 1.92	9:23–25	*Mos.* 1.118
7:12	*Migr.* 83, 85*; *Mos.* 1.93	9:29	*Leg.* 3.43*, 44; *Ebr.* 101*;
7:13	*Mos.* 1.94		*Mut.* 21*, 129
7:14–8:11	*Mos.* 1.144	9:30	*Mut.* 21
7:14–10:29	*Congr.* 118	9:34–35	*Mos.* 1.120
7:14–12:36	*Mos.* 1.96	10	*QE* 1.4
7:15	*Conf.* 29*, 30, 31*, 33;	10:1–20	*Prov.* 1.47
	Somn. 2.277*, 278, 300*	10:7	*Mos.* 1.122*
7:17	*Mut.* 20*	10:12–15	*Mos.* 1.121, 126, 145
7:19–21	*Mos.* 1.99	10:13	*Mos.* 1.120
7:20	*Det.* 177; *Somn.* 2.259	10:16–19	*Mos.* 1.122
7:21	*Somn.* 2.260	10:21	*Somn.* 1.114
7:22	*Migr.* 83; *Mut.* 208	10:21–23	*Mos.* 1.145
7:23	*Fug.* 124*	10:22–23	*Mos.* 1.123, 126
7:25	*Mos.* 1.101	10:23	*Somn.* 1.117*
7:26	*Conf.* 94*	11:5	*Somn.* 2.266
7:26–8:3	*Mos.* 1.103	11:7	*Somn.* 2.267*
7:26–8:11	*Sacr.* 69	12:1–2	*QE* 1.1; *Mos.* 2.222
8	*QE* 1.4	12:1–14	*Spec.* 2.145, 146
8:2	*Somn.* 2.259	12:1–20	*Decal.* 159
8:3	*Migr.* 83; *Mut.* 208	12:2	*QG* 2.45*; *QE* 1.1*;
8:4–9	*Mos.* 1.105		*Congr.* 161; *Spec.* 2.150,
8:5	*Sacr.* 69*		152
8:6	*Sacr.* 69*	12:3	*QE* 1.2, 3*; *Congr.* 89,
8:12–14	*Mos.* 1.107		106*

12:3–6	*Spec.* 2.148	12:48	*Virt.* 104
12:4	*QE* 1.5*, 6*; *Leg.* 3.165*;	12:45–50	*Decal.* 161
	Her. 193*	13:1–2	*Her.* 117*
12:5	*QE* 1.7*, 8*	13:2	*QE* 2.22; FR(M)15 =
12:6	*QE* 1.2, 9*, 10*, 11*, 12,		FR(P)22; *Her.* 118; *Spec.*
	13; *Mos.* 2.224; *Spec.*		2.134
	2.149	13:3–10	*Decal.* 161
12:7	*QE* 1.3, 12*	13:11	*Sacr.* 91
12:8	*QE* 1.13*, 14*, 15*, 18;	13:11–12	*Sacr.* 97*
	Congr. 162*; *Spec.* 2.158	13:11–13	*Sacr.* 89*
12:9	*QE* 1.14, 16*, 17*	13:12	*Sacr.* 102*, 103*, 104*
12:10	*QE* 1.18*	13:12–13	*Spec.* 1.135, 248
12:11	*QE* 1.4, 14, 15, 18, 19*;	13:13	*Sacr.* 112*, 114*; *Spec.*
	Leg. 3.154*; *Sacr.* 63*;		1.137, 138; *Virt.* 146
	Migr. 25*; *Her.* 255*	13:15	*Spec.* 2.134
12:12	*QE* 1.3, 20*	13:17–18	*Mos.* 1.164
12:14–24	*Spec.* 2.41	13:19	*Migr.* 17, 18; *Somn.*
12:14–27	*Decal.* 161		2.109
12:15	*Spec.* 2.156, 159, 161	13:21–22	*Mos.* 1.166
12:15–20	*Spec.* 2.150	14:2	*Mos.* 2.247
12:16	*Spec.* 2.157	14:5–8	*Mos.* 1.167
12:17	*QE* 1.21*	14:6–9	*Cher.* 130
12:21	*Spec.* 2.148	14:7	*Ebr.* 111
12:21–28	*Spec.* 2.146	14:9	*Mos.* 1.169; 2.248
12:22	*QE* 1.22*	14:10	*Mos.* 1.170; 2.249
12:23	*QE* 1.22, 23*; *Leg.* 2.34*	14:11–12	*Mos.* 1.171
12:29	*Sacr.* 134; *Somn.* 2.266;	14:13	*Cher.* 130*
	Mos. 1.135; *Spec.* 2.134	14:13–14	*Mos.* 1.173, 175; 2.252
12:29–30	*Congr.* 118; *Mos.* 1.134,	14:14	*Her.* 14*, 15*; *Somn.*
	145		2.265*
12:30	*QE* 1.3; *Mos.* 1.136	14:15	*Her.* 14*, 16, 19
12:33	*Mos.* 1.139	14:15–31	*Contempl.* 86
12:34	*Spec.* 2.158	14:16	*Mos.* 1.177
12:35–36	*Fug.* 19; *Mos.* 1.141	14:19–20	*Her.* 203*; *Mos.* 1.178
12:37	*Spec.* 2.146, 250	14:21	*Mos.* 1.176, 177; 2.253
12:37–38	*Mos.* 1.147	14:22–27	*Mos.* 2.254
12:37–41	*Hypoth.* 6.1 (427.10)	14:24–25	*Mos.* 1.178
12:38	*Migr.* 152*, 154, 163	14:26–28	*Mos.* 1.179
12:39	*Sacr.* 62*; *Spec.* 2.158	14:27	*Conf.* 70*

14:27–28	*Ebr.* 79; *Sobr.* 13; *Mos.* 2.255	16:4 *(cont.)*	167*; *Congr.* 173; *Fug.* 137*, 166; *Mut.* 259*; *Decal.* 16
14:28	*Leg.* 3.13	16:4–5	*Mos.* 2.258; *Spec.* 2.199
14:30	*Conf.* 36; *Somn.* 2.280*	16:12	FR(H) 106 B8
15:1	*Leg.* 2.102*, 103; *Agr.* 80, 82*, 94; *Ebr.* 111*; *Somn.* 2.269*	16:13	*Mos.* 1.209
		16:13–15	*Mos.* 1.200; *Decal.* 16
15:1–18	*Sobr.* 13	16:13–16	*Leg.* 3.169*
15:1–21	*Mos.* 1.180; 2.256; *Contempl.* 85, 87	16:14	*Leg.* 3.170, 172*
		16:15	*Leg.* 2.86; 3.175*; *Fug.* 137*, 138*, 139*; *Mos.* 1.201
15:4	*Ebr.* 111		
15:4–5	*Ebr.* 79	16:15–16	*Leg.* 3.173*
15:5	*Agr.* 89	16:16	*Her.* 191; *Fug.* 139*
15:8	*Leg.* 3.172*; *Deus* 60	16:16–18	QG 4.102
15:9	*Cher.* 74*, 75, 77*	16:17–18	*Decal.* 17
15:10	*Deus* 60; *Mos.* 2.252	16:18	*Her.* 191*
15:12	*Deus* 60	16:19	*Mos.* 2.259
15:17	*Plant.* 48, 50, 52, 53*, 54*, 55; *Congr.* 57*	16:19–20	*Spec.* 2.199
		16:20	*Mos.* 1.203; 2.260, 261, 262, 266
15:17–18	*Plant.* 47*		
15:18	*Plant.* 51*	16:20–21	*Mos.* 1.204
15:20	*Agr.* 80; *Mos.* 2.257	16:20–23	*Mos.* 1.207
15:21	*Leg.* 2.102*, 103; *Agr.* 82*; *Ebr.* 111*; *Somn.* 2.269*	16:21	*Mos.* 2.259
		16:22–25	*Mos.* 1.205
		16:22–26	*Mos.* 2.264
15:22	*Mos.* 1.181	16:23	*Cher.* 87; *Mos.* 2.219; *Abr.* 28
15:22–27	*Decal.* 15; *Spec.* 2.199		
15:23	*Post.* 155; *Mos.* 1.182	16:26	*Mos.* 2.268
15:23–25	*Congr.* 163*; *Decal.* 16	16:27	*Mos.* 2.269
15:24	*Mos.* 1.183	16:31	QG 4.102; *Det.* 118; *Fug.* 138; FR(H) 106 B7
15:25	*Post.* 156; *Migr.* 36*; *Congr.* 164*, 166*; *Mos.* 1.184, 185, 186, 211		
		16:32	FR(H) 106 B8
		16:32–34	*Congr.* 100; *Mos.* 2.97
15:26	*Praem.* 118, 119	16:35	*Mos.* 1.206; 2.258; *Spec.* 2.199; FR(H) 106 B3
15:27	*Fug.* 183*, 186; *Mos.* 1.188		
		16:36	*Congr.* 100*
16:3	*Post.* 155; *Mos.* 1.191, 193; *Hypoth.* 6.2 (428.1)	17:1–6	*Mos.* 1.210
16:4	*Leg.* 3.162*, 163, 166,		

17:1–7	*Spec.* 2.199; *Hypoth.* 6.2 (428.1)	19:18	*QE* 2.15, 28, 47; *Her.* 251*
17:6	*Leg.* 3.4*; *Sacr.* 67*; *Conf.* 138*; *Migr.* 183*; *Somn.* 1.241; 2.221*; *Decal.* 16	19:18–19	*Decal.* 33, 46
		19:19	*Her.* 17*, 19; *Decal.* 32; *Spec.* 2.189
17:8–9	*Mos.* 1.216	19:22	*QG* 4.4*
17:11	*Leg.* 3.186*	19:23	*QE* 2.47
17:11–12	*Mos.* 1.217	19:24	*Post.* 136*
17:12	*Leg.* 3.45*; *Prob.* 29	20:1–17	*QE* 2.49; *Congr.* 120; *Praem.* 2, 53, 55
17:13	*Mos.* 1.218		
17:14	*Leg.* 3.187*	20:2	*Mut.* 23*
17:15	*Mos.* 1.219	20:2–6	*Decal.* 65
18:1	*Ebr.* 36	20:2–12	*Decal.* 168
18:3–4	*Mos.* 1.150; *Virt.* 53, 59, 66	20:2–17	*Decal.* 51, 154
		20:2–18	*Decal.* 175
18:4	*Her.* 59*	20:3	*Decal.* 155; *Legat.* 115
18:7	*Her.* 44*	20:3–5	*Her.* 169; *Decal.* 59; *Spec.* 1.title
18:11	*Ebr.* 41*, 43, 45		
18:13–23	*Spec.* 4.173	20:3–6	*Spec.* 2.1
18:14	*Gig.* 50*	20:3–7	*Spec.* 2.258
18:16	*Ebr.* 37*	20:3–12	*Spec.* 2.224
18:17–23	*Ebr.* 37	20:3–17	*Her.* 168; *Decal.* 36; *Spec.* 1.1; 4.133, 134
18:20–26	*Mut.* 104		
18:21	*Spec.* 4.170, 171	20:4	*Gig.* 59
18:24–26	*Spec.* 4.174	20:4–5	*Decal.* 81
18:25	*Congr.* 110	20:4–6	*Decal.* 156
18:26	*Leg.* 3.197	20:5	*Deus* 60; *Sobr.* 48*
18:27	*Somn.* 1.214	20:6	*Spec.* 2.259
19:4	*Deo* 11*	20:7	*Decal.* 82, 157; *Spec.* 2.2, 27, 252; *Legat.* 353
19:6	*Sobr.* 66*; *Mos.* 1.149; *Abr.* 56*		
		20:7–11	*Her.* 170
19:8	*Conf.* 58*	20:7–12	*Spec.* 2.title
19:10–11	*Decal.* 45	20:8–10	*Cher.* 87; *Spec.* 2.56, 86; *Contempl.* 36
19:14–15	*Decal.* 45		
19:16	*Decal.* 32; *Spec.* 2.189	20:8–11	*Opif.* 128; *Decal.* 96, 98, 158; *Spec.* 2.39, 260; *Prov.* 1.84
19:16–19	*Decal.* 44		
19:17	*Somn.* 1.71*	20:8–17	*Decal.* 106
19:17–25	*QG* 4.29	20:9	*Mos.* 2.21; *Spec.* 2.60

20:9–10   *Abr.* 28; *Hypoth.* 7.12 (431.22); 7.15 (432.12); 7.20 (433.8)

20:10   *Cher.* 87*l *Mos.* 1.205; 2.22; *Spec.* 2.66, 69

20:11   *Mos.* 2.209; *Decal.* 97, 100, 101; *Spec.* 2.58

20:12   *Leg.* 1.99; *Det.* 52*; *Ebr.* 17; *Her.* 171; *Decal.* 118, 165; *Spec.* 2.223, 226, 235, 237, 261, 262; FR(H) 110 A16

20:12–13   *Decal.* 121

20:13   *Decal.* 36*, 131, 168; *Spec.* 3.title, 8*

20:13–15   *Spec.* 4.1

20:13–17   *Her.* 172

20:14   *Decal.* 36*, 135, 138, 171; *Spec.* 4.title; *Anim.* 49

20:15   *Decal.* 36*, 132, 170; *Spec.* 3.title

20:15–16   *Spec.* 3.49

20:16   *Decal.* 138, 141, 172; *Spec.* 4.41*, 42, 44

20:16–17   *Spec.* 4.title

20:17   *Ios.* 144; *Decal.* 142, 173; *Spec.* 4.78*, 80, 82, 83, 85, 86, 92, 95

20:18   *Migr.* 47*, 50; *Mos.* 2.213; *Decal.* 47*

20:19   *Post.* 143*; *Her.* 19*; *Somn.* 1.143*

20:21   *QE* 2.28; *Post.* 14; *Mut.* 7; *Mos.* 1.158

20:22   *Migr.* 47*, 50

20:23   *Leg.* 1.51*; *Congr.* 159; *Spec.* 1.22*, 25

20:24   *Leg.* 3.215*; *Somn.* 1.62*

20:24–25   *Spec.* 1.274, 287

20:25   *QE* 2.1*

20:26   *QE* 2.100; *Somn.* 2.67

21:2   *Spec.* 2.79, 84; 4.4; *Virt.* 122

21:5   *Leg.* 3.198*; *Cher.* 72*; *Her.* 186*

21:6   *Leg.* 3.199; *Cher.* 72

21:10   *Migr.* 105*

21:12   *Fug.* 54*, 64*; *Spec.* 3.84, 106, 182

21:12–14   *Fug.* 53*

21:12–27   *Decal.* 170

21:13   *QE* FR(M)6 = FR(P)1; *Sacr.* 133*; *Fug.* 65*, 75, 76, 77, 93*, 102, 107; *Spec.* 3.104, 120, 123, 128, 136

21:13–14   *Spec.* 3.129

21:14   *Conf.* 160*, 161; *Fug.* 77*, 78, 80, 83; *Spec.* 3.86, 88, 91, 130

21:15   *Fug.* 83*; *Spec.* 2.243*; 3.183

21:16   *Fug.* 83*; *Spec.* 2.248, 253; 4.13, 19

21:16–17   *Hypoth.* 7.1 (429.21)

21:17   *Hypoth.* 7.1 (429.16)

21:18–19   *Spec.* 3.106

21:19   *Spec.* 3.107

21:20–21   *Spec.* 3.141

21:21   *Spec.* 3.142, 143

21:22   *Spec.* 3.109, 110

21:22–23   *Congr.* 137*; *Spec.* 3.108, 117

21:23–25   *Spec.* 3.182

21:24   *Spec.* 3.195

21:26   *Spec.* 3.184, 196, 197

21:26–27   *Spec.* 3.201, 202

21:27	*Spec.* 3.198, 203	22:29–30	*Congr.* 89; *Spec.* 4.98
21:28	*Spec.* 3.144	22:30	*Spec.* 1.135; *Virt.* 126,
21:29–30	*Spec.* 3.145		129, 133, 142
21:32	*Spec.* 3.145	22:31	*Spec.* 4.119, 120
21:33–34	*Spec.* 3.148	23:1	*QE* 2.9*; *Conf.* 141*;
21:35–36	*Spec.* 3.146		*Spec.* 4.59, 60
22:1	*Spec.* 4.11, 12, 13	23:1–2	*Spec.* 4.44, 45
22:1–3	*Spec.* 4.7	23:1–3	*Decal.* 172
22:2	*Leg.* 3.33, 34	23:2	*Ebr.* 25*; *Migr.* 61*
22:2–3	*Leg.* 3.32*	23:3	*QE* 2.10*; *Spec.* 4.72, 76
22:3	*Leg.* 3.35; *Spec.* 4.3, 10	23:4	*QE* 2.11*, 12; *Virt.* 96,
22:3–4	*Spec.* 4.5		117
22:4	*Spec.* 4.2, 11, 13	23:4–5	*Virt.* 160
22:5	*Spec.* 4.22, 24	23:5	*QE* 2.12*; *Virt.* 116
22:5–6	*Spec.* 4.26	23:6–8	*Decal.* 172
22:6	*Leg.* 3.248*, 249; *Her.*	23:7	*Spec.* 4.44
	296*; *Spec.* 4.29	23:7–8	*Spec.* 4.64
22:7	*Spec.* 4.2, 33	23:8	*Spec.* 1.227; 4.62, 66
22:8	*Spec.* 4.34	23:9	*QE* 2.2
22:9	*Spec.* 4.2	23:10–11	*Decal.* 162; *Spec.* 2.86,
22:10–13	*Spec.* 4.36		87, 96, 104; 4.215; *Virt.*
22:14–15	*Spec.* 4.37		97, 98
22:16–17	*Decal.* 168; *Spec.* 3.65, 70	23:10–12	*Praem.* 153, 154
22:18	*Spec.* 3.94, 102	23:11	*Spec.* 2.105, 106, 108,
22:19	*Spec.* 3.49		109; *Hypoth.* 7.15
22:21	*QE* 2.2*; *Virt.* 103, 147,		(432.11); 7.19 (433.3)
	160	23:12	*Spec.* 2.41, 60, 69
22:22	*QE* 2.3*; *Congr.* 178*	23:13	*Spec.* 2.256
22:23	*QE* 2.4*	23:15	*QE* 2.7*
22:25	*Spec.* 2.74; *Virt.* 82	23:16	*Opif.* 116; *Decal.* 160,
22:26	*Somn.* 1.107, 112*		161; *Spec.* 1.183; 2.179,
22:26–27	*Somn.* 1.92*, 98, 100, 113		205
22:27	*Somn.* 1.99, 101*, 104,	23:16–19	*Legat.* 156
	107*, 109*	23:18	*QE* 2.14*, 15*
22:28	*QE* 2.5*, 6*; *Conf.* 154;	23:19	*QG* 4.110; *Sacr.* 72*;
	Spec. 1.53; *Hypoth.* 7.4		*Virt.* 142*, 144; *Anim.* 25
	(430.7)	23:20	*QE* 2.16; *Agr.* 51*; *Migr.*
22:29	*QE* 2.7*, 8; *Spec.* 1.134,		174*
	138, 248	23:20–21	*QE* 2.13*

23:21	*Migr.* 8, 174	25:8	*QE* 2.52*
23:22	*QE* 2.16*; *Sobr.* 66	25:9	*QE* 2.53*, 68, 69; *Leg.*
23:22–23	*Praem.* 79, 118, 126		3.102*
23:24	*QE* 2.17*	25:9–10	*QE* 2.54; *Mut.* 43
23:25	*QE* 2.18*; *Praem.* 99	25:9–21	*Mos.* 2.95
23:26	*QE* 2.19*, 20*; *Praem.*	25:10	*QE* 2.55*, 81, 83; *Ebr.* 85
	108*, 111*	25:10–13	*QG* 2.4
23:27	*QE* 2.21*, 22*, 23*;	25:11	*QE* 2.53, 56*
	Praem. 79, 95	25:12	*QE* 2.57*
23:27–32	*Spec.* 2.86	25:13	*QE* 2.58
23:28	*QE* 2.24*; *Praem.* 96	25:15	*QE* 2.59*; *Mos.* 2.97
23:29	*QE* 2.25*	25:15–17	*QE* 2.68
23:33	*QE* 2.26*	25:16	*QE* 2.60*, 61
24:1	*QE* 2.27*, 28*, 31; *Migr.*	25:16–19	*Fug.* 100
	168*, 201; *Mut.* 126	25:17	*QE* 2.62, 63
24:2	*QE* 2.29*; *Mos.* 2.163	25:17–18	*QE* 2.64
24:3	*Spec.* 2.14	25:17–19	*Mos.* 2.97
24:4	*QE* 2.30; *Mut.* 126	25:18–19	*Cher.* 25
24:5	*QE* 2.31, 32	25:19	*QE* 2.65*, 66
24:6	*QE* 2.33, 35; *Her.* 182*,	25:21	*QE* 2.67*, 68*; *Her.* 166*;
	184		*Fug.* 101*; *Deo* 5*
24:7	*QE* 2.34*; *Conf.* 148;	25:22	*QE* 2.69*; *Her.* 227; *Mos.*
	Spec. 2.14		2.104
24:8	*QE* 2.35, 36*	25:22–31	*Her.* 226
24:10	*QE* 2.37*; *Conf.* 96*, 99;	25:23	*QE* 2.70*, 81, 83
	Somn. 2.222*	25:28	*QE* 2.71*
24:10–11	*Deus* 60	25:29	*QE* 2.72*, 81
24:11	*QE* 2.37, 38*, 39*; *Conf.*	25:30	*QE* 2.73*, 74*; *Congr.*
	56*; *Mut.* 109; *Virt.* 44		168; *Fug.* 185; *Mos.*
24:12	*QE* 2.40*, 41*, 42, 52		2.104; *Spec.* 1.172
24:12–13	*QE* 2.43	25:30–31	*Her.* 227
24:14	*QE* 2.44	25:30–37	*Mos.* 2.102
24:16	*QE* 2.45*, 46*, 48, 52	25:31	*QE* 2.75*, 81; *Her.* 216,
24:17	*QE* 2.47*		225; *Congr.* 8
24:18	*QE* 2.48*, 49*	25:32	*QE* 2.76
25:1–2	*QE* 2.50*; *Her.* 113*	25:33–36	*QE* 2.77
25:2	*Her.* 117, 123	25:36	*Her.* 216*
25:3	*QE* 2.50	25:37	*QE* 2.78, 79*; *Congr.* 8
25:7	*QE* 2.51*	25:38	*QE* 2.80*

25:39	QE 2.81*	27:21	QE 2.104*, 105*, 106*;
25:40	QE 2.82*; Leg. 3.102*;		Spec. 1.296, 298
	Congr. 8	28:1	Somn. 2.186; Mos. 2.142;
26	Her. 112		Virt. 53, 59, 66
26:1	QE 2.83, 84, 85, 86, 88,	28:2	QE 2.107*
	92; Congr. 116*, 117	28:4	Ebr. 85; Mut. 43; Somn.
26:1–2	Mos. 2.84		1.214, 215; Spec. 1.85, 94
26:1–37	Congr. 89	28:5–8	Mos. 2.111
26:2	QE 2.87	28:6	QE 2.120
26:3	QE 2.86*	28:6–9	Spec. 1.86
26:6	QE 2.88*	28:7	QE 2.108*; Mos. 2.130,
26:7–13	Mos. 2.85		133
26:14	Mos. 2.88	28:9	QE 2.109*; Mos. 2.122,
26:15–17	Mos. 2.77		133; Spec. 1.94
26:16	Mos. 2.83	28:9–12	QE 2.109; Her. 176*
26:18	QE 2.89, 93	28:9–21	Mos. 2.112
26:18–25	Mos. 2.78	28:10	Mos. 2.123
26:20	QE 2.89, 93	28:12	QE 2.117; Spec. 1.86
26:26–27	Mos. 2.80	28:15	QE 2.110*; Mos. 2.112*;
26:28	QE 2.89*, 90		Spec. 1.88
26:30	QE 2.90*	28:15–21	Fug. 185
26:31	QE 2.91*, 92*, 96	28:15–30	Mos. 2.133
26:31–37	Mos. 2.87	28:16	QE 2.111*; Mos. 2.127
26:32	QE 2.93*, 97	28:17	QE 2.112*
26:33	QG 4.80; QE 2.91, 94*,	28:17–18	Leg. 1.81*
	104, 106; Mut. 43, 192	28:17–21	QE 2.112, 113, 117; Mos.
26:35	QE 2.95*		2.124; Spec. 1.87
26:36	QE 2.96*; Somn. 1.207	28:20	QE 2.113*
26:37	QE 2.97	28:21	QE 2.114*, 115
26:40	Mos. 2.116	28:22–28	Mos. 2.113
27:1	QE 2.98, 99, 100; Ebr. 85	28:26	QE 2.115*, 116*; Mos.
27:1–8	Mos. 2.106; Spec. 1.274		2.128; Spec. 1.88
27:2	QE 2.101*	28:27	QE 2.107, 117*; Mos.
27:3	QE 2.102*		2.118; Spec. 1.85
27:9	Mut. 190	28:28	QE 2.118*
27:9–15	Mos. 2.89	28:29	QE 2.119*; Migr. 103*
27:16	Mos. 2.87, 93	28:29–30	Mos. 2.119; Spec. 1.93
27:17–18	Mos. 2.90	28:30	QE 2.120*; Leg. 3.118*,
27:20	QE 2.103*		119, 120*, 123, 125, 128,

28:30 (cont.)

	129, 132; *Migr.* 103; *Her.*
	303*; *Spec.* 4.69
28:31	QE 2.120; *Migr.* 104*
28:32	QE 2.121*, 122*; *Migr.*
	103*; *Mos.* 2.132
28:32–35	*Mos.* 2.114
28:33	QE 2.120, 123*
28:33–34	QE 2.124
28:35	*Mos.* 2.131
28:36	QE 2.124
28:36–39	*Spec.* 1.83
28:38–39	*Mos.* 2.143
28:39	QE 2.107
29:4	*Somn.* 1.210
29:4–5	*Somn.* 1.214
29:4–9	*Mos.* 2.143
29:5	*Somn.* 1.215, 225
29:10–14	*Mos.* 2.147
29:15–18	*Mos.* 2.148
29:20	*Mos.* 2.150
29:25	*Mos.* 2.149
29:27	*Spec.* 1.145
29:29–30	QE 2.107
29:38	*Spec.* 2.42
29:38–39	*Her.* 174*
29:38–42	*Spec.* 1.169
29:40	*Congr.* 102
30:1	*Ebr.* 85
30:1–2	*Her.* 227
30:1–6	*Mos.* 2.101
30:1–7	*Spec.* 1.274
30:7	*Spec.* 1.276
30:7–8	*Spec.* 1.171
30:8	*Spec.* 1.296, 298
30:10	*Spec.* 1.72
30:12–13	*Her.* 186*
30:12–16	*Spec.* 1.77
30:13–15	QG 4.110

30:15	*Her.* 189*
30:18	*Mos.* 2.136
30:18–21	*Mos.* 2.138
30:19	QE 1.2; *Migr.* 98
30:20	QE 2.3
30:22–30	*Mos.* 2.146
30:34	*Her.* 198, 226*
30:34–35	*Her.* 196*
30:35	*Her.* 199
31:1–11	QG 1.90
31:2	*Plant.* 26*, 27; *Somn.*
	1.206
31:2–3	*Gig.* 23*; *Somn.* 1.207
31:2–5	*Leg.* 3.95
31:2–11	*Leg.* 3.102; *Plant.* 26
31:3	QG 1.90; *Gig.* 27, 47
31:12–17	*Prov.* 1.84
31:14–15	*Spec.* 2.249
31:17	*Spec.* 2.60
31:18	*Migr.* 85; *Decal.* 50
32:1–2	*Mos.* 2.161
32:1–6	*Ebr.* 95; *Mos.* 2.270;
	Spec. 1.79; 3.125
32:2–4	*Post.* 166
32:4	*Fug.* 90; FR(H) 106 B9
32:4–6	*Mos.* 2.162
32:7–8	*Mos.* 2.165
32:9–14	*Mos.* 2.166
32:15	*Her.* 167
32:16	*Her.* 167*
32:17	*Ebr.* 98*, 99*, 104
32:17–19	*Ebr.* 96*
32:18	*Ebr.* 105*, 121, 122,
	123*, 125
32:19	*Ebr.* 124*; *Mos.* 2.167, 271
32:20	*Post.* 158*, 162, 163, 164
32:25–26	*Mos.* 2.272
32:25–29	*Spec.* 1.79; 2.183; 3.124,
	126, 128; FR(H) 106 B7

32:26	*Mos.* 2.168*, 170; *Spec.* 3.127	34:25	*QE* 2.14
32:26–27	*Mos.* 2.273	34:26	*Spec.* 1.134, 248; 4.99; *Virt.* 142*, 144; *Anim.* 25; *Legat.* 156
32:26–28	*Sacr.* 130		
32:27	*Ebr.* 70, 71; *Fug.* 90*, 91; *Mos.* 2.171	34:28	*Leg.* 3.142*; *Somn.* 1.36; *Mos.* 2.69; *Decal.* 20
32:27–28	*Ebr.* 67*, 69	34:28–35	*Mos.* 2.70
32:28–29	*Mos.* 2.274	34:31–32	*Gig.* 54
32:28	*Fug.* 90; *Mos.* 2.172	35:2	*Spec.* 2.249
32:29	*Ebr.* 67*; *Mos.* 2.173; *Spec.* 3.127	35:3	*Mos.* 2.219; *Spec.* 2.65, 251
32:32	*Her.* 20*	35:22	*Migr.* 97*; *Mos.* 2.136
33:7	*Leg.* 2.54*, 55; 3.46*; *Det.* 160*; *Gig.* 54; *Ebr.* 100*	35:25–26	*Migr.* 97
		35:30	*Plant.* 27
33:7–11	*QG* 4.195f	35:30–31	*Gig.* 23*
33:11	*Leg.* 2.90; *Cher.* 49; *Sacr.* 77, 130; *Migr.* 67; *Her.* 21*; *Mos.* 1.156; 2.67; *Virt.* 55	35:30–35	*Plant.* 26
		35:30–36:1	*Leg.* 3.102
		35:31	*QG* 1.90; *Gig.* 27, 47
		36:1	*Plant.* 26
33:13	*QG* 4.8*; *Leg.* 3.101*; *Post.* 13, 16*; *Mut.* 8*	36:9–12	*Mos.* 2.111
		36:10	*Sacr.* 83; *Her.* 131*
33:15	*Migr.* 171*, 172	36:11	*Mos.* 2.130
33:17	*Deus* 109*, 116	36:11–13	*Mos.* 2.133
33:18	*Post.* 169; *Spec.* 1.41*, 42, 45	36:13	*Mos.* 2.122, 123; *Spec.* 1.94
33:18–23	*Det.* 86; *Post.* 13	36:13–14	*Spec.* 1.86
33:19	*Spec.* 1.43	36:13–21	*Mos.* 2.112
33:20	*QE* 2.3, 37; FR(M)1 = FR(P)3; *Spec.* 1.44	36:15	*Somn.* 1.202
		36:15–34	*Mos.* 2.133
33:22–23	*Spec.* 1.46	36:16	*Mos.* 2.127
33:23	*Post.* 169*; *Fug.* 165*; *Mut.* 9*; *Spec.* 1.49	36:16–21	*Mos.* 2.124
		36:17–21	*Spec.* 1.87
34:12	*Migr.* 8*	36:20–22[MT]	*Mos.* 2.77
34:14	*Deus* 60	36:21[MT]	*Mos.* 2.83
34:16	*Spec.* 3.29	36:22–29	*Mos.* 2.113
34:17	*Leg.* 3.22	36:30	*Mos.* 2.118; *Spec.* 1.85
34:19–20	*Spec.* 1.135, 248	36:32–34	*Mos.* 2.119; *Spec.* 1.93
34:22	*Opif.* 116; *Decal.* 160, 161; *Spec.* 2.41	36:38–39	*Mos.* 2.132
		36:38–40	*Mos.* 2.114

37:1–2	*Mos.* 2.84	1:3–4	*Spec.* 1.198, 239
37:2	*Mos.* 2.85	1:4	*Spec.* 1.202
37:3	*Mos.* 2.88	1:5	*Spec.* 1.205
37:3–6	*Mos.* 2.87	1:5–10	*Spec.* 1.199
37:6	*Mos.* 2.81	1:6	*Sacr.* 84*; *Abr.* 198; *Spec.*
37:6–14	*Mos.* 2.80		1.208
37:7	*Mut.* 190	1:9	*Leg.* 3.143, 144*, 159;
37:8–13	*Mos.* 2.78		*Spec.* 1.206, 245
37:10 [MT]	*Her.* 227	1:10	*Spec.* 1.163, 165, 198,
37:25[MT]	*Her.* 226, 227		200
38:1–8	*Mos.* 2.95	1:14	*Spec.* 1.162
38:2	*Ebr.* 85	2:1	*Somn.* 2.71*, 72, 73
38:6–8	*Fug.* 100; *Mos.* 2.97	2:2	*Somn.* 2.71*, 74
38:8	*Cher.* 25	2:11	*QE* 2.14; *Congr.* 169;
38:9	*Mos.* 2.104		*Spec.* 1.291, 293; 2.182
38:9–13	*Mos.* 2.89	2:12	*Spec.* 1.290
38:12–13	*Her.* 226	2:13	*QE* 1.3; *Spec.* 1.289*
38:13–15	*Her.* 216	2:14	*Sacr.* 76*, 80, 82, 86, 87
38:13–17	*Mos.* 2.102	3:1	*Spec.* 1.212
38:14–15	*Her.* 219	3:1–17	*Spec.* 1.194, 212, 222
38:14–17	*Her.* 220	3:1–4:35	*Spec.* 1.196
38:15–17	*Her.* 218*	3:3–4	*Sacr.* 136; *Spec.* 1.212,
38:17	*Her.* 219, 221, 225		216, 239
38:18–19	*Mos.* 2.90, 93	3:4	*Spec.* 1.218
38:22	*Ebr.* 85	3:6	*Spec.* 1.212
38:22–26	*Mos.* 2.106	3:9–10	*Spec.* 1.212, 216
38:26	*Migr.* 98; *Mos.* 2.137	3:10	*Spec.* 1.218
39:13	*Ebr.* 85; *Mos.* 2.110	3:14–15	*Spec.* 1.212, 216
39:18	*Congr.* 168	3:15	*Spec.* 1.218
40:6	*Mos.* 2.94	3:16–17	*Post.* 123*
40:18	*Mos.* 2.97	3:17	*Spec.* 4.123, 124
40:26	*Mos.* 2.94	4:1–35	*QE* 2.32; *Spec.* 1.194, 226
		4:3	*Spec.* 1.226, 228, 230*
		4:4–7	*Spec.* 1.231
Leviticus		4:7–10	*Spec.* 4.125
		4:8–9	*Spec.* 1.239
1:1	*Leg.* 3.101; *Plant.* 23, 26*	4:8–21	*Spec.* 1.232
1:1–17	*Spec.* 1.194, 195	4:11–12	*Sacr.* 139
1:2	*Spec.* 1.163, 165	4:12	*Spec.* 1.244
1:3	*Spec.* 1.200		

4:13–14	*Spec.* 1.226	6:36	*Spec.* 1.222, 240, 242
4:14	*Spec.* 1.228	6:36–38	*Spec.* 1.220
4:21	*Spec.* 1.244	6:37–38	*Spec.* 1.223
4:22–23	*Spec.* 1.226	6:38	*Spec.* 1.151
4:22–35	*Spec.* 1.233	6:40	*Her.* 195*
4:23	*Spec.* 1.228	7:9–11	*Prov.* 1.84
4:27–28	*Spec.* 1.226	7:11–14	*Spec.* 1.145
4:28	*Spec.* 1.228	7:13–15	*Spec.* 4.124
4:32	*Spec.* 1.226, 228	7:16–17	*Spec.* 4.123
5:1	*Spec.* 2.26	7:18–24	*Spec.* 2.183, 222
5:2	*Spec.* 4.119, 120	7:19–24	*Spec.* 1.152
5:4	*Somn.* 2.296*	7:21	*Leg.* 3.140
5:5	*Somn.* 2.296*, 299	7:34	*Leg.* 3.133*, 135, 136*,
5:6	*Mut.* 233*		137
5:6–7	*Mut.* 245	8:1–36	*QE* 1.10; *Praem.* 78
5:7	*QG* 2.38; *Mut.* 233, 247,	8:6–9	*Mos.* 2.143
	248, 250*	8:8	*Her.* 303; *Spec.* 4.69
5:11	*Mut.* 245, 249, 250*;	8:10–12	*Mos.* 2.146
	Spec. 1.271	8:13	*Mos.* 2.143
5:11–12	*Mut.* 234	8:14–17	*Mos.* 2.147
5:12	*Mut.* 249*	8:15	*Leg.* 3.130
5:15	*Spec.* 1.238	8:18–21	*Mos.* 2.148
5:15–16	*Spec.* 1.234	8:21	*Migr.* 67*
6:2	*Spec.* 4.31	8:22	*Mos.* 2.149
6:2–3	*Spec.* 1.235	8:23–24	*Mos.* 2.150
6:4	*Spec.* 4.31	8:29	*Leg.* 3.129*, 131, 135,
6:4–5	*Spec.* 1.236		147; *Migr.* 67*
6:6	*Spec.* 1.238	8:30	*Mos.* 2.152
6:6–7	*Spec.* 1.237	9:1	*Her.* 251
6:9	*Spec.* 1.285	9:1–22	*Mos.* 2.153
6:10	*Mut.* 43	9:1–24	*QE* 1.10
6:12–13	*Spec.* 1.285, 288	9:14	*Leg.* 3.141*, 144*, 147, 159
6:13–16	*Spec.* 1.256	9:23–24	*Mos.* 2.154
6:19	*Spec.* 1.240, 242	9:24	*Her.* 251*; *Mos.* 2.155
6:20	*Her.* 174*, 199; *Congr.*	10:1	*Fug.* 59
	103, 105	10:1–2	*Leg.* 2.57, 58; *Somn.*
6:22	*Spec.* 1.240, 242		2.186
6:32–34	*Spec.* 1.224	10:1–11	*Somn.* 2.67
6:35	*Spec.* 1.225	10:2	*Her.* 309*; *Fug.* 59*

10:3	*Fug.* 59*
10:5	*Leg.* 2.57, 58
10:8	*Ebr.* 128
10:8–10	*Ebr.* 127*
10:9	*Ebr.* 2, 129, 130, 131, 132, 134, 138*, 139, 140, 141; *Spec.* 1.98, 249; 4.191
10:10	*Spec.* 1.100*
10:14–15	*Spec.* 1.145
10:16	*Fug.* 157, 158*
10:19	*Fug.* 159*
10:20	*Fug.* 159*
11	*Prov.* 1.84; FR(H) 106 A23–24
11:3	*Spec.* 4.108, 206
11:3–4	*Agr.* 145
11:3–8	*Spec.* 4.106
11:4	*Agr.* 131*, 134, 142
11:7	*Agr.* 145*; *Spec.* 4.101
11:9–12	*Spec.* 4.110
11:10–12	*Spec.* 4.101; *Anim.* 31
11:13–19	*QG* 2.38; *Spec.* 4.116; *Anim.* 22
11:20	*Spec.* 4.113
11:21	*QG* 2.57; *Leg.* 2.105*; *Her.* 239*; *Opif.* 163*
11:21–22	*Spec.* 4.114
11:22	*Opif.* 163
11:23	*Spec.* 4.113
11:24	*Somn.* 1.81
11:27	*Legat.* 361
11:41–43	*Spec.* 4.113
11:42	*QG* 2.57; *Leg.* 3.139*; *Migr.* 64*, 65, 69
12:3	*Prov.* 1.84
12:6	*QG* 2.38
12:8	*QG* 2.38; 4.102
13:3	*Post.* 47

13:3–4	*Leg.* 1.49
13:9–17	*Leg.* 3.7
13:10–11	*Deus* 129
13:11	*Deus* 128
13:11–13	*Deus* 127
13:12	*Plant.* 111*
13:13	*Deus* 128, 130; *Plant.* 111
13:14–15	*Deus* 123, 129
13:15	*QG* 2.12; *Deus* 124*
13:16–17	*Deus* 130
13:22–23	*Sobr.* 49*
13:23	*QG* 2.29
14:37–42	*Det.* 16
14:34–35	*Deus* 131*
14:36	*Deus* 131*, 132, 133
15:18	*Spec.* 3.63
15:31	*Leg.* 3.15*
16:2	*Gig.* 52; *Ebr.* 135; *Legat.* 307
16:2–3	*Spec.* 1.72
16:2–4	*Leg.* 2.56
16:4	*Ebr.* 86; *Mut.* 43; *Somn.* 1.216; *Spec.* 1.84
16:5	*Spec.* 1.188
16:7–10	*Her.* 179; *Spec.* 1.188
16:8	*Leg.* 2.52*; *Plant.* 61*; *Her.* 179*, 187
16:10	*Post.* 70*
16:12–13	*Spec.* 1.72
16:16	*Her.* 113*
16:17	*Her.* 84*; *Somn.* 2.189*, 231*; *Legat.* 307
16:23–24	*Ebr.* 86
16:29–30	*Leg.* 3.174
16:29–31	*Mos.* 2.23; *Spec.* 1.186
16:31	*Spec.* 2.194
16:34	*Gig.* 52; *Ebr.* 136; *Spec.* 1.72; *Legat.* 306
17:3	*Virt.* 146

20:13	*Spec.* 2.50; 3.37, 39; *Hypoth.* 7.1 (429.19)	22:29	*Spec.* 1.224
20:14	*Spec.* 3.26	22:30	*Spec.* 1.225
20:15–16	*Spec.* 3.45, 49	23:2	*Spec.* 2.51*
20:17	*Spec.* 3.22, 24	23:3	*Spec.* 2.56
20:18	*Fug.* 188*, 189, 190*; *Spec.* 3.32	23:5	*Spec.* 2.145, 149, 150, 152
20:19–21	*Spec.* 3.26	23:5–8	*QG* 2.17; *Decal.* 159
20:27	*Spec.* 1.59, 60, 63	23:6	*Decal.* 161; *Spec.* 2.155, 156, 159
21:1–3	*Spec.* 1.112	23:10	*QE* 2.102; *Somn.* 2.75*, 76, 77*; *Spec.* 2.168, 175
21:5	*Spec.* 1.58		
21:7	*Spec.* 1.101, 102, 108, 109, 111	23:10–11	*QE* 1.1; *Decal.* 160; *Spec.* 2.171
21:10	*Fug.* 110*, 111*; *Spec.* 1.115	23:10–14	*Spec.* 2.162
		23:10–16	*Spec.* 2.176
21:11	*Fug.* 109, 113*; *Spec.* 1.113; 3.135	23:13	*QE* 2.102; *Congr.* 89
		23:14	*Spec.* 2.175
21:12	*Spec.* 1.115	23:15–16	*QG* 2.78; *Contempl.* 65
21:13	*Spec.* 1.109	23:15–21	*Spec.* 1.183
21:13–14	*Fug.* 114*; *Somn.* 2.185; *Spec.* 1.101, 105, 110	23:15–22	*Decal.* 160
		23:16–17	*Spec.* 2.179
21:14	*Spec.* 1.106	23:17	*Congr.* 89; *Spec.* 1.185; 2.182, 184, 187
21:17–21	*Spec.* 1.103		
21:17–22	*Spec.* 1.117	23:19–20	*Spec.* 1.184
21:17–23	*Agr.* 130; *Spec.* 1.80, 242	23:20	*Spec.* 1.185; 2.182, 183, 187
22:3–9	*Spec.* 3.135		
22:4	*Spec.* 1.80, 118	23:22	*Somn.* 2.23*, 29*; *Virt.* 90, 92, 149
22:4–7	*Spec.* 1.119		
22:6–7	*Somn.* 1.81*	23:23–32	*Decal.* 159
22:8	*Spec.* 4.119, 120	23:24	*Spec.* 1.186; 2.188, 192
22:10	*Spec.* 1.120, 122, 123	23:26–27	*Mos.* 2.23
22:11	*Spec.* 1.126, 128	23:26–32	*Spec.* 2.193, 197
22:13	*Spec.* 1.129	23:27	*Post.* 48; *Congr.* 89, 107; *Spec.* 2.200, 201
22:18–25	*Agr.* 130; *Spec.* 1.259		
22:19	*Spec.* 1.163, 165	23:27–32	*Spec.* 1.186; 2.86
22:19–20	*Cher.* 96	23:32	*Spec.* 2.194
22:19–24	*Spec.* 1.166	23:34	*Decal.* 161; *Spec.* 2.210; *Flacc.* 116
22:27	*Virt.* 126, 129, 133, 142		
22:28	*Virt.* 134, 136, 138	23:34–36	*Spec.* 1.189; 2.204

23:36	*Spec.* 2.211	25:8–12	*Spec.* 2.110
23:39	*Spec.* 2.205, 210	25:8–17	*QG* 2.5; *Virt.* 99
23:39–43	*Spec.* 2.204	25:8–55	*Decal.* 164
23:40–43	*Spec.* 2.41	25:9–10	*QG* 4.110; *Congr.* 89,
23:42	*Spec.* 2.206		108
23:43	*Spec.* 2.208	25:10	*QG* 3.39; 4.27; *Sacr.* 122;
23:44	*Spec.* 2.51*		*Her.* 273; *Congr.* 109;
24:3–4	*Spec.* 1.296, 298		*Mut.* 228; *Spec.* 2.111;
24:5–6	*Her.* 174, 175, 226;		*Virt.* 100
	Congr. 168; *Fug.* 185;	25:11	*Fug.* 170*, 171*
	Spec. 2.161	25:13	*Spec.* 2.111; *Virt.* 100
24:5–8	*Spec.* 1.172	25:14–16	*Spec.* 2.112, 113
24:5–9	*Contempl.* 81	25:23	*Cher.* 108*, 119*, 120,
24:7	*Mos.* 2.104; *Spec.* 1.175		121*, 124; *Spec.* 2.113,
24:10–11	*Mos.* 2.193, 196		173
24:12	*Mos.* 2.201	25:25–28	*Spec.* 2.114
24:13–14	*Mos.* 2.202	25:29–30	*Spec.* 2.117
24:15	*Mos.* 2.205; *Spec.* 1.53	25:29–31	*Spec.* 2.116
24:15–16	*Mos.* 2.203	25:32	*Sacr.* 127*, 128
24:16	*Mos.* 2.206; *Spec.* 2.252	25:32–34	*Spec.* 2.121
24:17	*Spec.* 3.84	25:35	*Virt.* 83
24:17–21	*Spec.* 3.182	25:35–37	*Spec.* 2.74; *Virt.* 82
24:17–22	*Decal.* 170	25:35–43	*Spec.* 2.122
24:20	*Spec.* 3.195	25:37	*Virt.* 86
24:21	*Spec.* 3.84	25:39–41	*Spec.* 2.79, 84; *Virt.* 122
24:23	*Mos.* 2.203	25:40	*Spec.* 2.82
25:1–5	*Decal.* 162	25:44–46	*Spec.* 2.123
25:2–5	*Spec.* 2.39	26:2	*Cher.* 87
25:2–7	*Spec.* 2.86, 87, 96, 104	26:3	*Praem.* 82
25:3–5	*Spec.* 4.215	26:3–5	*Praem.* 101
25:3–7	*Virt.* 97, 98	26:3–13	*Praem.* 79, 118, 126
25:4	*QG* 2.78; 3.39	26:4–5	*Praem.* 98
25:4–5	*Hypoth.* 7.15 (432.11);	26:5	*Virt.* 47
	7.19 (433.3)	26:6	*Praem.* 91, 93*
25:4–6	*Mut.* 260; *Spec.* 2.105	26:6–8	*Praem.* 85
25:6	*Fug.* 174*; *Spec.* 2.106,	26:7–8	*Praem.* 79
	108; *Virt.* 104	26:8	*Praem.* 94
25:7	*Spec.* 2.109	26:10	*Sacr.* 79*; *Her.* 279*;
25:8–10	*QG* 2.78		*Praem.* 98, 103

26:11–12	*Post.* 122		**Numbers**
26:12	*Sacr.* 87*; *Mut.* 266*;		
	Somn. 1.148*; 2.248*;	3:4	*Fug.* 59
	Praem. 123, 125	3:5–8	*Mos.* 2.159
26:13	*Praem.* 124	3:12	*Her.* 124*; *Congr.* 98
26:14–46	*Praem.* 126, 162	3:12–13	*Sacr.* 118*, 126
26:16	*Praem.* 127, 130, 136,	3:13	*Sacr.* 134*
	143	3:45	*Congr.* 98
26:19	*Praem.* 131*, 132	3:46–47	*Spec.* 1.139
26:20	*Praem.* 130	4:3	*Fug.* 37
26:22	*Praem.* 149	4:7	*Her.* 226
26:23	*Praem.* 148	4:23	*Fug.* 37
26:25	*Praem.* 147	5:2	*Leg.* 3.7
26:29	*Praem.* 134	5:2–3	*Leg.* 3.8*
26:31	*Praem.* 133	5:12–28	*Spec.* 3.53
26:31–32	*Praem.* 150	5:15	*Plant.* 108*; *Spec.* 3.55,
26:33–35	*Praem.* 153		57, 60
26:36–37	*Praem.* 148	5:17	*Spec.* 3.58, 59, 60
26:37	*Praem.* 94	5:18	*Cher.* 14*, 17*; *Spec.*
26:39	*Praem.* 149		3.56, 60
26:40–45	*Praem.* 163	5:19–20	*Spec.* 3.61
26:41	*Spec.* 1.304	5:19–28	*Cher.* 17
26:43	*Praem.* 157	5:22	*Spec.* 3.61
27:2–8	*Spec.* 2.32	5:23–28	*Spec.* 3.62
27:3–7	*Spec.* 2.33	5:27	*Leg.* 3.148*, 150*
27:9–10	*Spec.* 2.35	5:28	*Leg.* 150*
27:11–13	*Spec.* 2.36	6:2	*Leg.* 1.17; *Agr.* 175;
27:14–15	*Spec.* 2.37		*Somn.* 2.25*; *Spec.* 1.247,
27:16–21	*Spec.* 2.115		248
27:17–24	*Decal.* 164	6:2–3	*Ebr.* 2
27:30	*Congr.* 95*, 96	6:2–21	*Deus* 87
27:30–33	*Virt.* 95; FR(M)17 =	6:3–4	*Spec.* 1.249
	FR(P)17	6:5	*Deus* 88*; *Somn.* 1.253*
27:32	*Post.* 96*, 97; *Congr.* 94*,	6:5–7	*Spec.* 1.250
	95*, 96; *Spec.* 1.141	6:9	*Leg.* 1.17; *Deus* 89; *Agr.*
27:32–33	*Post.* 95*		175*, 176; *Fug.* 115*
27:33	*Leg.* 3.110*; *Post.* 94	6:12	*Leg.* 1.17*; *Deus* 90; *Agr.*
			175*, 176
		6:13–14	*Spec.* 1.251

6:14	*Spec.* 1.252, 253	9:7	*Mos.* 2.227
6:18	*Spec.* 1.254	9:8	*Mos.* 2.228
6:21	*Mut.* 220	9:9	*Mos.* 2.229
6:26	*Spec.* 2.192	9:10	*Mos.* 2.230
7	*Her.* 195	9:11–13	*Mos.* 2.231
7:10–11	*Congr.* 114	9:14	*Mos.* 2.232
7:13	*Migr.* 202	10:9	*Spec.* 2.190
7:14	*Congr.* 114*	10:10	*Decal.* 159; *Spec.* 2.188, 192
7:20	*Congr.* 114*		
7:26	*Congr.* 114*	10:29	*Ebr.* 39*
7:32	*Congr.* 114*	10:30	*Ebr.* 40*
7:38	*Congr.* 114*	11:4	*Migr.* 155*; FR(H) 106 B8
7:44	*Congr.* 114*		
7:50	*Congr.* 114*	11:4–5	*Mos.* 1.193
7:56	*Congr.* 114*	11:4–6	*Spec.* 4.126; *Hypoth.* 6.2 (428.1)
7:62	*Congr.* 114*		
7:68	*Congr.* 114*	11:5	FR(H) 106 B10
7:74	*Congr.* 114*	11:5–6	*Her.* 80*
7:80	*Congr.* 114*	11:6–9	*Spec.* 4.129
8:3	*Congr.* 8	11:7–8	*Det.* 118
8:5–26	*Sacr.* 120	11:8	*Sacr.* 86
8:14–16	*Fug.* 93	11:8–9	*Mos.* 1.208
8:15	FR(H) 108 A1	11:12	*Her.* 20*
8:16	FR(H) 107 B33	11:13	*Her.* 20*
8:16–18	*Congr.* 98	11:16	*Sacr.* 77*; *Gig.* 24; *Sobr.* 19*; *Fug.* 186
8:20–22	*Det.* 62		
8:21–22	*Sacr.* 132, 133	11:16–17	*Mos.* 1.189
8:24	*QG* 1.91	11:17	*Gig.* 24*, 26, 47, 55
8:24–25	*Det.* 66	11:20	*Spec.* 4.130
8:24–26	*QG* 4.151; *Det.* 63*, 68; *Fug.* 37	11:21	*Spec.* 2.146
		11:22	*Her.* 20*
8:26	*Det.* 64, 65, 66*	11:23	*Sacr.* 66*; *Mut.* 232*
9:1–2	*Mos.* 2.222	11:31	*Spec.* 4.128
9:3	*Mos.* 2.224; *Spec.* 2.145, 149	11:31–32	*Mos.* 1.209
		11:32–33	*Spec.* 4.129
9:6	*Mos.* 2.226	11:34	*Spec.* 4.130
9:6–7	*Mos.* 2.225	12:1	*Leg.* 2.67; 3.103
9:6–11	*Spec.* 2.145	12:1–2	*Leg.* 2.66
9:6–13	*Leg.* 3.94	12:3	*Mos.* 2.279; *Praem.* 77

12:6–8	*Leg.* 3.103*; *Her.* 262*	15:19–20	*Sacr.* 107*
12:7	*Leg.* 2.67*; 3.204*, 228*	15:19–21	*Spec.* 1.132
12:12	*Leg.* 1.76*	15:20	*Sacr.* 108, 111
12:14	*Leg.* 2.66*	15:30	*Spec.* 1.265*; *Virt.* 171*
13:2–4	*Mos.* 1.221	15:30–31	*Virt.* 174
13:3	*Mos.* 1.220	15:32	*Mos.* 2.214, 220; *Spec.*
13:18	*Mut.* 121, 224; *Mos.*		2.250
	1.222, 228	15:32–33	*Mos.* 2.213
13:18–21	*Somn.* 2.170	15:32–36	*Prov.* 1.84
13:19–21	*Mos.* 1.224	15:33–36	*Spec.* 2.251
13:21	*Mos.* 1.226	15:34–35	*Mos.* 2.217
13:23	*Post.* 60*, 62	15:35	*Mos.* 2.218
13:24	*Somn.* 2.171; *Mos.* 1.230,	16	*Fug.* 145
	231; *Spec.* 2.169	16:1–2	*Mos.* 2.276
13:24–25	*Mut.* 224	16:1–3	*Mos.* 2.175, 277
13:28	*Spec.* 2.169	16:1–35	*Praem.* 74
13:27–28	*Spec.* 2.170	16:3	*Praem.* 78
13:29	*Mos.* 1.229	16:5	*Leg.* FR(H) 8 B7
13:31–34	*Mos.* 1.233	16:8–9	*Fug.* 93
13:33–34	*Mos.* 1.229	16:8–14	*Praem.* 77
14:3–4	*Post.* 156; *Congr.* 164	16:15	*Conf.* 50*; *Mos.* 2.279
14:4	*Leg.* 3.175*	16:28–30	*Mos.* 2.281
14:6–9	*Mos.* 1.234	16:31–33	*Mos.* 2.282, 286
14:9	*QG* 1.100*; *Post.* 122*;	16:35	*Mos.* 2.283, 286
	Mut. 265*	16:47–48	*Her.* 201*
14:10	*Mos.* 1.235	16:48	*Somn.* 2.235*, 236*
14:11	*Migr.* 68*; *Spec.* 1.265	17:1–7	*Mos.* 2.178
14:12	*Migr.* 68	17:5	*Mos.* 2.97
14:18	*Sobr.* 48*	17:8	*Mos.* 2.179, 180
14:20	*Migr.* 122*	18:2	*Cher.* 18
14:23	*Leg.* 3.175	18:4	*Cher.* 18
14:24	*Mut.* 123*	18:8–20	*Spec.* 2.183
14:25	*Mos.* 1.237	18:9–19	*Spec.* 1.152
14:32–35	*QE* 2.49	18:12	*Spec.* 1.141; *Virt.* 95
14:33	*Mos.* 1.238	18:12–13	*Spec.* 1.134, 248; 4.98
14:36–38	*Mos.* 1.236	18:13	*Spec.* 4.99
14:44	*Gig.* 48*	18:15	*Spec.* 1.135, 248
15:3	*Prob.* 69	18:15–16	*Spec.* 1.139
15:14–16	*Virt.* 104	18:17	*Spec.* 1.135; *Virt.* 95

18:17–19	*Spec.* 1.248	20:19	*Deus* 167*, 168, 169*, 171, 179*
18:18	*Spec.* 1.145		
18:20	*Plant.* 63*; *Spec.* 1.131; 2.120, 222	20:21	*Mos.* 1.246
		20:25	*Leg.* 3.45
18:21–24	*Fug.* 93; *Spec.* 1.156	21:1	*Mos.* 1.250
18:21–32	*QE* 1.10	21:2–3	*Mos.* 1.252
18:26	*QG* 3.39; *Mut.* 2*	21:3	*Mos.* 1.253
18:26–28	FR(M)17 = FR(P)17	21:4–5	*Leg.* 2.77
18:26–29	*QG* 3.56	21:4–6	*Leg.* 2.84
18:26–32	*Spec.* 1.157	21:6	*Leg.* 2.77*, 87
18:28	*Mut.* 191	21:7	*Leg.* 2.78*
18:31	*Spec.* 4.98	21:8	*Leg.* 2.79*, 81*
18:32	*QG* 3.39	21:8–9	*Agr.* 95, 96, 97
19:2–6	*Spec.* 1.268	21:9	*Leg.* 2.80, 87, 93
19:9	*Spec.* 1.268	21:16–17	*Mos.* 1.255
19:11–13	*Spec.* 3.205	21:16–18	*Ebr.* 113
19:11–16	*Spec.* 1.261	21:17	*Somn.* 2.271*
19:14–15	*Spec.* 3.206	21:18	*Ebr.* 113*; *Mos.* 1.256
19:15	*Det.* 103*; *Conf.* 167*	21:21–23	*Mos.* 1.258
19:17	*Spec.* 1.264; 3.59	21:22	*QG* 4.226; *Gig.* 64; *Spec.* 4.168
19:17–18	*Spec.* 1.262		
19:19	*Spec.* 1.261; 3.206	21:24	*Mos.* 1.259
19:22	*Spec.* 3.208	21:25–26	*Mos.* 1.262
20:2–11	*Mos.* 1.210; *Hypoth.* 6.2 (427.22); 6.3 (428.5)	21:27	*Leg.* 3.226, 228
		21:27–30	*Leg.* 3.225*
20:2–13	*Spec.* 2.199	21:28	*Leg.* 3.229*
20:5	*Mos.* 1.192; *Decal.* 15	21:28–30	*Leg.* 3.233
20:11	*Decal.* 16	21:29	*Leg.* 3.231*
20:14	*Deus* 148	21:30	*Leg.* 3.234; *Migr.* 99*
20:14–16	*Mos.* 1.248	21:31	*Mos.* 1.262
20:14–21	*Deus* 180; *Mos.* 1.243	22:2–4	*Mos.* 1.263
20:17	*QG* 4.226*; *Post.* 101, 102; *Gig.* 64; *Deus* 148, 149, 152, 153, 157, 158, 159, 162, 164, 182; *Migr.* 146*; *Spec.* 4.168	22:4–20	*Mut.* 203
		22:5–6	*Conf.* 159
		22:5–13	*Mos.* 1.266
		22:12	*Mos.* 1.281
		22:14–17	*Mos.* 1.267
20:17–20	*Deus* 145*	22:20–21	*Mos.* 1.268
20:17–21	*Deus* 144	22:21–26	*Cher.* 32, 33
20:18	*Deus* 166*	22:22	*Mos.* 1.269

22:22–35	*Deus* 181, 183	24:11	*Mos.* 1.293
22:23	*Mos.* 1.270	24:16	*Mut.* 202*
22:24–27	*Mos.* 1.271	24:20	*Leg.* 3.187*
22:29	*Cher.* 32*	25:1	*Somn.* 1.89*
22:30–31	*Cher.* 35	25:1–2	*Mos.* 1.296; *Virt.* 35, 40
22:31	*Deus* 181*	25:1–3	*Mut.* 107; *Spec.* 1.56
22:31–34	*Mos.* 1.273	25:1–18	*Virt.* 34
22:35	*Mos.* 1.274	25:3	*Conf.* 55
22:36–40	*Mos.* 1.275	25:4	*Somn.* 1.89*, 90
22:41	*Mos.* 1.276	25:4–5	*Mos.* 1.303
23:1–3	*Mos.* 1.277	25:6	*Mos.* 1.302
23:1–24:25	*Conf.* 159; *Migr.* 113	25:6–7	*Mos.* 1.301
23:6	*Mos.* 1.277	25:6–8	*Spec.* 1.56
23:7	*Conf.* 72*	25:7	*Leg.* 3.242*; *Post.* 182
23:7–8	*Det.* 71; *Conf.* 65*	25:7–8	*Ebr.* 73; *Conf.* 57; *Mut.* 108
23:7–9	*Mos.* 1.278		
23:9	*Spec.* 4.179	25:8	*Leg.* 3.242; *Post.* 183;
23:10	*Mos.* 1.279		*Mos.* 1.302
23:11	*Mos.* 1.280	25:8–13	*Mos.* 1.304
23:12	*Mos.* 1.281	25:9	*Spec.* 3.126; *Virt.* 41
23:13–14	*Mos.* 1.282	25:11–13	*Spec.* 1.57
23:18–20	*Mos.* 1.283	25:12	*Conf.* 57; *Flacc.* 159
23:19	*QG* 1.55; 2.54*; *Leg.* FR(H) 8 A14, B2; *Sacr.* 94*; *Deus* 53*, 62*, 69; *Conf.* 98; *Migr.* 113*; *Her.* 113; *Somn.* 1.237*	25:12–13	*Leg.* 3.242; *Post.* 183; *Ebr.* 74; *Mut.* 108
		25:15	*Virt.* 104
		26:61	*Fug.* 59
		27:1	*Migr.* 205; *Mos.* 2.234
23:21–24	*Mos.* 1.284	27:3	*Migr.* 206*
23:24	*Migr.* 113	27:3–4	*Mos.* 2.235
23:25	*Mos.* 1.285	27:5	*Mos.* 2.237
23:26	*Mos.* 1.286	27:6–7	*Mos.* 2.238
23:27–28	*Mos.* 1.285	27:7	*Mos.* 2.239*, 242
23:28–24:1	*Mos.* 1.287	27:8	*Mos.* 2.243; *Spec.* 2.124
24:2	*Mos.* 1.288	27:8–11	*Spec.* 2.127, 129
24:3–6	*Mos.* 1.289	27:9–10	*Mos.* 2.244
24:7	*Praem.* 95*	27:10	*Spec.* 2.132
24:7–8	*Mos.* 1.290	27:10–11	*Mos.* 2.245
24:9	*Mos.* 1.291	27:16–17	*Post.* 67*; *Agr.* 44*, 48;
24:10	*Mos.* 1.292		*Virt.* 58

27:17	*Virt.* 63	29:25	*Spec.* 1.190
27:18–21	*Virt.* 66	29:28	*Spec.* 1.190
27:19	*Virt.* 70	29:31	*Spec.* 1.190
27:22–23	*Virt.* 67	29:34	*Spec.* 1.190
28:1–29:40	*Cher.* 85, 90	29:35	*Spec.* 2.211
28:2	*Leg.* 3.196*; *Cher.* 84*;	29:36	*Migr.* 202*
	Sacr. 111*; *Deus* 6*;	29:38	*Spec.* 1.190
	Migr. 142*	30:3	*QG* 4.132*; *Spec.* 2.9
28:2–3	*Spec.* 2.42	30:3–17	*Hypoth.* 7.5 (430.12)
28:3–8	*Spec.* 1.169	30:4–6	*Leg.* 2.63
28:5	*Spec.* 1.179	30:4–17	*Spec.* 2.24, 29
28:9–10	*Spec.* 1.170	30:10	*Leg.* 2.63*; *Det.* 147*,
28:11	*Spec.* 1.177, 180; 2.142		149; *Spec.* 2.25
28:11–15	*Spec.* 2.41, 140	31:1–18	*Virt.* 34
28:12–14	*Spec.* 1.179	31:2	*Virt.* 53
28:15	*Spec.* 1.190	31:3–6	*Virt.* 42
28:16	*Spec.* 2.150, 152	31:4–6	*Mos.* 1.306
28:16–17	*Decal.* 159; *Spec.* 1.181	31:5–8	*Virt.* 46
28:17	*Decal.* 161; *Spec.* 2.155,	31:7	*Mos.* 1.309
	156, 159	31:7–12	*Virt.* 43
28:19–24	*Spec.* 1.181	31:8	*Deus* 183*; *Mut.* 203*
28:22	*Spec.* 1.190	31:10	*Spec.* 4.223
28:26	*Spec.* 2.41, 179	31:15–18	*Mos.* 1.311; *Virt.* 43
28:26–31	*Spec.* 1.183	31:16	*Mos.* 1.296, 305
28:27	*Spec.* 1.184	31:19	*Mos.* 1.313
28:30	*Spec.* 1.190	31:25–31	*Mos.* 1.315
29:1	*Spec.* 2.186, 188, 192	31:26	*Leg.* 2.35*
29:1–6	*Spec.* 1.180	31:28	*Migr.* 139*; *Her.* 120*;
29:5	*Spec.* 1.190		*Somn.* 2.29*
29:7	*Spec.* 2.200, 201	31:29	*Migr.* 139
29:7–11	*Decal.* 159; *Spec.* 1.186;	31:47	*Mos.* 1.316
	2.86, 193, 197	31:48–54	*Mos.* 1.317
29:8	*Spec.* 1.188	31:49	*Ebr.* 115; *Conf.* 55*; *Mut.*
29:11	*Spec.* 1.190		109; *Virt.* 44, 46
29:12	*Spec.* 2.210	31:49–50	*Ebr.* 114*
29:12–34	*Fug.* 186	31:50	*Ebr.* 118*
29:12–38	*Spec.* 1.189	32:1–5	*Mos.* 1.320
29:13	*Migr.* 202*	32:6–7	*Mos.* 1.321
29:22	*Spec.* 1.190	32:8–9	*Mos.* 1.325

32:12–13	*Mos.* 1.325
32:13	*Migr.* 154
32:16–19	*Mos.* 1.330
32:20–21	*Mos.* 1.331
32:22	*Mos.* 1.332
32:23	*Mos.* 1.326
32:25–27	*Mos.* 1.333
32:25–29	*Spec.* 3.128
35:1–6	*Sacr.* 128
35:2–8	*Spec.* 1.158; 2.120
35:6	*Sacr.* 130, 133; *Ebr.* 94; *Fug.* 87, 94, 100; *Spec.* 3.123, 124, 128, 130; FR(H) 108 A7, B3
35:6–34	*Fug.* 86
35:8	*Her.* 194*
35:10–34	QG 3.52
35:11–15	*Fug.* 96, 97, 99, 102; *Spec.* 1.158; 3.123, 128, 130
35:12	*Spec.* 3.129
35:12–13	*Fug.* 100
35:13	*Fug.* 94
35:13–14	*Fug.* 87
35:14	*Fug.* 103
35:16–18	*Spec.* 3.92
35:16–21	*Spec.* 3.84
35:17	*Spec.* 3.106
35:21	*Spec.* 3.106
35:22–23	*Spec.* 3.92
35:25	*Fug.* 87, 106, 107, 110, 116; *Spec.* 3.123, 131, 133
35:25–26	*Spec.* 1.161
35:26–27	*Spec.* 1.160
35:26–28	*Spec.* 3.132
35:28	*Fug.* 87, 106, 107, 110, 116; *Spec.* 3.123, 131, 133
35:30	*Spec.* 4.53
35:30–31	*Spec.* 3.84

35:31–33	*Spec.* 3.150
36:6–9	*Spec.* 2.126
36:7	*Spec.* 2.113, 128
36:9	*Spec.* 2.113, 128
36:13	*Hypoth.* 6.8 (429.6)

Deuteronomy

1:16–17	*Spec.* 4.70
1:17	QE 2.10*; *Her.* 157*; *Mut.* 104; *Somn.* 2.24*; *Ios.* 72; *Spec.* 4.71*
1:31	*Sacr.* 101*
1:43–44	*Deus* 99*
1:44	*Deus* 100
4:1	*Mut.* 23*
4:1–8	*Decal.* 14
4:2	*Spec.* 4.143, 144, 147
4:4	*Fug.* 56*, 57; *Spec.* 1.31*, 345*
4:6	*Migr.* 56*, 58; *Praem.* 83
4:7	*Migr.* 56, 59; *Praem.* 84
4:9	*Migr.* 8
4:11	QE 2.28; *Decal.* 44
4:12	*Migr.* 48*; *Decal.* 32, 33, 46
4:13	*Decal.* 50
4:15	*Decal.* 33
4:19	*Conf.* 173; *Spec.* 1.15*, 16; 2.255
4:20	*Spec.* 4.180
4:24	*Deo* 7*
4:25–28	*Spec.* 2.170
4:28	*Spec.* 2.255
4:29	*Fug.* 142*
4:30	*Fug.* 141
4:39	*Leg.* 3.4*, 82*; *Migr.* 182*
5:1	*Decal.* 36
5:4	*Decal.* 32

7:13	Praem. 107	10:12–13	Spec. 1.300
7:14	Praem. 108*	10:14	Spec. 1.302*
7:15	Praem. 118, 119	10:15	Spec. 1.303
7:20	Praem. 96	10:16	QG 3.46*; Spec. 1.305
8:2–3	Congr. 170*, 172; Decal. 13; Spec. 2.199	10:17	Conf. 173*; Spec. 1.306; Prob. 43
8:3	Leg. 3.174*, 176*; Congr. 173*; Decal. 16	10:17–18	Spec. 4.177*
		10:17–19	Decal. 40
8:5	QG 1.55; 2.54; Leg. FR(H) 8 A15; Deus 54*, 69; Somn. 1.237*	10:18	Spec. 1.308, 309; 4.179; Virt. 104
		10:18–19	Spec. 1.51, 52
8:7	Spec. 1.303	10:19	Virt. 103, 147, 160
8:7–10	Spec. 2.169	10:20	Leg. 3.208*; Migr. 132*; Spec. 1.312
8:11–14	Virt. 163		
8:12–14	Sacr. 55*	10:21	Spec. 1.311
8:14–15	Mos. 1.192	10:22	Migr. 201*
8:15	Leg. 2.86; Somn. 2.222*; Mos. 1.210; Decal. 16	11:11	Spec. 1.303
		11:13	Praem. 82
8:15–16	Leg. 2.84*; Decal. 13	11:14–15	Praem. 101
8:15–18	Decal. 15	11:17	Praem. 101
8:17–18	Sacr. 56*	11:18	Spec. 4.137, 138
8:18	Agr. 172*, 173; Virt. 165*, 168	11:19	QG 4.154; Spec. 1.313; 4.141; Legat. 210
8:19–20	Spec. 2.170	11:20	Spec. 4.142
9:1–2	Spec. 2.170	11:22–25	Virt. 47
9:1–7	Virt. 47	12:2–3	Legat. 202
9:5	Sacr. 57*	12:5	Somn. 1.62*
9:9	Somn. 1.36	12:5–7	Spec. 1.67
9:10	Migr. 85	12:8	Spec. 4.131*; FR(H) 100 A11
9:18	Somn. 1.36; Mos. 2.69		
9:26	Prob. 43	12:11–14	Spec. 1.68
10:2	Fug. 100	12:17–18	Spec. 1.68
10:5	QE 2.41, 53; Fug. 100	12:23	Spec. 4.122, 123
10:8–9	Her. 124	12:25	Mut. 42
10:9	Leg. 2.51*; Sacr. 127; Plant. 63*, 69, 70, 72; Congr. 134*; Fug. 102; Somn. 1.159*; Spec. 1.131; 2.120, 183, 222	12:28	Mut. 42*
		12:29–31	Spec. 1.312
		12:31	Abr. 181*; Spec. 1.313
		12:32	Spec. 4.143, 144, 147
		13:1–11	Spec. 1.315, 316

13:4	*Migr.* 131*	16:9–10	*Spec.* 2.179
13:6	*Her.* 83*	16:9–17	*Opif.* 116
13:12–17	*Spec.* 1.55	16:10	*Spec.* 2.41
13:16	*Spec.* 4.223	16:13	*Spec.* 2.204, 205
13:18	*Spec.* 1.318*	16:13–15	*Decal.* 161
14:1	*Conf.* 145*; *Spec.* 1.58, 318*	16:16	*QG* 3.61; *Leg.* 3.11
		16:18–20	*Spec.* 4.64, 70
14:1–21	*Prov.* 1.84	16:19	*Spec.* 4.62
14:3–20	FR(H) 106 A23–24	16:19–20	*Decal.* 172
14:4	*Spec.* 4.206; *Virt.* 146	16:20	*Cher.* 15*; *Det.* 18*; *Spec.* 4.66, 169
14:4–5	*QE* 2.101; *Spec.* 4.105		
14:4–8	*Spec.* 4.106	16:21	*Leg.* 1.48*, 51*; *Spec.* 1.74
14:6	*Spec.* 4.108		
14:8–10	*Spec.* 4.101	16:22	*Somn.* 1.245*
14:9–10	*Spec.* 4.110	17:2–5	*Spec.* 2.255
14:11–19	*QG* 2.38	17:6	*Spec.* 4.53
14:11	*Spec.* 4.117	17:6–7	*Spec.* 1.55
14:12–19	*Spec.* 4.116	17:7	*Spec.* 2.251
14:19	*Spec.* 4.117	17:8–9	*Spec.* 4.190
14:20	*Spec.* 4.119, 120; *Virt.* 142*, 144	17:11	*Post.* 102
		17:15	*Spec.* 4.157*
15:1–2	*Spec.* 2.39	17:15–16	*Agr.* 84*
15:1–3	*Spec.* 2.71	17:16	*Agr.* 86, 88, 89
15:1–11	*Praem.* 154	17:16–17	*Spec.* 4.158
15:3	*Spec.* 2.73	17:18	*Spec.* 4.160, 163
15:6	*Praem.* 107	17:18–20	*Decal.* 40
15:7–11	*Spec.* 2.71	17:19	*Spec.* 4.161
15:8	*Post.* 142*	17:19–20	*Spec.* 4.165
15:10	*Spec.* 2.72; *Virt.* 83	17:20	*Spec.* 4.167, 169
15:12	*Spec.* 2.39, 79*, 84; 4.4; *Virt.* 122	18:1–2	*Plant.* 63; *Spec.* 1.131, 151
15:13–14	*Spec.* 2.85	18:1–5	*Spec.* 2.183, 222
15:14	*Hypoth.* 7.6 (430.18)	18:2	*Plant.* 69, 70, 72; *Congr.* 134; *Somn.* 1.159
15:18	*Spec.* 2.80, 82, 84		
15:19	*Spec.* 1.135, 248	18:3	*Spec.* 1.147, 150
16:3	*Congr.* 161*, 167; *Spec.* 2.158	18:4	*Spec.* 1.134, 141; *Virt.* 95
		18:4–5	*Spec.* 4.98
16:6	*Spec.* 2.145	18:10	*Spec.* 3.94, 102
16:9	*Decal.* 160; *Spec.* 2.176	18:10–12	*Spec.* 1.60; 4.48, 50

18:10–13	*Spec.* 1.63	21:17	*Post.* 63; *Sobr.* 25*; *Spec.*
18:15	*Spec.* 1.65		2.133, 138; *Legat.* 289
18:15–16	*Sacr.* 130	21:18	*Ebr.* 95
18:18	*Spec.* 1.65; 4.49; *Praem.*	21:18–21	*QG* 4.244; *Ebr.* 14*; *Spec.*
	53, 55		2.232, 234, 253
19:1–13	*Sacr.* 128; *Decal.* 170	21:19	*Ebr.* 33
19:4	*Sacr.* 130, 133	21:19–20	*Ebr.* 29
19:5	*Fug.* 77*	21:20	*Ebr.* 15, 17, 20, 23, 25,
19:14	*Post.* 89*; *Spec.* 4.149*		27, 93*, 94, 95; *Mut.*
19:15	*Spec.* 4.53		206*
19:16–20	*Spec.* 4.44	21:21	*Ebr.* 28*; *Spec.* 2.243
19:17	*Leg.* 3.65*	21:22	*Spec.* 3.151
19:21	*Spec.* 3.182, 195	21:23	*Post.* 26*; *Spec.* 3.152
20:1	*Agr.* 78*, 92, 124; *Migr.*	22:1	*Virt.* 117
	62*	22:1–3	*Decal.* 171; *Hypoth.* 7.6
20:5	*Agr.* 158; *Virt.* 29		(430.18)
20:5–7	*Agr.* 148*, 153, 157, 166;	22:1–4	*Virt.* 96
	Virt. 28, 30, 31	22:4	*Virt.* 116, 160
20:8	*Virt.* 23, 25	22:4–10	*Anim.* 25
20:9	*Virt.* 32	22:5	*Virt.* 18, 20, 21
20:10–11	*Spec.* 4.220; *Virt.* 160	22:6	*Anim.* 22; *Hypoth.* 7.9
20:11–15	*Virt.* 109		(431.8)
20:12–13	*Spec.* 4.222	22:8	*Agr.* 170*; *Spec.* 3.149
20:14	*Spec.* 4.223	22:9	*Spec.* 4.208, 211, 215,
20:19	*Spec.* 4.227; *Virt.* 150,		217, 218
	154	22:9–11	*Spec.* 4.203
20:19–20	*Spec.* 4.226; *Virt.* 149,	22:10	*Spec.* 4.205; *Virt.* 144,
	160		146, 160
20:20	*Agr.* 10*, 12*, 17, 19;	22:11	*Spec.* 4.207
	Spec. 4.229	22:13–23:1	*Decal.* 168
21:10	*Ebr.* 25	22:13–17	*Spec.* 3.80
21:10–13	*Virt.* 110	22:19	*Spec.* 3.81
21:12–13	*Virt.* 111	22:18–19	*Spec.* 3.82
21:13	*Virt.* 113	22:22	*Spec.* 3.11, 31, 52, 58;
21:14	*Cher.* 121; *Virt.* 115		*Anim.* 49
21:15	*Sobr.* 22*, 24; *Her.* 47	22:22–24	*Ios.* 43
21:15–16	*Leg.* 2.48*	22:23–24	*Spec.* 3.73
21:15–17	*Sacr.* 19*; *Sobr.* 21*; *Her.*	22:23–25	*Hypoth.* 7.1 (429.20)
	49*; *Spec.* 2.136	22:23–27	*Spec.* 3.74, 76, 78

22:24	*Spec.* 3.77	24:13–16	*Mut.* 104
22:27	*Spec.* 3.77*	24:14–15	*Virt.* 88
22:28–29	*Spec.* 3.65, 70	24:15	*Spec.* 4.195
22:30	*Spec.* 3.20	24:16	*Spec.* 3.153, 154, 168
23:1	*Deus* 111; *Ebr.* 213*;	24:19	*Virt.* 90, 92
	Migr. 69*; *Somn.* 2.184*;	24:20–21	*Virt.* 91
	Spec. 1.325, 328, 330;	25:2–3	*Spec.* 2.28
	3.42	25:4	*Virt.* 145, 146, 160;
23:1–2	*Leg.* 3.8; *Mut.* 205; *Spec.*		*Anim.* 25
	1.344	25:11–12	*Somn.* 2.69; *Spec.* 3.175,
23:2	*Conf.* 144*; *Migr.* 69;		177, 179
	Mut. 204; *Decal.* 8; *Spec.*	25:12	*Spec.* 3.180
	1.326, 332*	25:13–15	*Somn.* 2.193*; *Spec.*
23:3	*Post.* 177*; *Spec.* 1.333		4.194
23:3–4	*Leg.* 3.81*	25:13–16	*Her.* 162*; *Hypoth.* 7.8
23:4	*Migr.* 115		(431.3)
23:5	*Det.* 71; *Migr.* 115*	25:16	*Her.* 163
23:7	*Virt.* 106*	25:17	*Migr.* 143*
23:8	*Virt.* 108	25:17–19	*Mos.* 1.216
23:12	*Leg.* 3.151*	25:18	*Ebr.* 24; *Migr.* 144
23:12–13	*Leg.* 3.159	25:19	*Leg.* 3.187
23:13	*Leg.* 2.27*, 28, 29, 30;	26:1–4	*Spec.* 1.248
	3.153*, 157*, 158*	26:1–11	*QG* 1.64; *Spec.* 2.215
23:15–16	*Leg.* 3.194*; *Virt.* 124	26:1–15	*Virt.* 95
23:17	*Migr.* 224*; *Ios.* 43; *Spec.*	26:2	*QE* 2.102; *Somn.* 2.272;
	1.326; 3.38, 51; *Hypoth.*		*Spec.* 4.99; *Legat.* 156
	7.1 (429.21)	26:2–4	*Spec.* 1.134; 2.216
23:18	*Spec.* 1.104*, 280	26:4	*Somn.* 2.272; *Spec.* 2.222
23:19–20	*Spec.* 2.74; *Virt.* 82, 86	26:5	*Spec.* 2.168
23:21	*Sacr.* 53*; *Spec.* 2.38	26:5–6	*Spec.* 2.217
23:21–23	*Hypoth.* 7.5 (430.12)	26:7–9	*Spec.* 2.218
24:1–4	*Spec.* 3.30	26:10	*Spec.* 1.134, 248; 2.219
24:4	*Spec.* 3.31	26:10–11	*Spec.* 4.99
24:5	*Virt.* 28	26:13	*Somn.* 2.272*, 273
24:6	*Spec.* 3.204	26:17–18	*Virt.* 184*
24:7	*Spec.* 4.13, 19; *Hypoth.*	27:5–6	*Spec.* 1.274, 287
	7.2 (429.22)	27:9	*Her.* 10*, 13; *Somn.*
24:10–11	*Virt.* 89		1.193*; 2.263*
24:10–15	*Decal.* 171	27:11–13	*Her.* 177*

27:12–13	*Fug.* 73	28:42	*Praem.* 129
27:15	*Leg.* 3.36	28:43–44	*Praem.* 152
27:16	*Spec.* 2.248	28:44	*Praem.* 124
27:17	*Leg.* 3.107*; *Post.* 84*, 88	28:48	*Praem.* 138
27:18	*Leg.* 3.108*; *Spec.* 4.198,	28:49–57	*Spec.* 1.313
	200	28:53–57	*Praem.* 134
27:20	*Spec.* 3.20	28:56	*Praem.* 146
27:22	*Spec.* 3.22, 24	28:59	*Praem.* 143
27:24	*Leg.* 3.108*	28:61	*Praem.* 150
28:1–2	*Praem.* 82	28:65	*Post.* 24*
28:1–14	*Praem.* 79, 118, 126	28:66	*Post.* 24*
28:3–4	*Praem.* 107	28:66–67	*Praem.* 151
28:3–5	*Praem.* 101	28:67	*Flacc.* 167
28:3–6	*Praem.* 98	29:4	*Fug.* 123*
28:6	*Praem.* 113	29:20	*Deus* 68
28:7	*Praem.* 79, 94	29:20–21	*Deus* 60
28:8	*Praem.* 101, 104	29:23	*Abr.* 145, 165
28:8–14	*Praem.* 98	29:29	*Cher.* 16*; *Spec.* 3.52;
28:12	*Leg.* 3.104*; *Deus* 156;		*Prov.* 2.29
	Her. 76*; *Praem.* 101,	30:1–10	*Praem.* 163
	107	30:2	*Praem.* 82
28:13	*Praem.* 124	30:3–5	*Praem.* 164
28:14	*Post.* 102*; *Spec.* 4.167	30:4	*Conf.* 197*; *Praem.* 115
28:15–69	*Praem.* 126, 162	30:5–10	*Praem.* 168
28:16–18	*Praem.* 141	30:7	*Praem.* 79, 169
28:20	*Praem.* 136	30:9–10	*Somn.* 2.175*
28:22	*Praem.* 130, 136, 143	30:11	*Spec.* 1.299
28:23	*Praem.* 131	30:11–13	*Post.* 84; *Prob.* 68
28:24	*Praem.* 133	30:11–14	*Spec.* 1.301; *Virt.* 183;
28:25	*Spec.* 1.314		*Praem.* 80
28:27–28	*Praem.* 143	30:12–14	*Mut.* 237*; *Somn.* 2.180
28:28–29	*Her.* 250*	30:14	*Post.* 85*; *Mut.* 240;
28:30–31	*Praem.* 139		*Prob.* 68*
28:33	*Praem.* 127	30:15	*Leg.* FR(H) 8 A4, B10;
28:34	*Praem.* 139		*Deus* 50*; *Fug.* 58*;
28:35	*Praem.* 145	30:16	*Praem.* 79
28:36–37	*Spec.* 1.314	30:16–17	*Praem.* 82
28:38–39	*Praem.* 128	30:19	*Leg.* FR(H) 8 A4, B10;
28:40	*Praem.* 129		*Deus* 50*

Joshua

Judges

1 Kingdoms (1 Samuel)

1:13	*Ebr.* 146	7:23	*Congr.* 41
1:14	*Ebr.* 146*	9:17–34	*QE* 1.10
1:15	*Ebr.* 149*, 150, 151, 152*	9:19	*Praem.* 74
1:19–20	*Deus* 5	22:9	*Congr.* 177
1:20	*Ebr.* 144; *Somn.* 1.254	26:1–19	*QE* 1.10; *Praem.* 74
1:27–28	*Deus* 5	28:18	*Deo* 5
1:28	*Deus* 6; *Somn.* 1.254		

2 Chronicles

2:5	*Deus* 10*, 11, 13, 14; *Mut.* 143*, 144; *Praem.* 158*, 159	3	*Hypoth.* 6.6 (428.25)
2:18	*Ebr.* 144	4	*Hypoth.* 6.6 (428.25)

Esther

9:9	*QG* 4.138; *Deus* 139; *Migr.* 38*; *Her.* 78*; *Deo* 2	8:13	*Spec.* 3.140

Job

10:22	*Migr.* 196*	1:21	*Spec.* 1.295
10:23	*Migr.* 197*	14:4–5	*Mut.* 48*
16:7	*Prov.* 2.29	25:2	*Spec.* 2.192
		28	*Prob.* 65

3 Kingdoms (1 Kings)

		28:24	*QG* 1.69; *Det.* 61
6	*QE* 1.10; *Hypoth.* 6.6 (428.25)	38:4	*Migr.* 136

Psalms

8:6	*QG* 2.4		
15:11	*Conf.* 149	Title	*Conf.* 52; *Migr.* 157; *Fug.* 59
17:10	*Deus* 136	8:6–7	*Opif.* 84
17:18	*Deus* 138*	11:7	*Decal.* 48
22:17	*Virt.* 58	14:5	*Spec.* 1.204
		18:8	*QG* 4.195i*

4 Kingdoms (2 Kings)

		22	*Agr.* 51
2:11–12	*QG* 1.86	22:1	*Agr.* 50*, 52*, 54; *Mut.* 115*
18:3	*Conf.* 149	23:4	*Spec.* 1.204

1 Chronicles

		26:1	*Somn.* 1.75*
1:28	*Praem.* 58, 61	30:19	*Conf.* 39*
1:32	*Praem.* 58, 61		
1:34	*Praem.* 58, 61		
7:14	*Congr.* 41, 42, 43		

35:10	*Praem.* 46	6:6–8	*Prov.* 1.25, 51
36:4	*Plant.* 39*; *Somn.* 2.242*	6:9–11	*Spec.* 2.60
40:2	*Hypoth.* 7.6 (430.21)	8:22	*Leg.* 1.43; *Conf.* 146
41:4	*Migr.* 157*	8:22–23	*Det.* 54; *Ebr.* 31*; *Virt.*
45:5	*Somn.* 2.246*, 248, 250,		62
	253	9:1–5	*Somn.* 1.50
51:4	*Decal.* 63	9:1–6	*Prob.* 13
61:12	*Deus* 82*, 83	11:1	*Hypoth.* 7.8 (431.3)
64:2	*QG* 4.232	13:24	*Spec.* 2.232
64:10	*Somn.* 2.245*	16:11	*Hypoth.* 7.8 (431.3)
68:34	*QG* 4.147*	19:14	*QG* 4.129*
74:9	*Deus* 77*, 78, 81, 82	19:17	*Hypoth.* 7.6 (430.21)
77:49	*Gig.* 17*	19:18	*Ios.* 74
79:6	*Migr.* 157*	23:13–14	*Ios.* 74
79:7	*Conf.* 52*, 54	24:17–18	*Flacc.* 121
83:11	*Her.* 290*	24:33–34	*Spec.* 2.60
89:7	*QG* 1.92	30:30	*Anim.* 55
90:11–12	*Deus* 182	31:10–31	*QG* 1.26
93:9	*Plant.* 29*		
95:5	FR(H) 106 A28		

Ecclesiastes

98:5	*Conf.* 98		
100:1	*Deus* 74*	2:13	*Spec.* 1.288
104:4	*Virt.* 74	5:14	*Spec.* 1.295
106:1	*Aet.* 1		
111:1–3	*Spec.* 2.259		

Isaiah

113:12–16	*Decal.* 74		
113:16	*Spec.* 2.255	1:9	*QG* 2.43*
113:25	*Fug.* 59*	1:11	*Spec.* 1.271
113:26	*Fug.* 59	1:15	*Spec.* 1.277
134:15–18	*Decal.* 74	5:7	*Somn.* 2.172*
134:18	*Spec.* 2.255	6:1–2	*Deo* 6*
		6:2	*Deo* 9*

Proverbs

		6:9	*Ios.* 126
		11:2	*QG* 1.99
3:4	*Ebr.* 84*	11:6–8	*Praem.* 87, 88, 89
3:11–12	*Congr.* 177*	11:11–12	*Praem.* 165
3:13–14	*Cher.* 48	35:1	*QE* 2.76
3:19	*Det.* 54; *Fug.* 109	40:13	*Sacr.* 10
4:3	*Ebr.* 84*	41:8	*Cher.* 7

45:7	*Spec.* 2.192
46:5	*Leg.* 2.1
48:22	*Mut.* 169*
50:4	*Her.* 25*
51:2	*QG* 2.26*
54:1	*Praem.* 158
57:21	*Mut.* 169*
65:20	*Praem.* 110
66:1	*Conf.* 98; *Spec.* 1.66

Jeremiah

1:1–3	*Cher.* 49
2:3	*Spec.* 4.180
2:13	*Fug.* 197*, 199, 201
2:27	*Decal.* 8
3:1–11	*Decal.* 8
3:4	*Cher.* 49*, 51, 52
9:25	*Spec.* 1.304
10:12	*Fug.* 109
15:10	*Conf.* 44*, 49*, 51*
16:20	*Decal.* 8
34:9	*Spec.* 4.51
36:8	*Spec.* 4.51
38:9	*Conf.* 63
41:14	*Spec.* 2.79, 84

Ezekiel

44:10–11	*Spec.* 1.156
44:14	*Spec.* 1.156
44:21	*Spec.* 1.98, 249
44:22	*Spec.* 1.110
44:23	*Spec.* 1.100
46:13–14	*Spec.* 2.42

Daniel

4:32	*Flacc.* 177

Hosea

12:4	*Migr.* 200; *Her.* 252; *Mut.* 81; *Somn.* 1.171
14:6	*QE* 2.76*
14:9–10	*Plant.* 138*; *Mut.* 139*

Zechariah

6:12	*Conf.* 62*
12:10	*Conf.* 63

Wisdom of Solomon

3:6	*QG* 4.28
3:6–7	*Decal.* 48
4:8	*Her.* 290; *Spec.* 4.169
6:12	*Fug.* 139
7:26	*QG* 1.57; *Mut.* 223; *Ios.* 265
7:27	*Cher.* 7
10:6	*Abr.* 145, 147, 165
11:1	*Praem.* 53, 55
11:4	*Mos.* 1.210
11:17–19	*Mos.* 1.109
12:1	*Ios.* 265
12:27	*Ios.* 254
13:1–19	*Decal.* 66
13:2	*Spec.* 2.255
13:2–3	*Spec.* 1.13
14:1–11	*Decal.* 66
14:8	*Leg.* 2.3
15:7–19	*Decal.* 66
15:14	*Decal.* 69
15:15	*Decal.* 74
15:16–17	*Decal.* 69
15:18–19	*Decal.* 76
16:2	*Decal.* 17
16:20	*Congr.* 173

Sirach

Bibliography

Adams, Sean A. *Greek Genres and Jewish Authors: Negotiating Literary Culture in the Greco-Roman Era*. Waco, TX: Baylor University Press, 2020.

———. "Treatise Order in the Greek Codices of Philo of Alexandria: Lists, *Pinakes*, and Manuscripts." *SPhiloA* 34 (2022): 1–31.

Albrecht, Felix. "Report on the Göttingen Septuagint." *Text* 29 (2020): 201–20.

Allenbach, Jean, et al., eds., *Biblia Patristica: Supplément, Philon d'Alexandrie*. Paris: Centre National de la Recherche Scientifique, 1982.

Aucher, Johann Baptist. *Philonis Judaei paralipomena Armena: Libri videlicet quatuor in Genesin; Libri duo in Exodum; Sermo unus de Sampsone, alter de Jona, tertius de tribus angelis Abraamo apparentibus*. Venice: Lazari, 1826.

Barthélemy, Dominique. "Est-ce Hoshaya Rabba qui censura le 'Commentaire allégorique'? A partir des retouches faites aux citations bibliques, étude sur la tradition textuelle du Commentaire Allégorique de Philon." Pages 45–78 in *Philon d'Alexandrie: Lyon 11–15 Septembre 1966, colloques nationaux du Centre National de la Recherche Scientifique*. Edited by Roger Arnaldez, Claude Mondésert, and Jean Pouilloux. Paris: Centre national de la recherche scientifique, 1967. Repr. as pages 140–73, with additional notes on 390–91, in Dominique Barthélemy, *Études d'histoire du texte de l'Ancient Testament*. OBO 21. Göttingen: Vandenhoeck & Ruprecht, 1978.

Bogaert, Pierre-Maurice, Charles Perrot, Jacques Cazeaux, and Daniel J. Harrington. *Les Antiquités Bibliques*. 2 vols. SC 229–230. Paris: Cerf, 1976.

Böhm, Christiane. *Die Rezeption der Psalmen in den Qumranschriften, bei Philo von Alexandria und im Corpus Paulinum*. WUNT 2/437. Tübingen: Mohr Siebeck, 2017.

Burkhardt, Helmut. *Die Inspiration heiliger Schriften bei Philo von Alexandrien*. 2nd ed. TVG Monographien und Studienbücher 340. Giessen: Brunnen, 1992.

Cohen, Naomi G. *Philo's Scriptures: Citations from the Prophets and Writings; Evidence for a Haftarah Cycle in Second Temple Judaism*. JSJSup 123. Leiden: Brill, 2007.

Cohn, Leopold, et al., eds. *Philo von Alexandria: Die Werke in deutscher Übersetzung*. 7 vols. Berlin: de Gruyter, 1909–1964.

Earp, J. W. "Indices to Volumes I–X." Pages 189–520 in vol. 10 of *Philo in Ten Volumes (and Two Supplementary Volumes)*. Translated and edited by Francis H. Colson, George H. Whitaker, and Ralph Marcus. 12 vols. LCL. Cambridge: Harvard University Press, 1929–1962.

Fowler, Don. "On the Shoulders of Giants: Intertextuality and Classical Studies." *Materiali e discussioni per l'analisi dei testi classici* 39 (1997): 13–34.

Geljon, Albert C., and David T. Runia. *Philo of Alexandria, On Cultivation: Introduction, Translation, and Commentary*. PACS 4. Leiden: Brill, 2013.

Harris, James Rendel. *Fragments of Philo Judeaus*. Cambridge: Cambridge University Press, 1886.

Horst, Pieter Willem van der. *Philo's Flaccus: The First Pogrom; Translation, Introduction, and Commentary*. PACS 2. Leiden: Brill, 2003.

Katz, Peter. *Philo's Bible: The Aberrant Text of Biblical Quotations in Some Philonic Writings and Its Place in the Textual History of the Greek Bible*. Cambridge: Cambridge University Press, 1950.

Koskenniemi, Erkki. *Greek Writers and Philosophers in Philo and Josephus: A Study of Their Secular Education and Educational Ideals*. SPhA 9. Leiden: Brill, 2019.

Kowalski, Beate. *Die Rezeption des Propheten Ezechiel in der Offenbarung des Johannes*. SBB 52. Stuttgart: Katholisches Bibelwerk, 2004.

Lange, Armin, and Matthias Weigold. *Biblical Quotations and Allusions in Second Temple Jewish Literature*. JAJSup 5. Gottingen: Vandenhoeck & Ruprecht, 2011.

Leisegang, Hans. *Indices ad Philonis Alexandrini opera*. Vol. 7 of *Philonis Alexandrini opera quae supersunt*. Berlin: de Gruyter, 1926.

Leonard, Jeffery M. "Identifying Inner-Biblical Allusions: Psalm 78 as a Test Case." *JBL* 127 (2008): 241–65.

Leonhardt, Jutta. *Jewish Worship in Philo of Alexandria*. TSAJ 84. Tübingen: Mohr Siebeck, 2001.

Lewy, Hans. "Neue Philontexte in der Überarbeitung des Ambrosius: Mit einem Anhang; Neu gefundene griechische Philonfragmente." *SPAW* 4 (1932): 23–84.

Lincicum, David. "A Preliminary Index to Philo's Non-biblical Citations and Allusions." *SPhiloA* 25 (2013): 139–67.

Mangey, Thomas. *Philonis Judaei opera quae reperiri potuerunt omnia.* 2 vols. London: William Humphrey, 1742.

Marcus, Ralph, ed. and trans. *Questions on Exodus.* LCL 401. Cambridge: Harvard University Press, 1953.

Mayer, Günter. *Index Philoneus.* Berlin: de Gruyter, 1974.

Morgan, Teresa. *Literate Education in the Hellenistic and Roman Worlds.* CCS. Cambridge: Cambridge University Press, 1998.

Munnich, Olivier. "Les retouches faites aux lemmes bibliques dans le Commentaire allégorique de Philon d'Alexandrie: Bilan et proposition." Pages 137–83 in *Les études philoniennes: Regards sur cinquante ans de recherche (1967–2017).* Edited by Olivier Munnich and Sébastien Morlet. SPhA 13. Leiden: Brill, 2021.

Niehoff, Maren R. *Jewish Exegesis and Homeric Scholarship in Alexandria.* Cambridge: Cambridge University Press, 2011.

Petit, Françoise. *L'ancienne version latine des Questions sur la Genèse de Philon d'Alexandrie.* 2 vols. TUGAL 113–114. Berlin: Akademie, 1973.

———. *Catena Sinaitica.* Vol. 1 of *Catenae Graecae in Genesim et in Exodum.* 2 vols. CCSG 2. Turnhout: Brepols, 1977.

———. *Quaestiones in Genesim et in Exodum, Fragmenta Graeca: Introduction, texte critique et notes.* PAPM 33. Paris: Cerf, 1978.

Pick, B. "Philo's Canon of the Old Testament and His Mode of Quoting the Alexandrian Version." *Journal of the Society of Biblical Literature and Exegesis* 4 (1884): 126–43.

Rahlfs, Alfred, and Robert Hanhart, eds. *Septuaginta: Id est Vetus Testamentum graece iuxta LXX interpretes.* 2nd ed. Stuttgart: Deutsche Bibelgesellschaft, 2006.

Reister, Wolfgang. "Zur Problematik eines Philo-Index." *ZRGG* 27 (1975): 166–68.

Royse, James R. "The Biblical Quotations in the Coptos Papyrus of Philo." *SPhiloA* 28 (2016): 49–76.

———. "Some Overlooked Classical References in Philo." *SPhiloA* 32 (2020): 249–55.

———. *The Spurious Texts of Philo of Alexandria: A Study of Textual Trans-*

mission and Corruption with Indexes to the Major Collections of Greek Fragments. ALGHJ 22. Leiden: Brill, 1991.

Ruiten, Jacques T. A. G. M. van. "Der alttestamentliche Hintergrund von Apocalypse 6:12–17." *EstBib* 53 (1995): 239–60.

Runia, David T. *Philo in Early Christian Literature: A Survey.* CRINT 3. Assen: Van Gorcum, 1993.

———. "Philo's Reading of the Psalms." *SPhiloA* 13 (2001): 102–21.

Ryle, Herbert Edward. *Philo and Holy Scripture: Or, the Quotations of Philo from the Books of the Old Testament, with Introduction and Notes.* London: MacMillan, 1895.

Siegert, Folker. "Le fragment philonien *De Deo*: Première traduction française avec commentaire et remarques sur le langage métaphorique de Philon." Pages 183–227 in *Philon d'Alexandrie et le langage de la philosophie.* Edited by Carlos Lévy. Monothéismes et Philosophie 1. Turnhout: Brepols, 1998.

———. *Philon von Alexandrien: Über die Gottesbezeichnung "wohltätig verzehrendes Feuer" (DE DEO).* WUNT 46. Tübingen: Mohr Siebeck, 1988.

Sterling, Gregory E. "The People of the Covenant or the People of God: Exodus in Philo of Alexandria." Pages 404–39 in *The Book of Exodus: Composition, Reception, and Interpretation.* Edited by Thomas B. Dozeman, Craig A. Evans, and Joel N. Lohr. VTSup 164. Leiden: Brill, 2014.

———. "When the Beginning Is the End: The Place of Genesis in the Commentaries of Philo of Alexandria." Pages 427–46 in *The Book of Genesis: Composition, Reception, and Interpretation.* Edited by Craig A. Evans, Joel N. Lohr, and David L. Petersen. VTSup 152. Leiden: Brill, 2012.

———. "Which Version of the Greek Bible Did Philo Read?" Pages 89–127 in *Pentateuchal Traditions in the Late Second Temple Period: Proceedings of the International Workshop in Tokyo, August 28–31, 2007.* Edited by Akio Moriya and Gohei Hatta. JSJSup 158. Leiden: Brill, 2012.

Terian, Abraham. *Philonis Alexandrini De Animalibus: The Armenian Text with an Introduction, Translation, and Commentary.* Studies in Hellenistic Judaism 1. Chico, CA: Scholars Press, 1981.

———. "*Philonis De visione trium angelorum ad Abraham*: A New Translation of the Mistitled *De Deo.*" *SPhiloA* 28 (2016): 77–107.

Tov, Emanuel. "The Septuagint." Pages 161–88 in *Mikra: Text, Translation, Reading and Interpretation of the Hebrew Bible in Ancient Judaism and Early Christianity.* Edited by Martin Jan Mulder. CRINT 2.1. Assen: Van Gorcum, 1988.

Wendland, Paul. "Zu Philos Schrift *de posteritate Caini* (nebst Bemerkungen zur Rekonstruktion der Septuaginta)." *Phil* 57 (1898): 248–88.

Wevers, John W., ed. *Genesis*. SVTG 1. Göttingen: Vandenhoeck & Ruprecht, 1974.

Zaleski, Richard A. "Both Literal and Allegorical: Paraphrastic Biblical Exegesis in Gregory of Nyssa's and Philo of Alexandria's *Lives of
Moses*." PhD diss., University of Chicago, 2020.

Printed in the USA
CPSIA information can be obtained
at www.ICGtesting.com
LVHW040224090124
768326LV00040B/646

9 781628 374780